MW00718651

Modern Technology for Transportation Optimization

Steve Blough
Howard Troxler
MercuryGate International Inc.

www.mercurygate.com

MercuryGate International Inc.

Modern Technology for Transportation Optimization

Copyright © 2016 MercuryGate International Inc.

All rights reserved. No part of this book may be reproduced or transmitted in any form or by any means without the prior written permission of the copyright holder, except for the inclusion of brief quotations in a review.

The information in this book is provided on an as-is basis. While every effort has been made in the preparation of this book, the authors and MercuryGate International shall have neither liability nor responsibility to any person or entity with respect to any loss or damages allegedly arising from the information contained in this book.

MercuryGate International Inc.
Cary, North Carolina
www.mercurygate.com

First Edition
ISBN: 978-0-9965508-2-6
Library of Congress Control Number: 2016905316

Cover design by Stephen Bentley

Table of Contents

Foreword by Adrian Gonzalez

The word "optimization" is ubiquitous in the supply chain and logistics industry. "You have to optimize your [transportation, inventory, manufacturing, or other business process] to maximize your costs savings and benefits," is what industry analysts, consultants, academics, and solution providers have been preaching for decades. But what does that mean exactly? And if optimization technology is so beneficial, why aren't more companies leveraging it after all these years?

As an engineering student back in college, I remember feeling intimidated whenever I saw the pi symbol in an equation. "Don't be afraid of pi," my good friend Kevin once told me while we were doing our homework together, "it's just a number."

In many ways, I believe many supply chain and logistics professionals are intimidated by optimization. They see or hear optimization and they equate it with added complexity. "Don't be afraid of optimization," I tell them, "it's just a word."

A word that according Merriam-Webster means "to make as perfect, effective, or functional as possible."

When I speak with transportation executives, they tell me that the biggest challenge they face today is keeping pace with the rapid pace of change -- whether it's the rise of e-commerce and omni-channel fulfillment, with consumers expecting faster and cheaper deliveries; or it's the growing need to manage shipments across multiple modes and geographies; or it's having to respond more effectively to supply chain risks and disruptions; or it's staying informed of new regulations and how they might impact capacity and rates.

"We need the ability to make smarter decisions faster," is what shippers and logistics service providers tell me. They might not realize it, but what they're really saying is that they need optimization.

If the need to make smarter decisions faster -- that is, the need for optimization -- is greater than ever before, then why are so many companies still using spreadsheets, whiteboards, or nothing at all to plan and analyze their transportation operations?

"We don't need optimization," is the most common reason I hear from shippers and LSPs, especially small and mid-sized firms. "Our transportation operations are simple and straightforward." While this may be true for some (but a shrinking number of) companies, it doesn't take much added complexity -- whether it's an increase in orders, shipping locations, destinations, or modes -- before shippers start leaving money and other benefits on the table by not using optimization technology.

For example, in a recent exercise I conducted with MIT students, they were given a relatively simple transportation problem to solve using a spreadsheet: fulfill two orders for t-shirts, with two destinations, three potential ship-from locations, and a single truck carrier with a flat rate. Out of about 10 student teams, only two teams came up with the lowest-cost solution, meaning most teams were overpaying to deliver the t-shirts. While the cost difference was not large in some cases, when you multiply it by the number of shipments a company executes every day, every week, and every year, the money adds up quickly.

"Optimization solutions are too complicated to use," is another common excuse, along with "We don't have the right resources to use these tools effectively." These perceptions were realities in the past, but thanks to advancements in software architecture and user interfaces, optimization solutions are much easier to configure and use today than in the past. Simply put, you don't need a Ph.D. in mathematics or operations research to implement and use an optimization solution today; what you need is a good understanding of your transportation process flows and constraints and how they relate to other supply chain processes, as well as the ability to ask smart and important "What if?" questions.

Another misperception is that optimization solutions are too expensive to implement. Again, while cost might have been a barrier for some companies in the past, today's optimization solutions -- thanks to cloud computing and software-as-a-service -- are much more affordable.

In short, many companies still have an outdated perception and understanding of optimization, especially in transportation management. As this book illustrates, the scope of transportation optimization goes beyond load consolidation -- that is, aggregating less-than-truckload shipments into truckload shipments; it also plays an important role in procurement, zone skipping, mode conversion, what-if analysis, and various other applications outlined in this book.

And the business case for optimization goes well beyond cost savings too, although the opportunity to save 5 to 25 percent or more on transportation spend is certainly the most motivating factor. Progressive companies no longer view transportation as just a cost center; they view it as a competitive weapon to drive top-line growth, enhance customer loyalty, and increase market share. They look for ways to better align their transportation networks with those of their carriers, which creates more win-win opportunities and makes them "preferred shippers" in the eyes of carriers. And they also take a more proactive approach to supply chain risk management and continuous improvement by modeling, simulating and analyzing different "what-if" scenarios in order to find new opportunities to streamline and improve processes, and to respond more quickly and effectively to supply chain disruptions. The business case for optimization encompasses all of this and more.

Remember, optimization is just a word, so don't fear it, and don't let misconceptions about it get in the way of helping you make smarter decisions faster. May this book broaden your understanding of transportation optimization, and may it spark new ideas and opportunities to help you make your transportation operations as effective and functional as possible.

Adrian Gonzalez
President, Adelante SCM
Host, TalkingLogistics.com

Adrian Gonzalez is a trusted advisor and leading industry analyst with more than 17 years of research experience in transportation management, logistics outsourcing, global trade management, social media, and other supply chain and logistics topics.

In addition to launching Talking Logistics, an online weekly talk show featuring thought leaders in the supply chain and logistics industries, Gonzalez is the founder and president of Adelante SCM, a peer-to-peer learning and networking community for supply chain and logistics executives and young professionals.

Prior to his current roles, he held various leadership positions at ARC Advisory Group, Motorola, Polaroid, and Clare. He speaks frequently at industry events and conferences and is regularly quoted in industry publications. He is also a member of the Council of Supply Chain Management Professionals and is a LinkedIn Influencer with thousands of followers.

Gonzalez has a B.S. degree in Materials Science and Engineering from Cornell University. He also earned a Graduate Certificate in Supply Chain Management from Northeastern University.

Chapter 1: Introduction

This book is about the art and science of logistics *optimization* – the planning and execution of the movement of freight in a systematic way to produce a better result.

Even today, well into the 21st century, and despite all the tools at our command, optimization is hardly a universal priority – let alone a universal *practice* – in the logistics services provider industry.

In fact, listen and you'll hear some of the same themes of resistance over and over: "Look, we're just trying to get through today." "Optimization is too complicated." "It's for bigger players." "Maybe we'll consider something down the road."

On top of that, some resistance stems from tradition and long-standing manual practice. It wasn't <u>that</u> long ago, after all, that decisions about what got put on which truck depended on a paper route guide stapled to a bulletin board!

Today, maybe it's a spreadsheet instead of a piece of paper that somebody is using to build loads by hand. Maybe it's a matter of separate operating divisions or branches of the same organization that resist consolidation. In any case, the decision-making involved can be just as arbitrary. So here is a major theme of this book:

Most arbitrary and seat-of-the-pants criteria in logistics decision-making – inflexible assignment by weight break, by geographic boundary, by asset type, by personal preference – usually are at best a step away from an optimal result.

Therefore, part of our job as optimizers is to be relentless. We want the best result in the amount of time we have to produce that result, period. We want to decrease our costs, increase margins, save money, and satisfy our shippers and our consignees alike. As we will see in the chapter on private assets, if that means idling that trailer that happens to have our name on the side in big pretty letters - then that is exactly what we'll do.

How much difference does optimization make? How much money will it save?

There's no magic-bullet answer – this is not a book about the latest fad diet – but the potential optimized savings versus a non-optimized starting point can often reach double-digit percentage points. Savings of 6 to 8 percent against non-optimized practice is common among our clients; savings of 25 percent are not unheard of. The purpose of transportation optimization is to produce the most cost-effective routes in the amount of time given.

Planners often do battle against systemic optimizers and on given routes might be able to produce better results manually. However, given enough complexity and volume, the problem becomes impossible to manage manually in a reasonable amount of time. A transportation optimizer can produce consistent plans that will not violate any constraints for thousands of loads across multiple locations in only a few minutes. As the constraints mount and the shipments increase the human mind can no longer comprehend that complexity in a reasonable amount of time.

Approaches to Optimization – Rate, Route, Load, Network

In the very first paragraph we breezily defined "optimization" as the planning and execution of freight movement to achieve "a better result".

Which naturally leads to this question:

"Better" than <u>what</u>?

Doesn't the word "better" mean different things to different people? Can't it mean something besides the lowest rates? Can it mean using the fewest trucks, scheduling the fastest deliveries, or making the fullest use of a network?

Yes, yes, yes, yes and yes.

We're talking about different <u>kinds</u> of optimization, not a one-size-fits-all solution. In the real world, most business goals consist of some mix of these approaches.

Rate optimization is the most obvious and popular goal, of course – moving freight at the lowest possible cost, while still meeting our minimum goals. We might use actual historical experience, or we might calculate a theoretical direct-ship cost as our benchmark to "beat".

Route optimization means constructing routes, pickups and drops in the most efficient way possible. <u>Most</u> of the time this dovetails with rate optimization – but not always!

For example, take a look at Fig. 1-1, which isolates two loads created by a software optimizer:

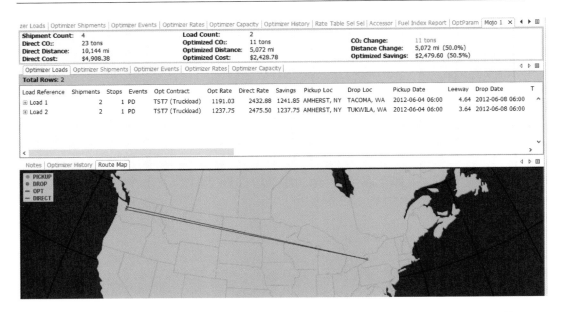

Fig. 1-1: *Why send shipments separately across the country on the same day, when they would fit on the same truck?*

In the above illustration, the optimization tool decided to send shipments on two separate trucks, to almost the same spot, at the same time, and on the same day -- all the way across the country! (You can almost hear spreadsheet users snickering.)

Yet in this case the optimizer relentlessly made its decision based on the fact the two-truck solution was the least-cost solution. A fine example of "rate" optimization versus "route" optimization! We'll see more about this theme in the chapter titled "Analysis & Improvement".

Load optimization approaches our problem with a focus on consolidation, maximizing weight, cube or pallet count on as few trucks as possible, while respecting other freight constraints. One of our main goals here is realizing the benefit of break ranges that give us an incentive to fill the truck. Again, of course, load optimization might dovetail nicely with rate or route optimization – or it might work in the opposite direction.

Network optimization is the driving factor for a lot of companies. "Network" optimization means you are driven by capacity constraints or the needs of your infrastructure. Maybe you have a pool-point system, warehouses or distribution centers. Maybe Product X has to go through Facility Y and not Facility Z. We might need to consider facility costs, capacity, operating hours and labor availability as we build routes.

We've just named four "philosophies" or approaches to optimization – rate, route, load and network. Sometimes you'll be pursuing one to the exclusion of all the others, and sometimes you'll naturally be achieving more than one kind of optimization at once.

Given the above -- what are your goals, or the goals of your organization, in optimization? It's worth some thought on the front end.

If the answer is, "We just want to save as much money as possible," well – that's a fine goal. Now we know. So in the following chapters you should emphasize the constraints and settings that give you the most room for saving money, above all other considerations.

If on the other hand, part of your goal is, "We want to make better use of our own trucks," or "We want to level out our docks," or "We need the tightest time windows possible," then you'll see how to do those things too.

Applications for Optimization

Naturally, the first question that occurs to most of us about optimization is whether it will save money and increase efficiency in actual execution.

But let's make this clear early on -- those aren't the <u>only</u> uses of an optimization tool. In fact, as with any useful tool, the more you use it, the more you'll think of other uses for it.

This book will demonstrate how transportation optimization tools can:

(1) Re-optimize our historical shipping data to test "what-if" scenarios (relocating a distribution center, for example), develop lane, volume and profitability data for route guides, conduct post-audit analysis, and look for patterns.

(2) Bring in external shipping data, such as from a sales prospect, to optimize that data against our own contracts and rates to demonstrate significant savings to the prospect.

(3) Bring in any external rate structure, such as from a carrier bid, to evaluate it against our own historical shipping data, or even against external shipping data from some other source.

(4) Create and share optimization "packages" with colleagues or prospects with shipment data, proposed loads, charts and graphs and other supporting output on demand.

(5) Tie <u>automated</u> optimization to an external warehouse or order management system, filtering out exceptions and otherwise generating execution loads on schedule.

About This Book

This book is published by MercuryGate International Inc., a logistics software company based in North Carolina. The concepts discussed in this book apply to our industry and to the theme of transportation optimization in general. Modern transportation optimization tools like MercuryGate's Mojo optimizer solve these industry problems efficiently with easy-to-use wizards and presentation methods.

The examples in this book will show scenarios and solutions using Mojo. Therefore the point is, "Here is a modern way to approach this optimization problem," and not "Mojo is really cool".

(But make no mistake -- Mojo is really cool.)

Here is how the rest of this book is structured:

Chapter 2, "What Are Your Constraints?" introduces us to this important word we'll use again and again. Constraints are the conditions and limits we have to obey in our optimization. That might mean a limit on truck capacity, on facility operating hours, on delivery time windows, or on freight types -- just to name a few. As we'll see, there can be dozens, even hundreds of possible constraints that govern the way we build our loads. As the numbers of constraints and shipments increase, the complexity of the optimization increases geometrically.

Chapter 3 introduces us to optimization software tools in general and discusses how transportation optimizers approach the problem.

We'll look at the kinds of data we need for transportation optimization, and how applying constraints impacts the optimization results, in chapters 4 and 5. We'll look at post-run results, analysis, and the benefits of re-optimization in chapters 6-7.

Then we'll look at more specific business use case scenarios. Some of the most important considerations in today's practical world are issues of carrier and lane capacity, which we'll look at in Chapter 8. We'll talk about facility constraints such as hours of operation and dock capacity in Chapter 9, and about pooling and cross-docking in Chapter 10.

Chapter 11 addresses how private or dedicated assets fit into optimization, especially when they are "competing" with third-party carriers. The key concept is to ensure that the assets are effectively utilized when compared to over-the-road carriers. Again, the point here is to be relentless in our decision-making and producing accurate plans as effectively as possible.

Chapter 12 talks about using optimization for other kinds of business scenarios, such as "continuous move" optimization.

Chapter 13 explores using the optimizer to understand the potential impact of what-if changes. One example shows how an optimizer can be used to see how changing conditions might make mode-shifting a viable option.

Chapter 14 presents ways a modern optimizer is actually used in a modern world. As orders are dropped into a TMS, the optimizer often runs in the background to build and consolidate loads automatically with no human interaction. As those loads begin to execute, quite often users must tactically adjust the routes to account for last minute changes. For complex routes these short-notice changes often are best accomplished by allowing the optimizer to re-plan the events and dates. This chapter also presents the concept of configuring the rules and constraints that drive the transportation considerations. This ability to apply unique rules is truly the next generation of the transportation optimizer.

So let's get started. Here's hoping you find our discussion of optimization useful – and, more importantly, profitable.

Discussion Questions

1. What is "optimization" in a logistics context? What are some of the reasons that small to mid-sized logistics service providers have not adopted it? What is the argument for retaining a manual method for building and routing loads, such as using a spreadsheet, as opposed to more elaborate software optimization?

2. What are the differences between an emphasis on "rate optimization" versus "route optimization", "load optimization" or "network optimization"? Can't we pursue more than one of these goals at a time?

3. The chapter claims that any "arbitrary" rule for building loads, such as an automatic assignment of a carrier mode, is usually a step away from an "optimal result". Does that mean that we should never have any restrictions on the way we build our loads, and that we should be open to any outcome as long as it is the lowest cost?

4. All too often, planners point out how on a given load they could save more money than the optimizer. Why should you use an optimizer if a planner could do better on a given load?

###

Chapter 2: What Are Your Constraints?

We'll use the term <u>constraints</u> throughout this book to mean the set of all rules or conditions that we have to obey when we build our loads.

The most direct "constraints", of course, are the basic requirements of place and time:

Pick it up here by 5 p.m. Tuesday.
Deliver it there by 5 p.m. Friday.

And if that were the whole story, then with a few single-pick, single-drop loads a day, and nothing to consider but geography and direction, creating loads by hand might be pretty manageable.

After all, if we just have one truck heading east and one truck heading west, it seems pretty clear which truck should get those deliveries to points east, and which should get those for points west.

("Seems" being an important word in that sentence, as we will see.)

But now let's change the rules just a little...

Suppose we have access to only one reefer (refrigerated unit) and one dry trailer. The refrigerated freight must go on the reefer but the dry freight can go on either trailer, regardless of direction. Our routes will look totally different.

Each new constraint adds exponentially to the possibilities.

What if certain freight types are never supposed to be on the same load?

What if some of the facilities that we're using for pickups, drops, pooling or cross-dock locations have conflicting operating hours?

What if some locations lie across a border with different national holidays? What if we need to take into consideration our estimated transit times, as well as facility load/unload service times and dock capacity?

Even a few such constraints can quickly overwhelm the best manual efforts to accommodate them all, for more than a few shipments at a time.

Which is the whole point of transportation optimization software. What we expect from an optimization tool is that it:

(1) Builds loads that obey all identified constraints.

and

(2) Reports back to us for the cases in which it can't.

That second point is vital, as well, and we'll spend some time on it. Enforcing constraints means that not every shipment can be optimized with every other shipment. Shipment consolidations that might look obvious are often not possible based on constraints. If the shipment says it must be picked up on Monday and delivered on Friday but is a one-day transit, the optimizer will not route it without a cross-dock. The optimizer knows that a truck will not drive around or sit somewhere for 4 days to do a 1 day move. But open up the pickup window from Monday to Thursday and the optimizer will determine the right day to pick up the load without violating any constraint.

The important thing in that case, as we will see in the chapters on analyzing our results, is to know which constraints are limiting the optimization results and to then decide how best to adapt to those constraints. Some constraints may be insurmountable, while others may have opportunities to minimize one aspect but adhering to other factors. For example, the date example above still enforced the delivery date but opened up the pickup window.

Categories of Constraints

So constraints are the main issue in optimization. Here are a few common categories of constraints (and the list could be a lot longer than this):

Date constraints are often the biggest limiting factor in optimization. Tight pickup and delivery ranges often result in limited consolidation opportunities. Shipment data sometimes has a pickup or delivery date but not a range, and often not a pickup date and a delivery date both.

Vehicle constraints: Max weight, quantity (pallet spaces/linear feet), cube.

Driver constraints: Duty and driving limits, how to handle estimated arrivals/departures outside of facility operating hours.

Route constraints: Required order of events (pickup/drop, no pickup after 1st drop, e.g.); maximum "out-of-route" limits (degree of zig-zag of the proposed route).

Freight constraints: Compatible and incompatible cargo types, temperature min/max, stackability, required loading priority (last in-first-out, e.g.), mode restrictions (e.g., truckload only).

Service and equipment requirements such as limited-access locations requiring inside delivery or residential deliveries requiring a lift gate.

Carrier capacity constraints: Number of available vehicles per day, per lane, per origin or dest, per origin-dest pair, by day, by optimization run.

Dock and facility constraints: Number and location of facilities, operating hours, allowance for service times, requirements for arrival times (e.g., must complete unload before closing time), facility restrictions by mode or by preferred or owner SCAC.

Pooling constraints: Required or preassigned pool locations, whether to force, require, or consider pool points. Pool hold time is also a consideration since short or long hold times may limit when a pool may be used.

Asset type constraints: Possible requirements to use privately owned or dedicated assets "in the mix" of optimization in competition with common over-the-road carriers, whether to restrict by geographic area, equipment type, etc.

Keep these categories of constraints in mind as we explore our software optimization tool. They will start to feel very familiar.

An Optimization Exercise

Here's an edited version of a college-level optimization exercise supplied by MercuryGate to a leading university's logistics program – which had rejected an earlier attempt for being too complicated. We're including it here as an illustration of the challenges of optimizing manually with even just a few constraints. An optimal solution is found at the end of the exercise.

MercuryGate University
Transportation Optimization Exercise

Exercise Aims and Outcomes

The aim of this exercise is to demonstrate the complexity of transportation optimization. While optimization is simple in concept, constraints quickly raise the level of complexity to a point where manual manipulation of data is no longer feasible or cost effective.

While individual routes may be more effectively planned manually by transportation personnel the consolidation challenges grow as complexity increases and quickly bypasses the individual's ability to manage the problem.

Quite often system optimizers are challenged by manual planners who demonstrate on a given route that they could have done "better." While this simplistic view may be true for a given load, the argument goes away as the complexities and volumes increase.

Assumptions

For this exercise there will be limits of weight, cube, and pallets on the movements being considered. While users may use any tools such as a spreadsheet, etc. the purpose is not to develop an optimizer but rather understand the complexities of consolidations and ultimately the challenges with using a transportation optimizer. The reduction of transportation costs can be significant to corporations since up to 60% of the budget for logistics is typically the cost of moving the goods or raw materials.

Exercise Description

This exercise will examine 139 shipments moving out of a facility in Laurel, Maryland to multiple points on the east coast of the United States. A spreadsheet is provided for this exercise. The 139 shipments in this spreadsheet all basic information such as weight and cube of the total shipment. Figure 1 below graphically shows all the destinations for the 139 shipments from Laurel, MD. Obviously there are a lot of common destinations.

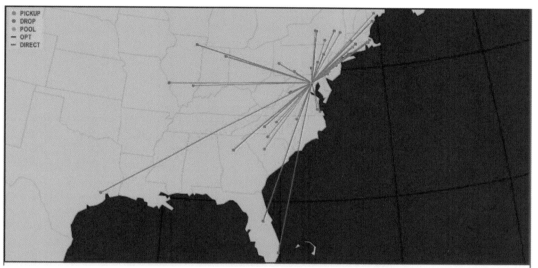

Figure 1: Map showing shipment destinations from Laurel, MD

The spreadsheet contains a worksheet entitled "Shipment – Laurel MD" which contains shipments from Laurel to 44 different destinations.

The column definitions are as follows:

Column Name	Description
Pallets	Total number of pallets on the shipment.
Weight	Total weight of the shipment
Cube	Total cube of the shipment
Dest Zip	Postal code of the destination location

Exercise: Consolidate based on origin/destination pairs

Take the shipments listed on the worksheet "Shipment – Laurel MD" (see following pages) and attempt to consolidate them based on like-destination locations. For this exercise, you really only need to consider the shipment worksheet but constrain your loads to the following.

1. Weight – 45,000 lbs
2. Cube – 3,600 cubic feet
3. Quantity (pallets) – max of 60

Results:

1. How many loads did you end up with?

2. What were the major constraints that you encountered? For example were most loads you considered constrained by weight, cube, or pallets?

3. What real-world processes might be violated by your transportation plan? (An example to think of would be a process consolidating parcel shipments where it is not feasible to stage thousands of packages around a warehouse.)

Dest Zip	Weight	Cube	Pallet
02382	15600	780	24
06084	16900	845	26
06084	16900	845	26
06084	16900	845	26
07008	16900	845	26
07008	16250	812.5	25
07008	15600	780	24
10451	13000	650	20
10451	13000	650	20
10451	14300	715	22

13201	15600	780	24
15044	15600	780	24
28601	15600	780	24
02780	16900	845	26
04072	16900	845	26
04072	16900	845	26
18424	29900	1495	46
07083	1300	65	2
08831	16900	845	26
15044	16250	812.5	25
28601	15600	780	24
30042	19500	975	30
02382	14950	747.5	23
06084	16250	812.5	25
06084	16900	845	26
06084	16900	845	26
07008	16900	845	26
07008	16900	845	26
08831	16900	845	26
10451	13000	650	20
10451	14300	715	22
10451	14950	747.5	23
10451	13000	650	20
13201	15600	780	24
17128	2600	130	4
19172	3900	195	6
22801	3250	162.5	5
22841	17550	877.5	27
22942	7150	357.5	11
27536	9750	487.5	15
29211	650	32.5	1
30042	19500	975	30
32801	19500	975	30
60137	19500	975	30
04072	16250	812.5	25
08085	15600	780	24
08085	15600	780	24
08085	15600	780	24
18424	14300	715	22
18424	11700	585	18
46802	19500	975	30
77002	16250	812.5	25
77002	18200	910	28

02382	5200	260	8
02382	15600	780	24
02382	15600	780	24
04240	6500	325	10
06067	6500	325	10
06084	16900	845	26
06084	15600	780	24
06084	10400	520	16
07008	16900	845	26
07008	16900	845	26
07008	16250	812.5	25
08831	16900	845	26
08831	16900	845	26
10451	13000	650	20
10451	13000	650	20
10451	13650	682.5	21
10451	13000	650	20
12065	1950	97.5	3
12095	4550	227.5	7
12095	10400	520	16
13164	4550	227.5	7
13201	15600	780	24
13201	15600	780	24
15044	14950	747.5	23
20781	15600	780	24
30042	19500	975	30
32801	19500	975	30
32801	19500	975	30
33301	19500	975	30
60137	13650	682.5	21
60137	19500	975	30
62450	3250	162.5	5
63045	17550	877.5	27
04072	16250	812.5	25
08085	15600	780	24
18424	14300	715	22
18424	14300	715	22
18424	14300	715	22
18424	15600	780	24
18424	11050	552.5	17
46802	19500	975	30
46802	19500	975	30
02766	5850	292.5	9

06084	7150	357.5	11
06084	16250	812.5	25
06084	16900	845	26
06084	16900	845	26
07008	16900	845	26
10451	13000	650	20
10451	13000	650	20
10451	14950	747.5	23
10451	14300	715	22
15522	6500	325	10
15522	5850	292.5	9
23501	7800	390	12
27101	1300	65	2
28601	16250	812.5	25
29730	650	32.5	1
60137	19500	975	30
60137	19500	975	30
01085	18200	910	28
06604	8450	422.5	13
08085	15600	780	24
08085	15600	780	24
08085	15600	780	24
13838	16250	812.5	25
17901	12350	617.5	19
18424	14300	715	22
18424	11700	585	18
18424	9750	487.5	15
23601	14950	747.5	23
46802	19500	975	30
46802	19500	975	30
77002	17550	877.5	27
06084	16900	845	26
06084	16900	845	26
30042	16250	812.5	25
30042	17550	877.5	27
32801	19500	975	30
32801	19500	975	30
33301	17550	877.5	27
60137	18200	910	28
63045	19500	975	30
18424	14300	715	22
46802	17550	877.5	27
46802	18200	910	28

Solution

The most common error made in attempting to solve this exercise concerns the number of trucks needed. The most common incorrect answer is 80. The correct answer is 83. This is a non-trivial matter if you have just stranded three truckloads of pallets on a loading dock!

It's tempting to add up total number of pallets by destination, divide by 60 (the pallet capacity of a truck) and round up to determine the number of trucks needed for that destination.

However, this does not consider the actual pallet organization of the consolidated shipments. For example, if there are 3 shipments of 40 pallets each going to the same destination, the simple approach would yield 3 x 40 = 120 / 60 = 2 required trucks. However, a single truck cannot transport 2 shipments of 40 pallets because it exceeds the 60 pallet truck limit. Three lanes in the exercise, highlighted below, had pallet distribution issues and required an additional truck. Therefore, the correct answer with these considerations is 83 trucks.

Zip code	Pallets	Pallets / 60	Theoretical Trucks	Actual Trucks	Difference
07008	230	3.83	4	5	1
08085	168	2.80	3	4	1
18424	270	4.50	5	6	1
Total			80	83	3

Discussion Questions

1. What is your understanding of the definition of the word "constraint"? Why do we care about constraints in the first place, when it comes to building loads?

2. What are some of the general categories of constraints that affect the way loads can be built? Do you think some of these are more critical than others? Name some constraints that might be considered more important than others.

3. Why is a discussion of constraints relevant to the question of whether to use a software logistics optimization tool, as opposed to traditional, manual load building and routing?

###

Chapter 3: Software Tools for Optimization

We've talked about the need for a transportation optimizer that can handle the constraints we throw at it, while giving us a clear idea of what it's doing and why. Ideally we need a software tool that can:

- Accept shipment data from any internal or external source or even both internal and external at the same time.
- Apply rates from any internal or external source.
- Map the above imported data into the exact fields and purposes that we want to use.
- Accept and use a wide range of constraints on the loads that it builds.
- Return a list of proposed loads with detailed analysis and provide the ability to "drill down" into those results to learn more.
- Allow users to adjust, re-run and compare optimization results based on changed parameters and constraints.
- Export results to an external system either for actual execution or for further analysis.

There are a variety of software tools on the market for optimization. The one we'll be using as our example in this book is named <u>Mojo</u>, which is a product of MercuryGate International Inc.

Mojo does all the things listed above, and more, as we'll see again and again. But let's start with something that it <u>doesn't</u> do.

"An optimizer," you might hear someone say, "considers every possible combination, and then chooses the best one."

Just to be clear here:

No, it doesn't.

The key phrase that should set off warning bells is "every possible combination". Even a basic shipment record in the MercuryGate TMS (TMS = transportation management system) contains more than 100 fields.

Add to that all the possible variables for time windows, routes, and load permutations, and even today's fastest computers would be overwhelmed as such combinations increased exponentially:

* 10 shipments ~ 5 minutes
* 22 shipments ~ 4 billion years (age of the Earth)
* 23 shipments ~ 80 billion years (5 x age of the universe)
* 1000 shipments ~ 10^{55} years (incomprehensible!)

So let's forget the idea of considering "every possible combination". Instead, transportation optimizers make optimization decisions *heuristically*. That means using common sense, sound rules of thumb and educated decision making.

Example: We're starting in Kansas, we have plenty of truck choices, and we have some shipments going to New York and some to California. It's pretty clear (even the spreadsheet load-builder would agree) that we're <u>not</u> going to send the same truck to both New York and California!

In more precise terms, such a crazy Kansas-to-coast-to-coast gambol would constitute a "max out-of-route" violation, and so it immediately disqualifies this proposed load from the start. No need to consider all the possible other combinations down the line.

Fortunately, a transportation optimizer's heuristic decision-making can knock a little time off the optimization process. (After all, most shipments probably need to be delivered some time before the end of the known universe.)

Optimizer Results

To start in the middle of the story, below is a screen of transportation optimization results from Mojo (Fig. 3-1). We've fed a few hundred shipments into the optimizer and set our constraints. The optimizer has built recommended loads, which are presented in list view and on an interactive map.

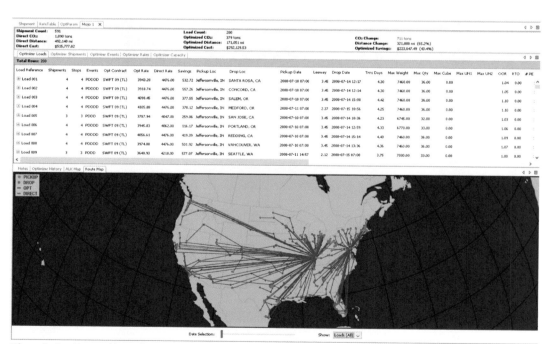

Fig. 3-1: Results of an optimization run in Mojo with statistical summary, drill-down list results and interactive map display.

Looking more closely at the statistical summary (Fig. 3-2), we see that in this example the optimizer took nearly 600 proposed shipments on behalf of customers and recommended their consolidation into 200 execution loads, with a tremendous savings.

Shipment Count:	591	**Load Count:**	200
Direct CO₂:	1,090 tons	**Optimized CO₂:**	379 tons
Direct Distance:	492,140 mi	**Optimized Distance:**	171,051 mi
Direct Cost:	$515,777.02	**Optimized Cost:**	$292,129.53

Fig. 3-2: Detail of results screen showing original shipment data versus the effects of a recommended consolidation upon carbon emissions, mileage and freight spend.

The optimizer gives us a series of tabs filled with list information (we'll look at each in more depth in Chapter 6) for the recommended loads, the original shipment data, a summary of recommended pickup, drop and pool events, rating information and a tab of data about how this optimization uses carrier capacity.

Direct Distance:	492,140 mi							Optim
Direct Cost:	$515,777.02							Optim

Optimizer Loads | Optimizer Shipments | Optimizer Events | Optimizer Rates | Optimizer Capacity

Total Rows: 200

Load Reference	Shipments	Stops	Events	Opt Contract	Opt Rate	Direct Rate	Savings
⊞ Load 001		4	4 PDDDD	SWFT 09 (TL)	3943.28	4476.00	532.72

Fig. 3-3: Tabs of data with drill-down details of optimization run.

A row of more tabs at the bottom of the screen give us access to <u>notes</u> about the optimization run, a <u>history</u> tab for comparing one run to another (once we start re-optimizing), and the choice of <u>map views</u> with a variety of overlays and viewing and mark-up options.

Fig. 3-4: Mapping for optimizer results. Maps are interactive; highlighting a route on the map selects its related loads in the results list and vice-versa.

On the right side of the results screen we'll find a series of commands for performing re-optimization, opening additional analysis screens, running different "what-if" scenarios against our results, and of course, sending the recommended loads to an external system (in this case the MercuryGate TMS) for actual creation and execution.

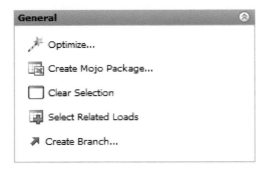

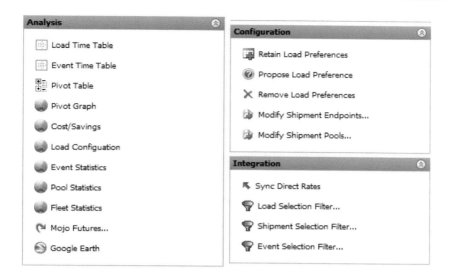

Fig. 3-5: Options for creating and testing post-run adjustments, launching re-optimization runs and conducing other analysis tasks.

That's a quick look at the kind of results we'll be working with. In the next two chapters we'll talk about what kinds of data we need to perform optimization, and how to go about setting the constraints ("parameters") that we want the optimizer to obey.

Discussion Questions

1. Discuss the following statement: "A software optimizer builds loads out of individual shipments by considering every possible combination and choosing the best one."

2. What is an "out of route violation" and why is it one of the most common reasons that certain combinations get rejected as the optimizer builds its recommended loads?

3. Why should we care whether our optimizer allows us to bring in data from external sources, such as shipments or rates? Why would we want to combine data from internal and external sources?

###

Chapter 4: Preparing the Data

Accurate data is the heart of a solid optimization run. The adage "garbage in, garbage out" is never more evident than it is in optimization. With bad data even the best-planned constraints cannot produce a solution that works in the real world.

One great trait of the modern transportation optimizer is that it will tell you when it has insufficient data. If you are missing a rate for a lane going into a cross-dock, the optimizer will tell you that. If your date window constraint is too tight, the optimizer will tell you that.

So as we examine the data for optimization, remember we have made great strides in identifying data issues -- but bad data is still bad data. The optimizer can build really bad plans really fast with bad data.

At a bare-bones minimum, two kinds of data are required to conduct an optimization:

(1) The shipments that we want to optimize.
(2) The rate tables of the carriers we want to consider.

Later, as we look at more complicated optimization scenarios, we'll require additional kinds of data such as:

- Data about locations – identifying codes, physical location, operating hours, available services, restrictions.
- Lists of accessorial rates that might be charged for additional or special services on our load.
- Fuel indexes containing necessary information for fuel adjustments.
- Facility, equipment, driver and schedule information for private-fleet optimization scenarios.

In the rest of this chapter, first we'll learn more about the exact information we need for shipments and rates, and then we'll see how to get that data into our optimizer.

Shipment Data

The minimum that we need to know about a shipment to be able to use it for optimization is:

- A unique identifier, such as a shipment or order number.
- A pickup location.
- A pickup date window.
- A delivery location.
- A delivery date window.
- Something about the freight itself.

What do we mean by "something" about the freight itself? For starters, Mojo requires at least a <u>weight</u> for each shipment. But depending on our rate tables, a weight value alone might not be enough to get back a rate.

Some carrier rates are based on weight, but others are based on distance, on volume, on quantity, or on freight class. We also need to make sure that our shipment data has <u>geodata</u> (precise latitudes and longitudes). See the section at the end of this chapter titled "Shipment GeoData and Mileage".

Beyond these basics, there can be dozens of additional columns in shipment data. We might need some of these depending on how our rate tables work and what our shipments require. Here are a few more:

Location Codes:	A unique code to use for each location. Required for location-related optimization, such as specifying a required pool point.
Quantity:	A numerical quantity used for rating – a contract might rate by pallet count, for example.
Cube:	A volume-based measurement of each shipment. Some contracts rate by a shipment's cube value.
Freight Class:	A standard industry classification of freight tied to density and other attributes such as ease of handling. Rating by freight class is prevalent in LTL (less than truckload) scenarios.
Services: Equipment:	Any required services or equipment for this shipment, e.g. refrigerated.

That's still not all the possible fields of shipment data. A list of possible fields (at least those possible in Mojo) is in the appendix. We'll talk more about shipment data in the next chapter.

Rate Tables

The other minimum requirement for optimization is a rate structure for our carriers – a rate table that the optimizer uses to build loads.

Rates usually come from carrier contracts. A logistics services provider might have just a few contracts with carriers – or thousands. So the list of rates used in optimization can come from one carrier contract, or many, and a rate table can contain just a few lines, or hundreds, or even thousands.

Each line of the rate table defines a rate and the lane and conditions for which that rate will apply. That means that each row of the table will contain, at the least, fields for:

- An identifier for the contract that supplies this rate.

- The carrier SCAC (Standard Carrier Alphanumeric Code, a unique identifier issued to carriers in the U.S).

- The mode for this rate, such as "Truckload", "Less Than Truckload", "Rail", "Air" or "Ocean".

- The contract service that applies for this rate, such as "Standard", "Overnight", "2d Day Air", etc.

- Effective and expiration dates for this rate.

- A lane calculation method ("lane calc") for this rate. A "lane" can be city to city, zip to zip (5-digit or 3-digit group), state to state, zone to zone, location code to location code, or even country to country. A lane of "USA" to "USA" covers any origin and destination pair in the United States.

- In our optimizer example, Mojo, the lane calculation method is declared by a pair of values for origin and destination separated by a hyphen. For example, the term "5ZC-3ZC" means this lane covers any origin within a five-digit zip code, going to any destination within an area covered by a three-digit zip code. See the list of allowed values in the chart below.

- Next come columns about the origin and destination that "satisfy" the zone calculation. This can be origin and destination city, state, zip, zone or location code (if used). A country code is always required.

- The <u>rate field</u>, meaning the basis on which the rate will be calculated. This value can be "Mileage, "Cube", "Class", "Quantity" "ItemCount", "Stops", "Weight C" (for hundredweight), or "Weight ST" for short ton.

- The <u>rate calculation method</u>, which can be "Per", "Pct" or "Flat". If the method is "Per" and the rate field is "Mileage", then a rate is calculated per mile. If the method is "Flat", then a flat rate is applied to any shipment that qualifies for this lane.

- The actual <u>rate</u> to apply, for example, "1.00". For a rate field of Mileage, a rate calc of "Per" and a rate of "1.00", the rate to charge is $1 per mile. For a rate calc of "Flat" and a rate of "100", a rate of $100 is applied to any shipment that qualifies for this lane.

Here's a chart that recaps these fields:

REQUIRED FIELDS FOR RATE TABLES		
Contract Id	<String>	Name of contract to which this lane belongs
SCAC	<String>	Carrier SCAC
Mode	<String>	LTL, TL, Truckload, etc.
Service	<String>	Standard, e.g.
Effective Date	yyyy-mm-dd	First day the rate is effective
Expiration Date	yyyy-mm-dd	Last day the rate is effective

REQUIRED FIELDS FOR RATE TABLES		
Lane Calc	<val1-val2>	ZONE,LOC,5ZC,3ZC,CSC (city-state),SC (state),CTRY,ANY - so the lane calc value would look like "CTRY-CTRY" or "3ZC-3ZC" for origin and destination.
Origin & Destination Columns		These will be several columns next that supply the kind of information needed to satisfy the lane calc method – zone, city, state, zip. Country is always required.
Rate Field	<constant>	Possible values include: Weight, Mileage, Class, Quantity, Cube, ItemCount, Stops, Weight C (hundredweight), Weight ST (short ton).
Rate Calc	<constant>	Per, Pct, Flat, Flat-Conditional
Rate	<numeric>	Actual rate to apply, e.g. "1.00"

Here are some other commonly used rate table columns:

Carrier Services: A column with the names of services available on this lane ("Saturday Delivery", "White Glove", "Lift Gate"). If we are enforcing service requirements, then shipments that require a certain service will only be rated on a lane that offers that service.

Carrier Equipment: Same for specific equipment types, for example, "Reefer" (refrigerated).

Transit Method:
Transit Value: Information about transit times on this lane, which Mojo uses in its calculations.

There are many other possible columns in a rate table. We'll discuss more in the coming chapters, and a full list is included in the appendix.

Rate Table 'Break Ranges'

Each line in a rate table optionally can declare one or more break ranges for which that rate applies.

For example, a line of the rate table might declare a rate for a certain geographic lane – but only for shipments of up to 100 pounds. Then in the next line, the rate table might provide the rate that applies to shipments in the next weight range of 100-200 pounds, and so on. Any numerical range can be specified.

As another example, a carrier might charge a certain rate per pallet for shipments that have up to 30 pallets, but then a lower per-pallet rate for shipments of 30-60 pallets. (In other words, this is a volume discount that creates an incentive to fill up the truck.)

This is one of the ways Mojo looks to save money – by consolidating individual shipments into loads that take advantage of break ranges.

One, two or even three break ranges for different factors can be defined for a lane in a single row of the rate table. Here, for illustration, are two break ranges on distance and weight being used together. Lines of the rate table might cover shipments of:

```
0-100 pounds    and  0-100 miles
0-100 pounds    and  100-200 miles
0-100 pounds    and  200+ miles
100-200 pounds  and  0-100 miles
100-200 pounds  and  100-200 miles
100-200 pounds  and  200+ miles
200+ pounds     and  0-100 miles
200+ pounds     and  100-200 miles
200+ pounds     and  200+ miles
```

Here are the actual columns used to define a break range in a line of the rate table. (Change the column title to "Break 2" or "Break 3" as needed.)

Break 1 Field	Constant	Break ranges can be declared by these options: Weight, Mileage, Class, Quantity, Cube, ItemCount, ItemUOM (unit of measure), ItemId, Stops, Equipment or Services.
Break 1 Min	Numeric	Starting value for the range for which this rate applies. Initial ranges often start at 0.
Break 1 Max	Numeric	First value <u>beyond</u> the range to which this rate applies. In other words, a range of "0-100" means that 99.99999 falls within the range, but 100 falls into the next range.

NOTE that break range max values in Mojo are <u>exclusive</u> of the range being defined. That means ranges should be defined like this: "0-100" "100-200", "200-300" and NOT with constructions such as "0-100", "101-200" – the latter scheme will not capture and rate a value of 100 because no range covers it!

	A	B	C	D	E	F	G	H	I	J	K	L	M	N	O	P	
1	Contract Id	Lane Calc	From LocCode	From City	From State	From Zip	From Country	To LocCode	To City	To State	To Zip	To Country	SCAC	Service	Mode	Break 1 Field	Br
2	SWFT 09	CTRY-CTRY					USA					USA	SWFT	Standard	TL	Weight	
3	ARBS 09	CTRY-CTRY					USA					USA	ARBS	Standard	TL	Weight	
4	ODFL 09	CTRY-CTRY					USA					USA	ODFL	Standard	LTL	Weight	

Fig. 4-1: Example of a rate table spreadsheet.

Matching Shipments with Rates

So we're feeding our shipment data to the rate table to see whether we can find rates that apply to each shipment. If the rate table doesn't get the information that it needs from the shipment data, then it doesn't return a rate for that shipment!

Example: Let's say our shipment data does not contain a quantity column, yet we have a rate table that only rates on quantity. We won't get back any rates – an empty list!

The same is true for a cube contract but no shipment cube values, or a freight-class contract and no shipment freight classes, and so on. (For more on this topic see the "Troubleshooting" chapter.)

The more thought and preparation we put in on the front end for the data to be used in optimization, the better the results will be. In the next chapter we'll see how to put our data and our constraints to work by launching our first optimization.

Getting Data into a Modern Transportation Optimizer

Modern optimizers allow the user to feed data into the optimizer via spreadsheets to simplify use. Of course when combined with a TMS, the data can feed directly from the TMS to the optimizer seamlessly. However, since optimization often is more than just the operational view of the movements, an open architecture allowing loading of data from industry standard formats like a spreadsheet is essential.

MercuryGate's Mojo tool runs its optimizations from data contained in at least two open spreadsheets. (Why at least two spreadsheets? Because one holds the list of shipments, and one holds the list of rates.)

Each spreadsheet is called a "report" and it contains one kind of data. A list of shipments is called a "shipment report"; a list of rates is called a "rate table report", and so on. There are several other report types, although we'll see that a few are used over and over in optimization.

Fig. 4-2: An open spreadsheet used in Mojo. The type of this report is 'Shipment' and it contains shipment data needed to run an optimization.

Where does the information in these spreadsheets come from? For Mojo, it can come from one of two places:

(1) We can import an external spreadsheet. This means we can use any data supplied from any external source. That's one of the things that makes Mojo such a powerful tool.

(2) MercuryGate clients can bring in their own live data into Mojo directly from the MercuryGate Transportation Management System (TMS).

Importing Shipments & Rate Tables into Mojo

We can import any spreadsheet file to use for optimization. Select the menu command File > Import and a standard dialog opens to choose a file from the local system.

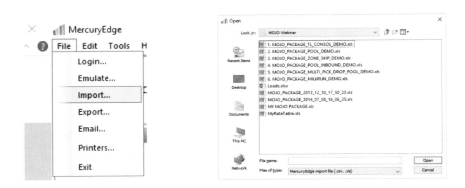

Fig. 4-3: Any external spreadsheet can be imported for use in a Mojo optimization.

After you choose the file to import, there's one small twist: You'll be asked whether the file has a "header row", meaning that the first row of the spreadsheet contains titles for its columns.

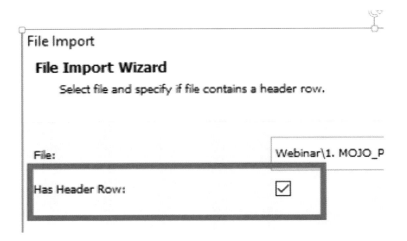

Fig. 4-4: Dealing with column headers in an imported spreadsheet.

It's better to use files with column headers. Mojo will look at those headers to try to match the columns to the right fields, for example, "Origin City" or "Weight". Without headers, Mojo provides an easy tool to map columns in a spreadsheet into the known fields in the optimizer but naming the columns the standard names automates this step.

Here's another Mojo tip: The <u>tab name</u> of the spreadsheet should start with the report <u>type</u> it applies to in Mojo, For example, "Shipment 2016-03-31", or "RateTable February", or just "Shipment" or "RateTable". The application will automatically assign the correct report type when it opens the spreadsheet. (Otherwise you can set the report type yourself with the drop-down menu in the open spreadsheet.)

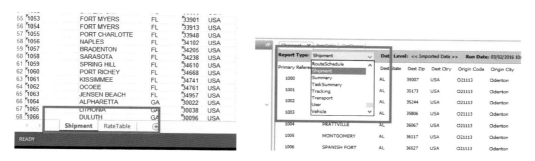

Fig. 4-5: If the spreadsheet tab name starts with the correct report type, it will be recognized automatically. Otherwise the generic report type will be "Import", and you can change it yourself.

When we import a spreadsheet, how does Mojo know which column is which? What if our imported file has columns arranged in every-which-order, with odd or missing column names? How do we sort the jumble of external data into something that makes sense for optimization?

For shipment data, the twofold answer is: (1) Mojo makes a pretty good guess as to which column contains what, based on the column headers, and then (2) asks us to take a look and make any corrections and new selections before the optimization run starts. We'll see how this works in the next chapter.

As for rate tables, their columns can be in any order, and non-essential columns can be omitted. But the column headers from the imported file <u>must be exact</u> as listed in this chapter and in the appendix. That means <u>exact</u>: "Zip" mean "Zip", not "ZIP".

Another Option – Data from the TMS

As noted earlier, besides using imported spreadsheets, modern transportation optimizers can open their shipment data and contract rate tables from directly and seamlessly from the TMS.

That means live shipments can be passed to the optimizer for actual execution. Historical data may be used for what-if analysis. Actual contract rates may be used to evaluate external shipment data.

For example, in Mojo to open TMS shipment data, the user clicks in the left-hand "Reports" window, under the tabs labeled "Main" and "Shipment". Here the user can open an existing TMS shipment report, or create a new report and open it. A TMS "report" is a format saved under a name ("Shipments Ready to Optimize", for example) that is used to retrieve data from the TMS.

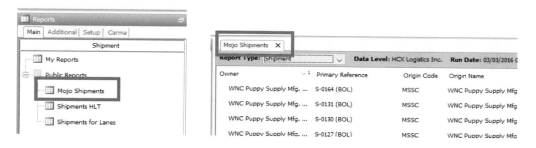

Fig. 4-6: The 'Reports' window gives clients access to their data in the TMS. Users simply click a report name – this one is 'Mojo Shipments' - to open it in a spreadsheet.

Opening contract <u>rates</u> from the TMS is a two-step process – first get a list of contracts, then open a rate table report from the contracts that you choose.

(1) In the "Reports" window, choose "Additional" and "Contract" to see available contracts. Choose the list you want and it opens as a spreadsheet of type "Contract".

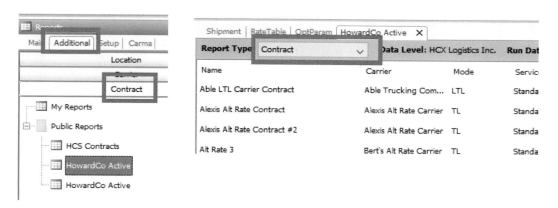

Fig. 4-7: Opening a TMS contract report.

(2) Select the contracts that contain the rates you want, and in the right-hand task window, select the command "Open Rate Table Report". Another tab opens, this one of type "RateTable".

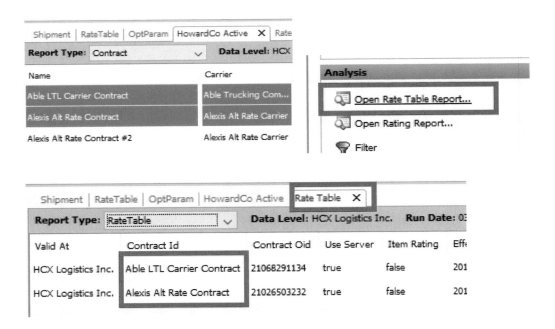

Fig. 4-8: Select the contracts to use in the optimization and open a rate table with the rates from those contracts.

Chapter Addendum: Adding Shipment 'GeoData' and Mileage

Most if not all optimizers require <u>geodata</u>, or precise latitude and longitude coordinates, for the origins and destinations in shipment data.

But if our shipment data doesn't have those coordinates, the modern transportation optimizer has the ability to determine and add geodata columns automatically, based on zip code or valid city-state combinations in the shipment file (so you do need at least that).

Here's how to add geodata using in Mojo:

From an open Shipment report that is currently selected (the front tab): look to the right side of the screen for a command labeled "Add GeoData...". Click this command, and you'll see a window asking you to confirm which columns contain the information needed to calculate geocodes:

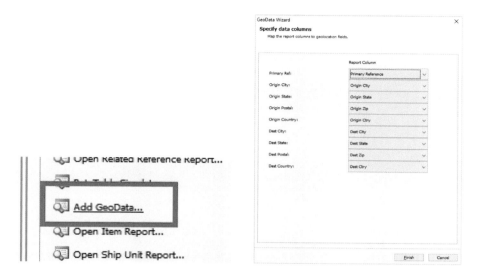

Fig. 4-9: You can add precise latitude and longitude with the "Add GeoData" command. Mojo asks you to confirm which columns contain the right information for making the calculation.

The application will add columns to your shipment data with the new values, one for origin and one for destination:

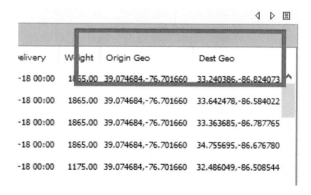

Fig. 4-10: 'Geodata' is automatically added to the shipment data to use in the optimization.

Mojo relies on its own distances for optimization. But if you need, you can add explicit mileage data directly to your shipments. From an open shipment report, choose the right-hand command "Add Mileage".

Fig. 4-11: 'Add Mileage' command. The user is asked to confirm which columns contain location information to use in the calculation.

We will discuss later how the modern transportation optimizer identifies questionable data to the user to help ensure accurate and realistic optimization plans.

Discussion Questions

1. The text says that to optimize, we need two things – shipments and rates. Why do we need rates to optimize?

2. What are some of the different ways in which we can state the measure of a shipment? Why are there various options, and why are some better than others? What is the relationship between a shipment's unit of measure and the rate table?

3. How do rate tables work? What is going on in each line of the rate table? What is a rate table "break range"?

4. How do we deal with the problem of bringing in outside, "messy" data such as shipments and rates into the optimization tool? How do we even know how basic information is arranged?

###

Chapter 5: Creating the Models

Modern transportation optimizers allow the user to create one or many models that can be used to create load plans. These models consist of the aforementioned components of constraints, shipments (orders), and rates. Users can evaluate the different models to see which one really works best with the soup of shipments submitted. Models are often set up, tested, and then automated.

So in this chapter we'll bring together all the components of optimization that we've discussed so far:

- The <u>constraints</u> under which we want our loads to be built.
- The <u>shipments</u> we will use to build optimized loads.
- The <u>rates</u> for the lanes on which our loads can move.

This is a three-way dance. The optimizer looks at the fields of each shipment, searches for rates and lanes that qualify, and decides whether this shipment can be consolidated and routed with others to some optimized advantage, according to the rules of the optimization – that is, within the specified constraints.

Keep in mind that these high-level model constraints could be overridden by specific constraints. For example a generic weight constraint of 45,000 pounds might be overridden for a specific type of equipment to 48,000 pounds. Default hours of operations of 8 a.m.-10 p.m. Monday to Friday might be overridden to a 24-hour, 7-day operation for a specific location. The generic constraints are discussed here, but specific data will override when provided. The generic is a fallback if nothing more unique is specified.

Optimizing on Location and Date/Time

The most obvious (and unforgiving) requirements are for place and time. For each shipment, we must pick up at location X and deliver to location Y within a given time frame. Can we consolidate on loads to save money yet still obey these requirements?

As the optimizer considers combinations, it calculates transit and service times and tries to build loads that (1) gain an optimized advantage while (2) still respecting the required time constraints.

To build a model the optimizer needs to understand what data is being loaded. For example, Mojo first asks users to confirm a "map" of the information in the shipment data. Which columns in the spreadsheet should be used to supply which values?

Here's how that mapping looks for location information (Fig. 5-1). The user confirms which columns in the shipment spreadsheet should be used to supply the origin and destination address fields.

Fig. 5-1: Selection of columns in the shipment data that hold information about origins and destinations. The right-hand selections are the actual names of columns in the shipment spreadsheet.

Since the dates and times of the shipment are a critical constraint the optimizer asks the user to name four required columns in the shipment data that will supply time windows – earliest and latest pickup, earliest and latest delivery:

Fig. 5-2: These settings declare which columns in the shipment data contain pickup and delivery date ranges.

But the matter of time windows brings up a problem: Sometimes our shipment data doesn't have columns for all four of these dates. For example, historical data sometimes only has one date column – the actual ship date. What then?

A common solution is to map the <u>same</u> date column to as many of these four settings as necessary (Fig. 5-3):

Fig. 5-3: There is only one date column available in our shipment data. No problem -- we'll map the same column and then 'stretch' these date windows in a later setting.

By itself, this solution <u>does not work</u>. Technically speaking we are telling the optimizer to schedule pickups and delivery at the exact same point in time! Mojo will not find an optimized solution for an "instantaneous" pickup and delivery and zero transit time.

Since data often has very limited date/time information, the optimizer must allow us to "stretch" the time constraints, both for achieving more optimized loads overall, and for dealing with cases such as the no-time-window just described. Mojo has settings that allow the date windows to be extended earlier or later as necessary:

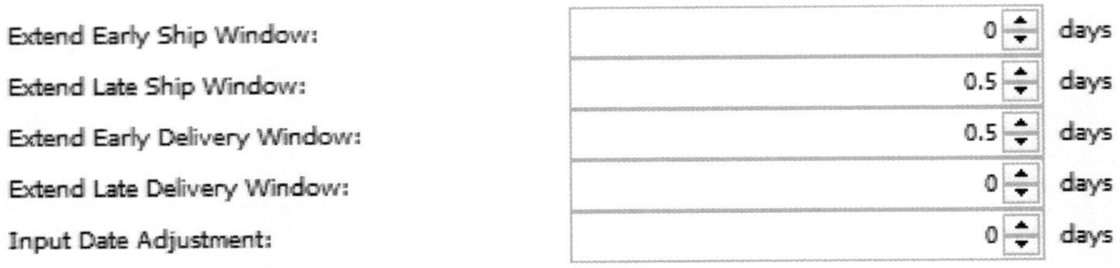

Extend Early Ship Window:	0 ⬍	days
Extend Late Ship Window:	0.5 ⬍	days
Extend Early Delivery Window:	0.5 ⬍	days
Extend Late Delivery Window:	0 ⬍	days
Input Date Adjustment:	0 ⬍	days

Fig. 5-4: Option to extend our pickup and delivery time windows, or move all dates and times in the shipment time by a global offset.

The "extend" options will give the optimizer more leeway in building loads, a half-day at a time in either direction, early or late.

In real life, of course, customers and carriers will only put up with so much stretching. But even in live execution, a common practice is to extend the <u>inner</u> windows, allowing later "late" pickups, and earlier "early" deliveries, as long as the delivery can still be made on time. This flexibility can greatly improve the result.

The "extend" option also solves our problem of historical shipment data that does not supply time windows. Given the date fields that we do know, we can extend the windows to give the optimizer enough breathing room to build a load. Keep in mind that dates also must allow some leeway for the hours of operations of a location.

By the way, the final setting in the section shown above, "Input Date Adjustment", allows us to offset every date in the shipment file by the specified number of days. An example usage would be to bring historical shipment data into the effective date range of a current contract in the rate table.

Optimizing on Freight – Weight, Quantity, Cube, Class

Some of the most common constraints in creating optimized loads deal with vehicle capacity and the nature of the freight itself. We should be able to provide this kind of information to the optimizer.

Besides weight, these fields in the shipment data might include a quantity (like a pallet count), a cube or volume-related measurement, a freight class, or certain other frequently used fields for rating such a rating count.

Assuming that the optimizer knows these values for each individual shipment, it will be able to obey its constraints on the per-truck limit as it builds its loads.

Here what our settings might look like for these constraints:

Vehicle Max Weight:	45,000
Vehicle Max Quantity:	36
Vehicle Max Cube:	3,500
Truckload Max Stops:	5

Fig. 5-5: Setting limits on what the optimizer can allow per truck.

"Max Weight" in this example is set to 45,000 pounds, a typical standard, but the user can adjust it by vehicle type or for other reasons.

"Max Quantity" is an arbitrary number – it is the number of "somethings" that will fit on a truck. If we are using quantity, we expect each shipment in our data to include a value for how many "somethings" that shipment contains. Again, a good example is a pallet count.

"Max Cube" is a measure related to cubic volume, e.g. feet.

"Max Stops" is not a direct limit on vehicle capacity, but indirectly affects it by limiting the number of stops the optimizer can require a single truck to make on a route. This number might depend on what carrier contracts and rate tables allow.

Putting it all together, in the following example let's say that we have mapped columns from our shipment data for weight, quantity (a pallet count in this example) and cube:

Fig. 5-6: Columns selected from the shipment data inform us of each shipment's weight, quantity and cube value.

Now in the constraints, let's set new limits on these values for what will be allowed per vehicle:

Fig. 5-7: Specifying different per-truck limits for weight, quantity, cube, stops.

When we run our results, we will see that the optimizer "respected" these limits and that no optimized load contains more than 30,000 pounds, more than 50 units (pallets), no cube value of more than 500, and never has more than three stops.

rns Days	Max Weight	Max Qty	Max Cube	Stops	Ma
3.20	28000.00	11.00	33.00	3	
4.15	23767.50	9.00	33.00	3	
4.12	26041.00	10.00	33.00	3	
3.93	25766.00	10.00	33.00	3	
3.18	21310.50	8.00	22.00	2	

Fig. 5-8: In this snippet of results, we see that the optimizer has obeyed the new limits that we set on per-truck weight, quantity, cube and stop count.

Of course, there are many other kinds of constraints besides vehicle capacity, as we will continue to explore.

An Example of Creating an Optimization Model

So far we've talked in general terms about identifying the fields to use from our shipment data, and setting constraints based on factors such as weight, quantity and cube.

Let's see exactly how all this works in our example of a modern transportation optimizer, Mojo. As we discussed in the last chapter, Mojo needs at least an open shipment report and an open rate table report.

So either we've brought this information in from imported spreadsheets, or we have opened it directly from the MercuryGate TMS.

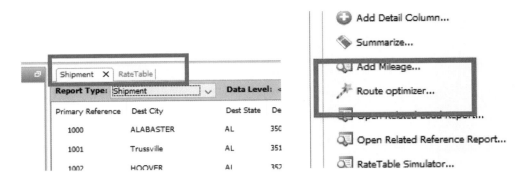

Fig. 5-9: A shipment report and a rate table report are open, ready for optimization. The user chooses the 'Route optimizer...' command to launch.

The "Route optimizer..." command launches a series of screens presented to the user called the <u>Mojo Optimization Wizard</u>. This wizard has two main purposes:

(1) To let us tell Mojo which columns to use from the shipment data.

(2) To let us set the constraints and options that we want for the optimization model.

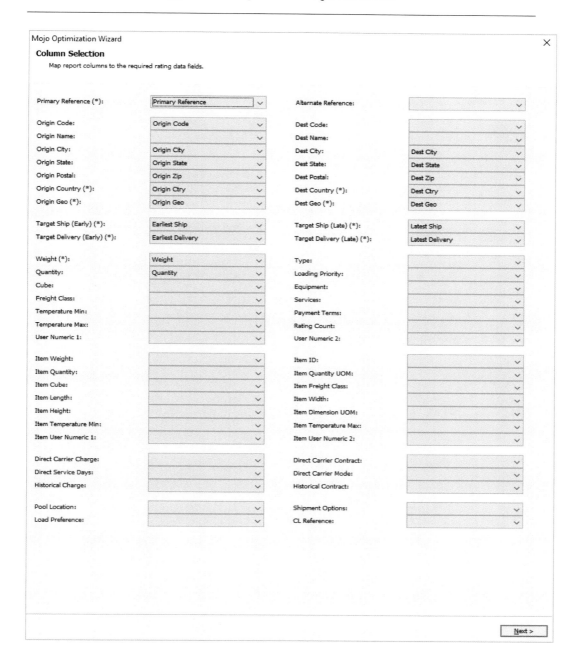

Fig. 5-10: The first screen of the Mojo Optimization Wizard, used to map the correct columns from our shipment data.

At first glance, the series of four "wizard" screens of settings might seem complicated. But we have three things working in our favor.

1. We probably will never change more than a few settings at a time.

2. We can easily save and recall setting settings without having to re-set them every time. So repeat runs of the optimizer will just take a mouse click.

3. You'll quickly get familiar with the "usual suspects" for settings that you need most often in your own work. So despite all the bells and whistles and switches, it's actually pretty easy.

First Wizard Screen – Column Mapping

The purpose of the entire first screen of the wizard (Fig. 5-10) is to let us choose columns from the shipment spreadsheet to use in Mojo.

A few of these fields are marked with an asterisk – these are the ones required for Mojo to run at all. They correspond to the "bare bones minimum" that we said we needed to know about shipments to be able to optimize them.

The first setting, "Primary Reference", names a column in the shipment report that should hold a unique identifier for each shipment. In this example, this is a column in the shipment data that is named (by an amazing coincidence) "Primary Reference."

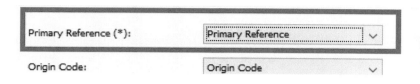

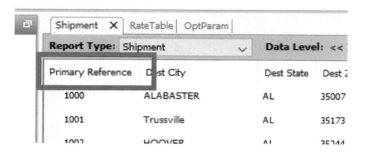

Fig. 5-11: We're using a column from the shipment report named "Primary Reference" to get our shipment numbers.

By the way, there are no rules for shipment IDs. Call them "Shipment 001", "Shipment 002" and so on if you like. Or "1, 2, 3", etc. In the screen above the numbers start at "1000". In actual execution, these numbers might have been generated by a warehouse or order system or a TMS. For test data, it's common to use spreadsheet formulas just to populate a "Primary Reference" column downward.

As for <u>selecting</u> this column – Mojo has pre-selected a column in the spreadsheet named "Primary Reference". Makes sense based on the name! But we could choose a different column. And if our imported file did not have a column that Mojo recognized, we'd have to choose one ourselves anyway.

To illustrate that last point, here's an example where we renamed the "Primary Reference" column as "Random Title" and re-imported the spreadsheet. Now Mojo doesn't have a good idea as to which column to use for primary reference, so it leaves the selection blank and leaves it up to us. (If you leave a required field blank, Mojo will tell you that it can't run.)

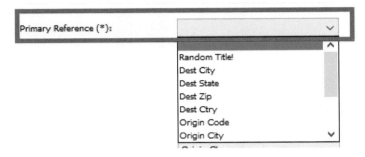

Fig. 5-12: Choosing a column from our shipment data when Mojo does not know which column to use.

The rest of the first wizard screen works the same way. Mojo takes a stab at suggesting a column from the shipment report, and is right a lot of the time. Otherwise we choose the right column. For a numerical field, Mojo asks us to choose from all the columns that contain only numbers; for a date column, columns containing dates; otherwise, all remaining columns.

We've already seen how this works for declaring which columns to use for locations, dates, and freight quantities.

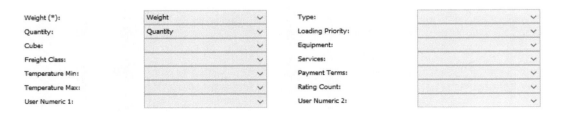

Fig. 5-13: Selection of columns from the shipment data to use for rating and optimization. The right-hand selected values are the names of columns from the shipment spreadsheet.

Besides the fields already discussed, notice that we can choose columns that specify the names of required <u>services</u> or <u>equipment</u> for each shipment. (Remember that each lane in the rate table has a column declaring which services it provides.)

"Type" is a catch-all value that we can use in a lot of ways – we'll see more about it later. "Loading Priority" can be a value indicating that this shipment needs to be loaded on the truck first.

"Rating Count" is a column that contains an arbitrary number that we can use for rating. When we say "arbitrary" -- that means the number can stand for <u>anything</u>, or have no independent meaning at all. Maybe a shipment has a rating count of "3" and our rate table just says: "If a shipment is a '3', then charge this much."

If all the above options aren't enough, notice that there are more possible column choices labeled "User Numeric 1" and "User Numeric 2". These are two more columns than can contain a number that means anything we want, to match against lanes in the rate table.

Item-Level Columns and Rating

The next area of the first wizard screen seems to repeat itself with more options for "Weight", "Quantity" and so on – but notice that all these fields are preceded with the word "Item".

Fig. 5-14: We can supply information to the optimizer at the level of individual items, rate those items separately, and then "roll up" the results for the overall load.

The way that Mojo shipment data works is that if multiple lines share the same ID, each line is treated as <u>a separate item in the same shipment</u>. This gives users the power to rate at a more "granular" item if desired, item by item, and then to "roll up" the results for the overall load.

If these "item" columns are mapped, Mojo knows to rate item by item. If they are NOT mapped but there are multiple lines in the shipment data with the same primary reference anyway – Mojo only uses the <u>first item with the unique ID</u> and treats it as the value for the overall load. That might not be what you want, so be sure to map the "Item" columns if you are using line-by-line item rating.

'Direct' and 'Historical' Columns

The column choices for "Direct" and "Historical" rates can hold values that tell Mojo what to try to "beat" when it optimizes. This might be the actual rate paid in historical shipment data, for example.

We can supply our own "direct" values in these columns. We also will see that Mojo can calculate and install its own "direct" values for future use. A "direct" value means a <u>non-optimized</u> rating, before Mojo has performed any improvements. Typically this rate is the least cost rate if shipped individually that meets or exceeds the date constraints.

Fig. 5-15: Columns for "direct" (non-optimized) and "historical" charges for each shipment that Mojo will try to beat. For example, we might be optimizing a sales prospect's historical data and trying to improve on the rates they previously paid.

Remaining Columns – First Wizard Screen

Fig. 5-16: Bottom of the first wizard screen for column mapping.

The setting "Pool Location" lets us choose a column in the shipment spreadsheet that contains a pre-assigned pool point through which this shipment must travel. We'll see how it's used in the chapter on pooling.

"Shipment Options" can contain a short text command that overrides Mojo's normal behavior <u>for this shipment only</u>. The options for that command are listed in the appendix.

"Load Preference" is a value that we can use to <u>require</u> certain shipments to be placed on the same load. The actual value can be anything. We'll see that we can create and remove our own load preferences on the fly as we re-analyze Mojo's results.

"CL Reference" refers a column that contains a unique identifier – like a load number – for a MercuryGate TMS *customer load*. A "customer load", like a shipment, represents a customer order or requested movement. TMS loads are either "customer" loads or they are "execution" loads – meaning the loads we hire carriers to move, like the ones we'll create in Mojo. Shipments with matching CL references move on the same execution load.

Remember that everything we have seen on the first screen of the Mojo "wizard" deals with mapping columns from our shipment data. When we're done, we can click "Next" and go to the next screen of the wizard. (We also can come back to this screen if we need to.)

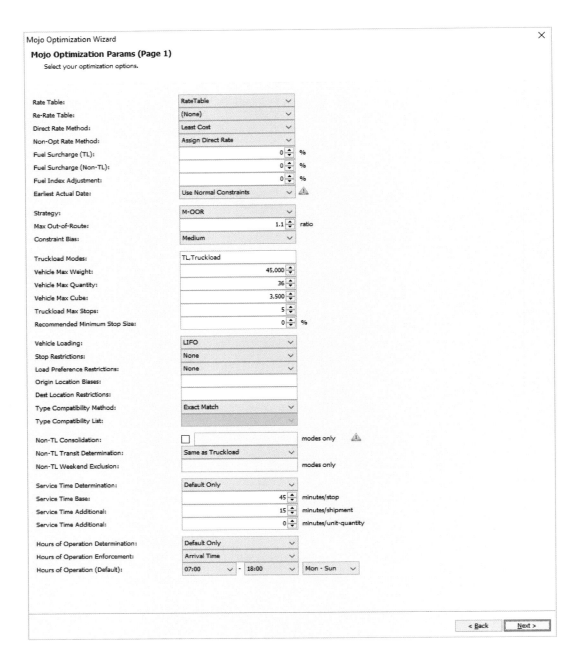

Fig. 5-17: Second screen of the optimization wizard, where users can start setting constraints for the run.

Mojo Wizard Screen 2

The next wizard screen is titled "Mojo Optimization Params (Page 1)". That's because this is the first screen in which we start to set the constraints for the run.

We're going to mention just a few of these settings here. Every setting is described in detail in later chapters or in the appendix. But the overall theme is that we're using the settings on these screens to set the <u>constraints</u> for our optimization.

Modeling Fuel Cost Changes

Fig. 5-18: We can tell Mojo to assume hypothetical fuel increases to test their effect on optimizations.

The fuel settings allow us to test the impact of fuel increases by truckload versus non-truckload modes, or by bumping up an overall "fuel index" if one is being used in the optimization.

'Earliest Actual Date' (For Real-time Execution)

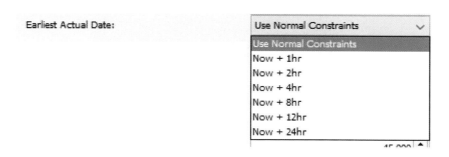

Fig. 5-19: Options for 'Earliest Actual Date' parameter.

The point of the "Earliest Actual Date" setting is that we might be running data from the past for analysis – or we might be running live data to create new execution loads. In that case, we want to tell Mojo to create pickups and drops <u>only in the future</u>.

Non-TL Consolidation

The setting labeled "Non-TL Consolidation" is important – it determines whether our optimization model is allowed to consolidate non-truckload modes, as well as truckload:

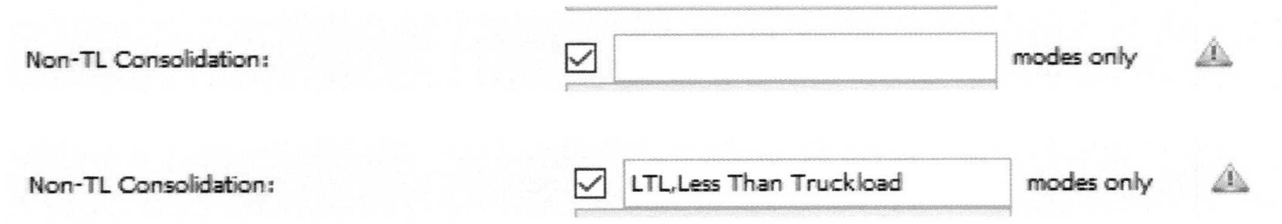

Fig. 5-20: Ways to set the "Non-TL Consolidation" parameter.

This is a setting that some Mojo users routinely enable every single time, or just save their setting to make sure it is enabled.

By default, Mojo consolidates for <u>truckload</u> modes. This checkbox enables consolidation by other modes at well.

Once you check this box, you can enter a <u>list</u> of other modes you want to consolidate, separated by commas. Or if you check the box, and leave the space blank, Mojo will look consolidation opportunities on <u>all</u> non-truckload modes.

A little lower on this wizard screen, notice there are settings for "Service Time" and "Hours of Operation". We'll look at how those work in the chapters on locations, pool and cross-dock strategies.

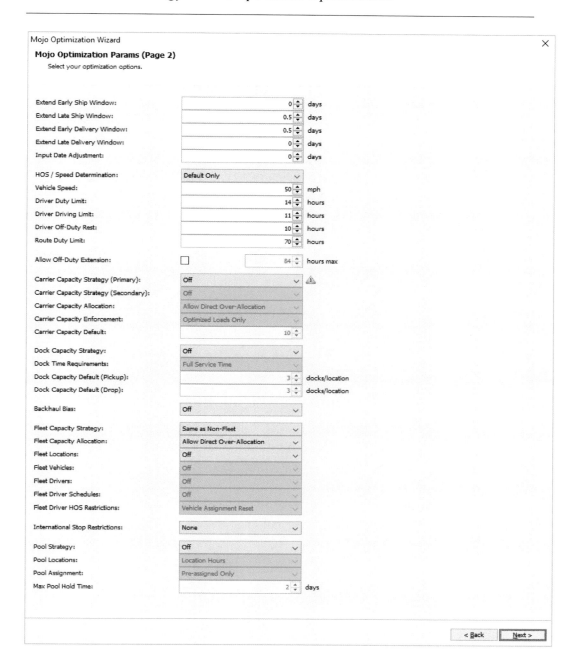

Fig. 5-21: Third screen of the optimization wizard.

Mojo Wizard Screen 3

The next wizard screen (Fig. 5-21) lists more options for setting constraints for the optimization. We've already talked about the options at the top of this screen for extending time windows.

We'll cover the rest in later chapters – carrier capacity, dock capacity, private fleet optimization and pool and cross-docking.

Final Mojo Wizard Screen

The last screen of the wizard (Fig. 5-23, next page) starts with options to enforce the requirements for <u>equipment</u> and <u>services</u> as specified in columns in the shipment data.

Equipment Enforcement: ☐   ⚠

Services Enforcement: ☐   ⚠

Fig. 5-22: Check one or both of these boxes to require that equipment and services listed in the shipment data must match only lanes in the rate table that provide them.

Services and equipment are <u>not</u> enforced by default, since many users are simply looking to build routes and test assumptions.

Notice the section of settings related to "green" factors for carbon emission. Mojo calculates an estimated carbon savings for each optimization run, based on the factors set here. The default values are based on U.S. Department of Energy and international scientific standards. For details see the appendix.

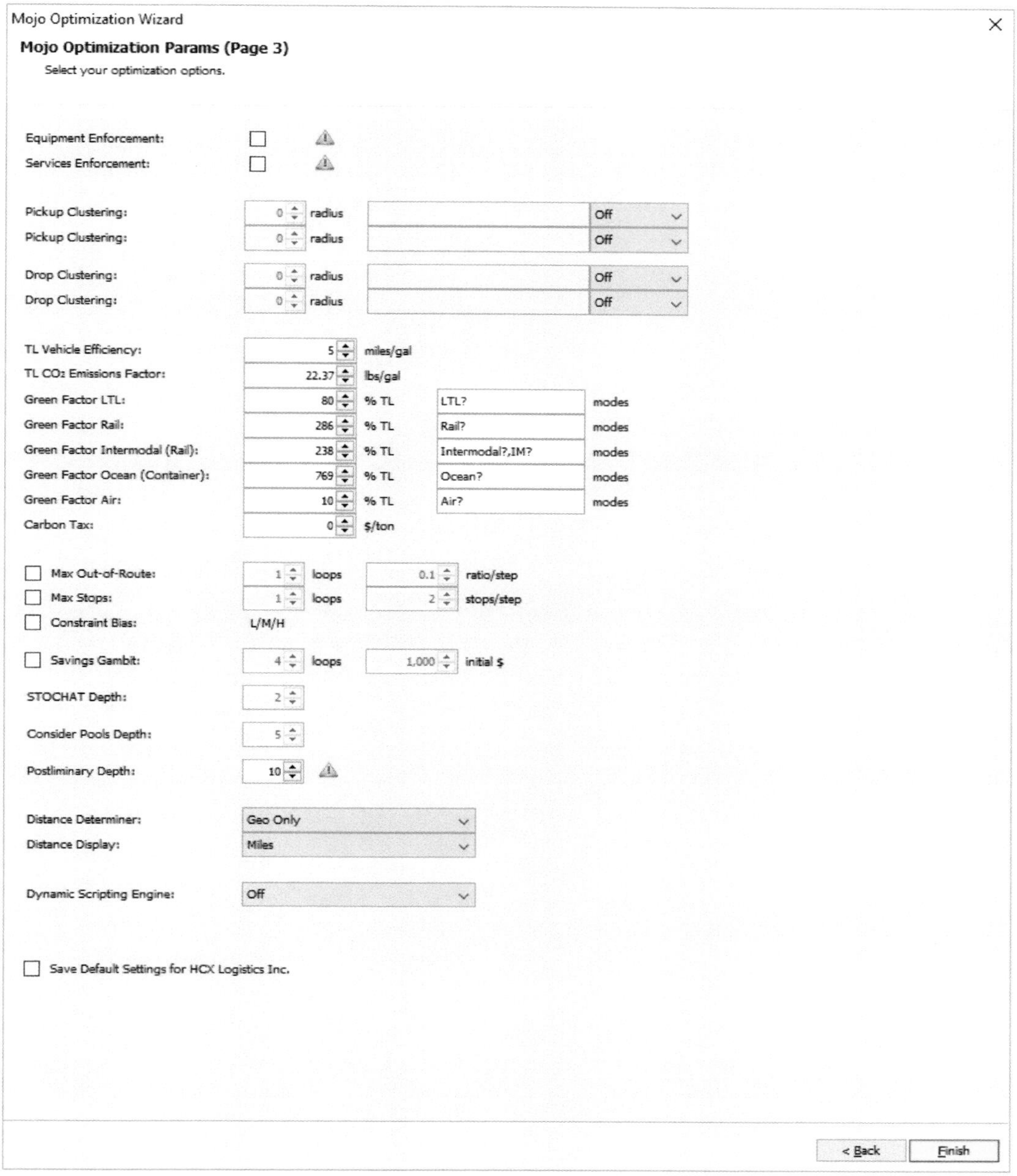

Fig. 5-23: Final screen of optimization wizard.

Of the remaining settings on the final screen, some deal with "looping" scenarios – running Mojo repeatedly to test different values for the same setting – and <u>depth</u> settings for how deeply to conduct optimization calculations. Again, see the appendix.

Notice the checkbox at the bottom of the final screen: "Save Default Settings". Now that we've been through all four screens to set things up the way we want, we might want to save them as our default, to be set automatically the next time Mojo runs.

At the bottom of the first three wizard screens, we've had the option to proceed to the next screen or to go back to the previous one. On this final screen, the button named "Next" is now named "Finish".

At the bottom of the first three wizard screens, we've had the option to proceed to the next screen or to go back to the previous one. On this final screen, the button named "Next" is now named "Finish".

Once we've given the optimizer everything we have, we tell it to go run the optimization. Now we'll see what the results look like and the kinds of things we can do with them.

Modern transportation optimizers such as Mojo allow you to save your settings in reusable models for facilitating execution and for automating operational creation of loads. These screens allow tweaking and evaluation of changes to hone the model to be as effective as possible.

Discussion Questions

1. The optimization wizard discussed in this chapter is really showing the user how to create optimization models. Why would a user want to create multiple models?

2. The text in the chapter tried to stress that the optimization wizard looks more complicated than it actually is. What were the reasons cited for making such a claim and why do you think the author thought it was necessary?

3. Discuss the application of concept of generic parameters/constraints vs. specific parameters/constraints?

4. In setting up an optimization, we have the option of mapping a "Direct Cost" column from our shipment data. What does this information represent, and how does the optimizer try to use it? What's the difference between the "Direct Cost" and "Historical Cost" columns?

###

Chapter 6: Using the Models

Understanding what the optimizer model is doing starts with the results. A list of loads alone is not enough to understand what the tool is presenting. The modern transportation optimizer not only creates the loads but provides key metrics in reports to help understand what is happening with the results.

Time window reports and others show the validity of the model and allow users to understand if the loads can actually be executed. The latest optimizer tools must allow sharing of this information with or without utilization of a TMS. These tools must also show quickly why a given shipment could not be combined with another shipment, something that is many times very difficult to figure out manually.

In this chapter we'll look at the scope of the results we expect back from the optimizer, the nature of the "direct cost" that we using as a benchmark, and what to do about shipments that could not be optimized. In the chapter that follows this one, we'll talk about post-run analysis and searching for further improvements.

The results that we get back from an optimization should include information such as:

- The loads, routes, schedules and rates that the optimizer proposes, with the ability to drill into details of each load and to understand why it was built.

- A savings calculated against a benchmark. The benchmark could be actual historical cost or values supplied in the shipment data, or could be the optimizer's own calculation of non-optimized cost.

- A report of any shipments that could <u>not</u> be optimized according to the given constraints, with options for what to do about it.

- The ability to execute the recommended loads (if we are optimizing for execution) or to save and share our results for analysis, demonstration and other purposes.

Let's take another look at the results screen we saw earlier from the Mojo optimizer. This is the screen that appears after the user has approved the four screens of the optimization wizard and clicked "Finish" to run the calculation.

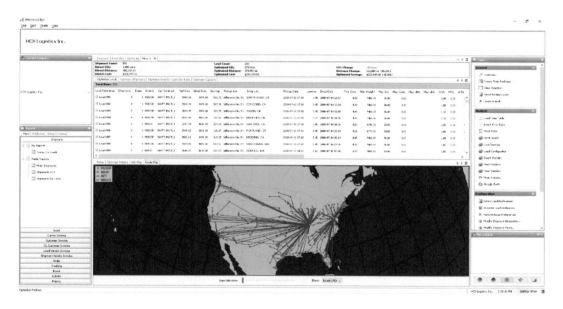

Fig. 6-1: Results screen with summary statistics, lists of recommended loads and routes, graphical output of the run, supporting notes and metrics, and commands for running additional analysis.

The three columns of results at the top summarize the input data, the recommended output, and the estimated savings in terms of distance, cost and carbon emissions.

Shipment Count:	591	Load Count:	200
Direct CO₂:	1,090 tons	Optimized CO₂:	379 tons
Direct Distance:	492,140 mi	Optimized Distance:	171,051 mi
Direct Cost:	$515,777.02	Optimized Cost:	$292,129.53

CO₂ Change:	711 tons
Distance Change:	321,088 mi (65.2%)
Optimized Savings:	$223,647.49 (43.4%)

Fig. 6-2: The optimizer proposes consolidating 591 input shipments into 200 loads, at considerable savings of total distance and cost.

About 'Direct Cost'

The "direct cost" benchmark represents the cost the optimizer was trying to "beat". This might be a proposed or historical rate supplied in the shipment data. Or if no direct cost was supplied, the optimizer can calculate its own direct, non-optimized cost.

Direct Carrier Charge:		Direct Carrier Contract:	
Direct Service Days:		Direct Carrier Mode:	
Historical Charge:		Historical Contract:	

Fig. 6-3: On the first page of the optimizer wizard, we can map a "Direct Carrier Charge" column name from our shipment data to use as the benchmark to beat – for example, the rates actually paid in historical shipment data. This column might or not be the same column used for "Historical Charge", if any.

If we are calculating the direct charge, the normal method is to use the least-cost rate that is found before any optimization. There are two variants: Using the least-cost rate that also meets on-time delivery (otherwise falling back to the least cost rate anyway), or requiring an on-time delivery to find a direct rate at all. If no direct rate is found, the shipment is not optimized.

These options are found in the "Direct Rate Method" setting on the second wizard screen.

Fig. 6-4: Wizard options for calculating direct rates for the optimization benchmark. A simple least-cost rating often is fine, but there also are options to try to comply with transit-time constraints.

If our direct-rate calculation is based on time-consuming calls to an outside server (carrier web service rating, for example), we can <u>save</u> our direct-cost results after the first lookup, and re-use them in future runs. This can save a lot of time. The command "Sync Direct Rates" stores the calculated values as columns in the optimizer's shipment data for re-use.

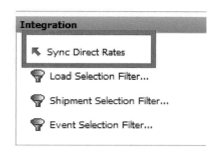

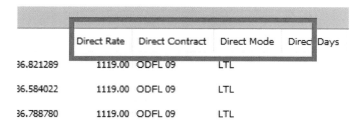

Fig. 6-5: Option to save calculated direct-cost instead of doing the same calls to an outside server again and again.

Load, Shipment and Event Results

Each load that is proposed in the optimization results consists of one or more of the original shipments, consolidated when possible while obeying the required constraints.

In Mojo, load results are found in the "Optimizer Loads" tab:

Fig: 6-6: The 'Optimizer Loads' tab in optimization results.

The level of detail in these results is extensive. Here are the columns of information displayed for each load in the list:

Load Reference	ID assigned for this load
Shipments	# shipments consolidated on this load
Stops	# stops planned for this load
Events	A string of characters: P = pickup, D = drop, I = inbound pool, O = outbound pool, R = return to origin, < > = departure/arrival at equipment domicile
Opt Contract	Name of contract used for optimized rate
Opt Rate	Optimized contract rate
Direct Rate	Direct ship cost, either from shipment data or from calculation
Savings	Direct rate minus optimized rate
Pickup Loc	First pickup event location
Pickup Date	First pickup planned date
Leeway	Estimate of how long (in fractional days) pickup could be delayed and still achieve on-time delivery – can be useful in continuous optimization scenarios, e.g., this has to move now, could wait until next run this afternoon, etc.
Drop Date	Last drop planned date
Trans Days	Total planned transit time
Weight/Qty/Cube	Totals of these values for all shipments on this load
Max UNI1, UNI2	Max value of any one shipment on this load for the "user-defined" columns in the shipment data

OOR	"Out of route" calculation – the ratio of the sum of all legs to the direct distance between origin and dest - the "zig-zag factor" of the route
RTO	Distance of any return-to-origin leg, for example, if required in private fleet scenarios
#PE, #DE	Number of pickup and drop events
Equipment, Services	Names of any equipment or services specified for this load
Type	Shipment type, if used for grouping
Temp Min, Temp Max	If these values were set and used
Opt Distance	Sum of legs for this route
Direct Distance	Sum of non-optimized shipment distances
Distance Diff	Direct distance minus optimized
CO2 Change	Estimated carbon savings vs direct ship
Payment Terms	If specified, e.g. "Prepaid", "COD"
Flags	Messages for loads that violate constraints
Server Rate	If a server rating was performed
Hist Rate	Value from historical data, if it was mapped in wizard

The "plus-sign" icon next to each load expands its display to show additional "drill-down" categories of detail for this load: detailed views of its shipments, events, and any related loads (for example, the next legs in a pooling scenario), as well as details about the rates and rating process for this load.

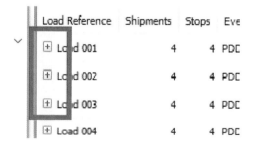

Fig. 6-7: The plus sign opens an expanded display for "drilling down" into new sections of details about the proposed load.

Fig. 6-8: Drill-down detail of individual <u>shipments</u> on the load.

Fig. 6-9: Drill-down detail of each <u>event</u> on the optimized load.

Fig. 6-10: Drill-down of all _related loads_. There might be entries here for each shipment's next leg in a pooling scenario, for example.

Fig. 6-11: Drill-down detail of _rating results_ for this optimized load.

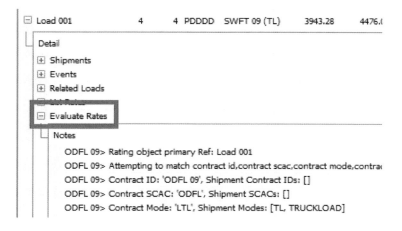

Fig. 6-12: Line-by-line explanation of the _rating process_ performed on each load for each contract considered.

The previous few examples and images dealt with details in the "Optimizer Loads" tab. The next tab, labeled "Optimizer Shipments", lets us look through the "other end of the telescope" from the point of view of each shipment.

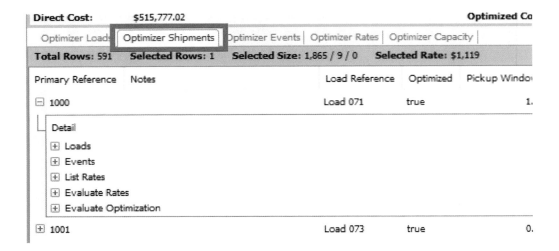

Fig. 6-13: The 'Optimizer Shipments' results tab lets us drill into details for each original shipment – the loads on which it is placed, its sequence of events and drops, and rating information.

For shipments, the drill-down option labeled "Evaluate Optimization" shows a glimpse into the optimizer's decision-making. This section when expanded shows why the optimizer <u>could not put this shipment on any other load in the run.</u>

Load Reference	Shipments	Stops	Events	Max Weight	Max Quantity	Max Cube	Out-of-Route	New Load Notes	Orig Load
Load 001	5	6	PPDDDD	9325.00	45.00	0.00	1.20	Stop-constrained	
Load 002	5	6	PPDDDD	9325.00	45.00	0.00	1.20	Stop-constrained	
Load 003	5	6	PPDDDD	9325.00	45.00	0.00	1.35	Stop-constrained	
Load 004	5	6	PPDDDD	9325.00	45.00	0.00	1.32	Stop-constrained	
Load 005	4	5	PPDDD	8610.00	41.00	0.00	1.20	MOOR-constrained	
Load 006	5	6	PPDDDD	8635.00	42.00	0.00	1.30	Stop-constrained	
Load 007	5	6	PPDDDD	9325.00	45.00	0.00	1.25	Stop-constrained	
Load 008	5	6	PPDDDD	9325.00	45.00	0.00	1.31	Stop-constrained	
Load 009	4	5	PPDDD	8895.00	42.00	0.00	1.26	MOOR-constrained	

Fig. 6-14: The optimizer explains why no other load or route worked for this shipment. The most common reasons are that adding this shipment would have violated a stop limit, or taken the route too far out of its way ('MOOR' = 'Max out Of Route').

The remaining results tabs are labeled "Optimizer Events", showing the results of the run as a list of events, "Optimizer Rates", showing rating details for each load, and "Optimizer Capacity", showing utilization of carrier trucks for each <u>day</u> of the time period covered by the optimization. We'll come back to the last tab in the chapter on carrier capacity.

Direct Cost: $515,777.02

Optimizer Loads | Optimizer Shipment | **Optimizer Events** | Optimizer Rates | Opti

Total Rows: 791   Selected Rows: 5

Load Reference	Type	Seq Num	Distance	Weight	Quantity	Cube	U
⊟ Load 001	Pickup	1	0.00	7460.00	36.00	0.00	

    Detail
    ⊞ Hours of Operation
    ⊞ Shipments

| ⊞ Load 001 | Drop | 2 | 2364.53 | 1865.00 | 9.00 | 0.00 | |
| ⊞ Load 001 | Drop | 3 | 2400.80 | 1865.00 | 9.00 | 0.00 | |

Direct Cost:	$515,777.02								Optimized (

Optimizer Loads | Optimizer Shipments | Optimizer Events | **Optimizer Rates** | ptimizer Capacity

Total Rows: 200   Selected Rows: 1

Load Reference	Contract	SCAC	Mode	Service	Lane	Total	Item	Accessorial
Load 001	SWFT 09	SWFT	TL	Standard	USA to USA	3943.28	3718.28	225.00
Load 002	SWFT 09	SWFT	TL	Standard	USA to USA	3918.74	3693.74	225.00
Load 003	SWFT 09	SWFT	TL	Standard	USA to USA	4098.45	3873.45	225.00

Direct Cost:	$515,777.02				Optim

Optimizer Loads | Optimizer Shipments | Optimizer Events | Optimizer Rate | **Optimizer Capacity**

Total Rows: 8

Date	^ 1	Day	SCAC	Origin Code	Capacity Used
2008-07-10		Thu	SWFT	47310	7
2008-07-11		Fri	SWFT	47310	17
2008-07-12		Sat	SWFT	47310	8
2008-07-12		Sat	SWFT	O21113	2
2008-07-13		Sun	SWFT	47310	27
2008-07-13		Sun	SWFT	O21113	17
2008-07-14		Mon	SWFT	47310	51
2008-07-14		Mon	SWFT	O21113	51

Fig. 6-15: Optimization results displayed by views of all created events, rating details by load, and day-by-day usage of carrier capacity.

The optimizer also offers a variety of charts and graphs about the optimization result. These include Gantt-style workflow charts displaying load and event times, pivot-table analysis, load configurations and statistics for events, pool and private fleet scenarios, if they are involved.

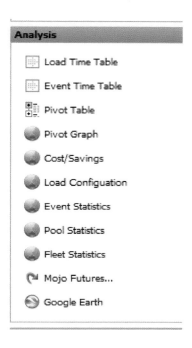

Fig. 6-16: More options for viewing optimization results.

Lastly, the map options allow the highlighting and selection of loads. Pickups are marked in green; drops in red. Optimized routes are marked in blue and loads with shipments that could not be optimized are displayed in red. If pool points are used, they are marked in light blue.

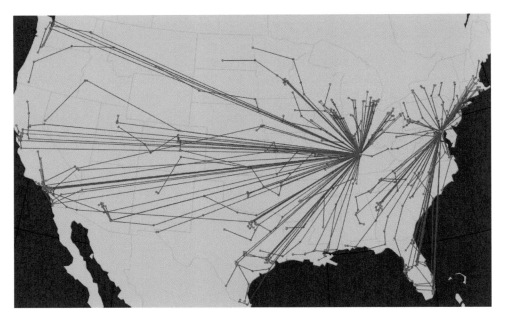

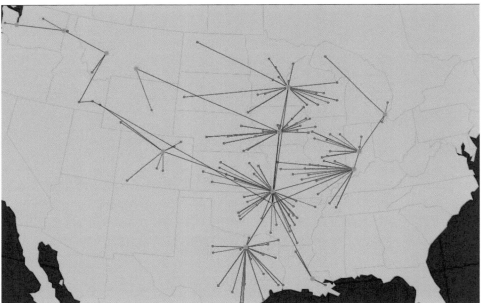

Fig. 6-17: Examples of mapping output from optimization runs.

Non-Optimized Shipments

So far we've talked about viewing the optimized loads that resulted from the run. It's time to stress a key point:

Some shipments might not be optimized.

Or at least, in some cases, an improvement on direct cost cannot be found under the given conditions and constraints. There's something about the requirements or time windows that made this shipment incompatible with any other shipment or load.

One of the beauties of modern transportation optimizer is the ability to show the user why the shipment could not be optimized. One of the first things to check after an optimization run is which shipments were not optimized. In Mojo, the "Optimized" true/false result for each shipment is found under the "Optimizer Shipments" tab. (Remember that you can click in the column header to sort the list, so we can see all our "true" or "false" results at the top as we wish.)

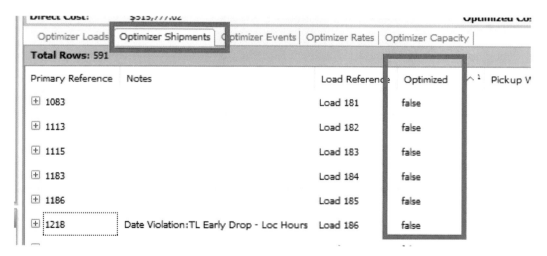

Fig. 6-18: The 'Optimizer Shipments' tab informs us that these shipments could not be optimized, at least not under the given constraints and conditions.

Remember too that any shipment row may be expanded to review its sub-section labeled "Evaluate Optimization" to tell us why the shipment did not work with any other proposed load. The most common reasons are that trying to combine this load would violate the stop limit, the load size, or the route's "out of route" ratio.

Notice in the "Optimizer Shipments" tab the presence of a column labeled "Notes". The presence of a note tells us not only could the shipment not be optimized, but it could not be put on a load at all without violating the given constraints!

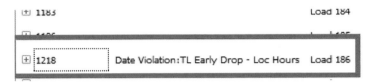

Fig. 6-19: It is not possible to optimize this shipment under the given constraints on hours of operation.

We also will see a warning attached to the loads that the optimizer tries to build from these "trouble" shipments. The loads are there – but they carry their own warning that they break the rules of the constraints. Look at the "Flags" column of the load list (again you can click to sort and bring all the trouble spots to the top):

Direct Cost:	$515,777.02						Optimiz

Optimizer Loads	Optimizer Shipments	Optimizer Events	Optimizer Rates	Optimizer Capacity

Total Rows: 200

t	Max Qty	Max Cube	Flags	∨ ¹	Ma	UN1	Max UN2	OOR
00	9.00	0.00	SV(Date Violation:TL Early Drop - Loc Hours)					1.00
00	15.00	0.00	SV(Date Violation:TL Early Drop - Loc Hours)					1.00
00	36.00	0.00						1.04
00	36.00	0.00						1.05

Fig. 6-20: These loads, like their related shipments, are flagged for a violation. They cannot be executed without violating the specified time constraints.

What should we do with non-optimized shipments? Depending on your business practice, you might:

(1) Throw them "back into the pool" for the next run. This assumes the business is optimizing often enough for the time windows to work. We'll touch on this kind of "continuous optimization" approach in chapter 12.

(2) Try to find improvements to our optimization using the analysis data we have at our fingertips, and re-running the optimizer. More about this is covered in the next chapter.

(3) Execute them as non-optimized loads, using the direct-ship cost. For those shipments that are "merely" non-optimized because there was no better solution, we can console ourselves that at least we gave it a shot. As for loads that violate constraints, it's up to you to decide whether that is an acceptable business practice. (Besides, we might be optimizing simply for analysis, in which the flagged loads are merely informational.)

On the second screen of the optimizer wizard, there's a setting named "Non-Opt Rate Method" that sets a preference for calculating the direct rate for non-optimized shipments. The options are similar to those described for the "Direct Rate Method" – assign the least-cost rate regardless, or try to assign one that still obeys transit time requirements. In the chapters on carrier capacity and fleet management, we'll see settings for whether to make non-optimized shipments "obey" limits on capacity anyway.

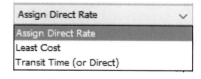

Fig. 6-21: Wizard setting for how to assign direct cost shipments that could not be optimized.

Note that while this section describes how to review non-optimized loads, the same technique described can be used to review any shipment. If a user is trying to understand why a given shipment did not get combined on a given load, reviewing the optimization results will show the reason.

Saving and Sharing Results

A <u>Mojo package</u> is a saved, multi-tabbed spreadsheet that preserves the result of the run, including any additional charts and graphs.

You have options for what you save: All content, input or output only (if all you need to do is show results in a presentation), and as a "flash" package that preserves Mojo's last calculations so that they do not have to be re-run.

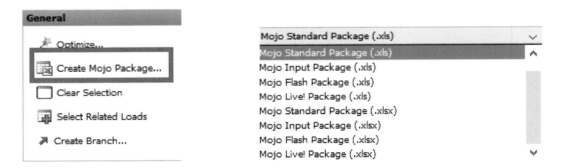

Fig. 6-22: Command and options for saving a 'Mojo package'.

One of the tabs in a saved Mojo package is of special note: It has a label, "OptParam" (short for "Optimizer Parameters") that lists all the wizard settings used in this run. When the Mojo package is re-imported and run, Mojo obeys the settings in this tab. In other words, a report of type "OptParam" that is open will control the settings for the optimizer – very useful.

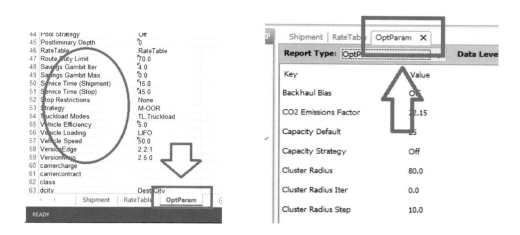

Fig. 6-23: In a saved Mojo package, a tab named 'OptParam' remembers all wizard settings. When the package is re-loaded, the "OptParam" report type tells Mojo which settings to use.

Let's run through some of the other commands available in the task lists on the right side of the screen:

Clear Selection	Un-highlight the selected entries in a Mojo list of shipments, rates, etc.
Select Related Loads	"Related loads" include other legs on which these shipments should move in a pooling scenario. Make sure related loads are included for actual execution.
Create Branch...	Launch a new optimization only for the selected entries. Often used in analysis.
Mojo Futures...	We'll see this used in a later chapter. Runs repeated loops on staggered variables to test the effect of projected changes.
Retain/Propose/Remove Load Preference	Force/unforce shipments onto the same load. Often used in analysis, see next chapter.

Modify Shipment Endpoints/Pool…	Another way to reach into the result and force an outcome. See next chapter.
Sync Direct Rates	Discussed earlier in this chapter. Installs the current direct-cost calculations as columns in the shipment data for re-use.
Load/Shipment/Event Selection Filter	Launch a small "wizard" for filtering these lists. Example usage: Before creating actual execution loads, filter out any non-optimized shipments or loads with warning flags.
Create Server Loads	See following discussion.

Actual Execution – 'Create Server Loads'

If the shipments used in optimization came from the TMS, then the optimization results can be sent back to the TMS for the creation of live execution loads via the command labeled "Create Server Loads".

Fig. 6-24: 'Create Server Load' command uses optimizer results to create actual execution loads in the TMS.

Once the user confirms the command, several things happen:

- The TMS generates its own "real" primary references for each newly created load, according to the company's TMS settings.

- A server re-rating is added to the "Server Rate" column in Mojo's "Optimized Loads" tab.

- The carrier and rate on the load are determined by the Mojo contract ID – if the contract exists in the TMS, the load is auto-re-rated and its status is set to "Rated." Otherwise, a rate from the Mojo data is created and the status is set to "Edge Rated." (The implication is that there is some exception process for tendering the load manually to a carrier with a non-TMS contract.)

- The plan dates are set according to rules set up during your implementation.

- A column headed "Run ID," with a unique run identifier, is added to Mojo's Load and Shipment reports. This is a reportable field in the TMS as well, and shows the load was created from a Mojo run.

Once loads are created in the TMS, they can be tendered – or auto-tendered, if set up – in the usual workflow.

It can be a good practice, before "Create Server Loads", to make sure that (1) any related loads in a pooling scenario are included in the loads to create, via the "Select Related Loads" command described above, and (2) any screening of undesirable entries has been performed by the "Selection Filter" commands, for example, loads with non-optimized shipments or those with flags for violations. See also the chapter on the "Mojo Dark" feature for automating this process.

In the next chapter we'll talk about analysis, re-optimization for improvement, and troubleshooting.

Discussion Questions

1. In the statistical summary of the optimization run presented at the top of the results screen, what do the terms "optimized" versus "direct" indicate? Why is the direct rate such an important concept?

2. A section of this chapter discusses at some length what to do about "non-optimized" shipments. Why do they still exist, if the whole point of the software is to "optimize" our shipments? What can we do about them?

3. Sometimes it appears that the optimizer did something wrong in not combining something with another although both optimized. Why could that happen? What tools are available to understand why it happened?

4. One of the options for an optimization result is the command "Create Server Loads". This allows clients of the software to send their optimization results to the server to create as "real" loads for actual execution. Is this a good idea?

###

Chapter 7: Tuning the Models

Once optimization models are created, they can be used and tuned as needed for the best results. The modern transportation optimizer will show the user what the model is doing. Not only do the results indicate the success of the optimizer, the model statistics also show what is constraining the model as well as where there are issues. The optimizer allows running multiple results and saving those for comparison. These tools combine to give a never-before-seen arsenal for the planner to understand what is happening during the optimization routines.

In designing any optimization, whether for live execution or for business intelligence, we're unlikely to sit down for the very first time, throw everything together, and declare:

"Exactly perfect! These are the settings and parameters we'll use from now on."

There's almost always room for improvement – there are usually ways to "optimize the optimization", so to speak.

So if some of our shipments are still routinely not getting optimized, we might look for chances to tweak the constraints while still meeting our overall requirements.

If we're saving X percent against direct cost, that's great – but should we at least look to see whether we can save X-plus-Y?

Or we might even want to move in the opposite direction – we might consider "spending" some of our optimization savings back in the direction of a desired network result such as using fewer trucks, leveling the use of facilities, meeting pool requirements, or other considerations. (In other words, better network optimization is not always least-cost optimization.)

The beauty of these kinds of questions is that *they don't cost anything to answer*. All we have to do is change the rules – our constraints – and test the results. It would be all the better if our optimizer keeps track and tells us what is changing, and why.

Where's the Pinch?

For starters, we can ask our optimizer to tell us where our constraints are the "tightest". In the results of a run, look at the "Notes" tab at the bottom of the screen, and scroll to the section titled "Limiting Constraints". The statistics in Fig. 7-1 are illuminating:

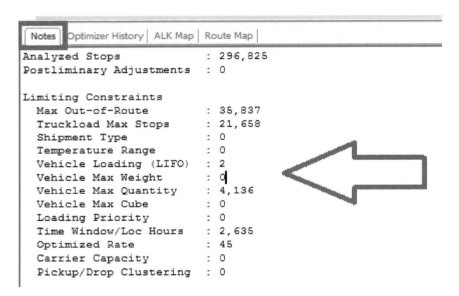

```
Notes   Optimizer History   ALK Map   Route Map

Analyzed Stops              : 296,825
Postliminary Adjustments    : 0

Limiting Constraints
  Max Out-of-Route          : 35,837
  Truckload Max Stops       : 21,658
  Shipment Type             : 0
  Temperature Range         : 0
  Vehicle Loading (LIFO)    : 2
  Vehicle Max Weight        : 0
  Vehicle Max Quantity      : 4,136
  Vehicle Max Cube          : 0
  Loading Priority          : 0
  Time Window/Loc Hours     : 2,635
  Optimized Rate            : 45
  Carrier Capacity          : 0
  Pickup/Drop Clustering    : 0
```

Fig. 7-1: Explanation of which constraints in the optimization became the most common basis for rejecting proposed combinations.

In the above example, the optimizer considered nearly 300,000 possible stops, and of course rejected the vast majority. In the "Limiting Constraints" section, we can see the most common reasons <u>why</u> particular combinations did not work.

The most common limiting constraint (as often is the case in practice) was "Max Out-of-Route". This is the "zig-zag factor" of the route allowed by the optimizer.

Typically we're not going to allow the legs of a route to add up to more than about 1.3 or 1.4 times the direct distance between first pickup and last drop(and that's already pushing it). We can build routes with more zig-zag than that, but in the real world our carriers are going to start rejecting them.

Let's test the effect of tweaking this constraint. Using the same data as in the run above, choose "Optimize" from the right-hand menu (this really means we're going to re-optimize). But this time, in the second wizard screen, let's bump our Max Out-of-Route by a couple of tenths. The default setting is 1.1, so let's go to 1.3.

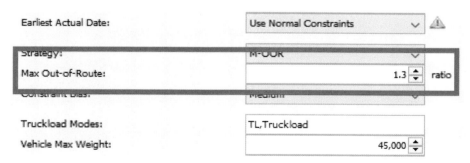

Fig. 7-2: We'll re-optimize, and this time allow routes that zig-zag a bit more.

As it turns out, if we can have a little more zig-zag, we can build a slightly smaller number of loads – in this example we went from 200 loads down to 195, although it didn't save much money.

But now in the 'Limiting Constraints" list under the Notes tab, we can see that Max Out-of-Route is no longer the tightest "pinch" on our load-building (Fig. 7-3). The new "most enforced" constraint is the number of max stops on a route.

```
Analyzed Stops            : 329,049
Postliminary Adjustments  : 0

Limiting Constraints
 Max Out-of-Route         : 26,058
 Truckload Max Stops      : 29,008
 Shipment Type            : 0
 Temperature Range        : 0
 Vehicle Loading (LIFO)   : 340
 Vehicle Max Weight       : 0
 Vehicle Max Quantity     : 10,536
 Vehicle Max Cube         : 0
 Loading Priority         : 0
 Time Window/Loc Hours    : 4,950
 Optimized Rate           : 78
 Carrier Capacity         : 0
 Pickup/Drop Clustering   : 0
```

Fig. 7-3: Allowing more wiggle room in the 'Max Out-of-Route' constraint meant that fewer loads were rejected for that reason.

Notice some of the other most frequent reasons that loads were rejected – max stops on a route, max quantity per vehicle, and after that, time windows and location operating hours. We even lost some opportunities because we had a "Vehicle Loading" requirement of Last In, First Out. If you don't <u>have</u> to have that setting, why impose the condition?

It's up to your own business practices to decide which constraints can be loosened and which can't. Obviously, we can't wave a magic wand and make trucks bigger. But we might be able to create elbow room for the optimizer in settings such as Max Out-of-Route, Max Stops or Vehicle Loading, and several others.

One friendly warning: It's easy to get addicted to playing with parameters to achieve a better and better result. But trying to squeeze everything out of the "Limiting Constraints" list is like trying to squeeze a balloon – there's usually going to be the NEXT "most common reason" no matter how many constraints you widen. And there's always a tradeoff between widening constraints and real-world practicality.

Adjusting Time Windows

One of the most effective and frequently used tweaks is to extend the allowed time windows for shipments. After all, the most significant date usually is the end of the expected delivery range – known in Mojo as "Target Delivery (Late)".

So if we can still get it there by that date, do we have any room to adjust the other time windows – early and late pickup, early delivery? If it helps us build a more convenient route, can we...

- Pick up even earlier than the earliest stated pickup time?
- Pick up later than the latest pickup time, as long as we can still deliver on time?
- Deliver even earlier that the earliest requested delivery time?

Of course, your answer to one of all of these questions might be, "Absolutely not," and we'll have to live with the time windows we have. The pickup might not be ready until X, and absolutely cannot be picked up later than Y, and cannot be delivered until at least Z when the recipient can receive it.

But it's a common practice to extend at least the inner time windows, when (1) we don't care how late the pickup is, as long as it gets delivered on time, and (2) it's acceptable to deliver to a fixed location even earlier than the earliest stated delivery window.

Mojo Optimization Wizard

Mojo Optimization Params (Page 2)

Select your optimization options.

Extend Early Ship Window:	0 ⬍	days
Extend Late Ship Window:	0.5 ⬍	days
Extend Early Delivery Window:	2 ⬍	days
Extend Late Delivery Window:	0 ⬍	days
Input Date Adjustment:	0 ⬍	days

Fig. 7-4: Telling the optimizer it can allow pickups up to a half-day later, and deliveries up to two days earlier, than the time windows in the shipment data.

If the optimizer does take advantage of "stretched" time windows, it will report that fact under the "Optimizer Shipments" results tab. Notice the columns titled "Pickup Window" and "Delivery Window". In Fig. 7-5 we can see that the optimizer routinely took advantage of "earlier than early" delivery.

Shipment | RateTable | OptParam | Mojo 1 ✕

Shipment Count:	591	**Load Count:**	202
Direct CO₂:	1,090 tons	**Optimized CO₂:**	389 tons
Direct Distance:	492,140 mi	**Optimized Distance:**	175,675 mi
Direct Cost:	$515,777.02	**Optimized Cost:**	$298,824.93

Optimizer Loads | Optimizer Shipments | Optimizer Events | Optimizer Rates | Optimizer Capacity

Total Rows: 591

Primary Reference	Notes	Load Reference	Optimized	Pickup Window	Delivery Window	Direct Rat
⊞ 1000		Load 071	true	0.00	-0.53	1119.
⊞ 1001		Load 073	true	0.00	-1.46	1119.
⊞ 1002		Load 073	true	0.00	-1.40	1119.
⊞ 1003		Load 073	true	0.00	-1.58	1119.
⊞ 1004		Load 071	true	0.00	-0.43	705

Fig. 7-5: The 'Optimizer Shipments' tab reports how much the optimizer stretched an early or late time window for that shipment.

Other Possible Adjustments

Load Preference Restrictions is a setting on the second wizard screen that determines how tightly to enforce the "Load Preference" column in shipment data. The possible settings are "None", "Single Only" and "Allow Group".

The "Single Only" setting means that only shipments with the same load preference can be on the same truck. The more permissive "Allow Group" means that shipments the same type must be grouped, but can be on the same load as another type.

Service Time Determination is a setting on the second wizard screen. The settings include a "base" time allowed per stop, plus additional allowances on a per-shipment or per-quantity basis. This can be important depending on the nature of the freight – the default allowance is an additional 15 minutes per additional shipment, but what if a truck consists of many small shipments?

See more about service time in the section below titled "Analysis Tools".

Analysis Tools

'Optimizer History' Tab

The modern transportation optimizer provides tools to compare the runs of different models showing the impact of altering parameters. Each time that we re-optimize and change settings, the 'Optimizer History' tab at the bottom of the results will contain an entry for the new run, a note about which settings were changed, and how the results compare from run to run, model to model. (Fig. 7-6).

Notes	Optimizer History	Route Map												◁ ▷ ▤
Total Rows: 3														
#	Run Date	Elapsed	Savings/Sec	Direct Cost	Opt Cost	Savings	% Sav	Input Ship Legs	Opt Ship Legs	PL Adj	Total Loads	Opt Loads	Direct Miles	
1	2013-06-27 14:56:38	3.96	55911.87	515777.02	292129.53	223647.49	43.36	591	571	0	200	180	492139.71	⌃
2	2013-06-27 15:49:26	2.41	72317.36	515777.02	298824.93	216952.09	42.06	591	572	0	202	183	492139.71	
		-1.55	+16405.49		+6695.40	-6695.40	-1.30		+1		+2	+3		

Fig. 7-6: 'Optimizer History' tab compares the results of each run to the previous.

To restore to a previous run/model, double-click on its entry in the list and the optimizer wizard will re-launch with those parameter values loaded. This feature is useful when you want to experiment with changing one or more parameters to evaluate the alternatives. In the illustration above, for instance, the change made for the second run resulted in smaller savings – in this case, the history tab shows us that we were better off with the first model.

Note: Be sure you are re-optimizing with the "Optimize" command in the Tools menu in Mojo that is present when a Mojo tab is currently selected (Fig. 7-7). The alternative is going back to the original Shipment report and choosing the "Route optimizer..." command. That launches a new, separate run that has its own history tab starting from scratch.

Fig. 7-7: Use the "Optimize..." command from a tab of Mojo results to launch the wizard using the same data and settings. The re-optimization will be recorded in the Optimizer History tab.

'Modify Endpoints/Pools' Commands

It's possible to change the origin or destination for selected shipments. This is useful for running "what-if" scenarios for warehouse sourcing, considering new distribution centers or network facilities, or for planning in-transit, multi-pool traversal.

Let's jump ahead a bit and use a pooling scenario, where our shipments are being picked up, taken to pre-assigned required pool points, and then sent on an outbound leg to their final destination. (We'll learn more about pooling in a coming chapter.)

Here's our starting optimization (Fig. 7-8). The light blue dots represent pool points.

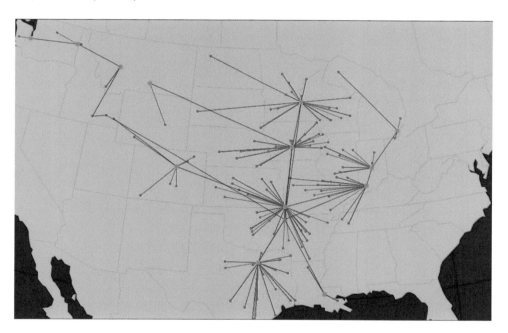

Fig. 7-8: Initial results of a pooling scenario.

It so happens that if we have to obey the preassigned pool points, then we have two in the state of Indiana, in Indianapolis and in Jasper (Fig. 7-9). What might be the impacts of closing Jasper, in terms of sheer transportation costs?

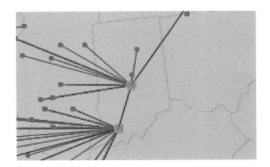

Fig. 7-9: We'll use the 'Modify Shipment Pools' command to test the effect of closing one of the two locations in this state and redirecting to the other.

In the 'Optimizer Loads' tab, select any loads inbound to and outbound from Jasper (sorting the list and using shift-click and control-click as needed), and choose the right-hand command "Modify Shipment Pools".

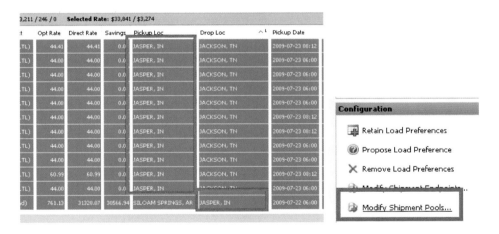

Fig. 7-10: Selecting loads inbound to or outbound from our target location, then choosing the 'Modify Shipment Pools' command.

This opens a list of available options and new locations to use as a pool point (Fig. 7-11). Notice the option at the bottom to change the pool location for <u>all</u> pools, or just the current selection.

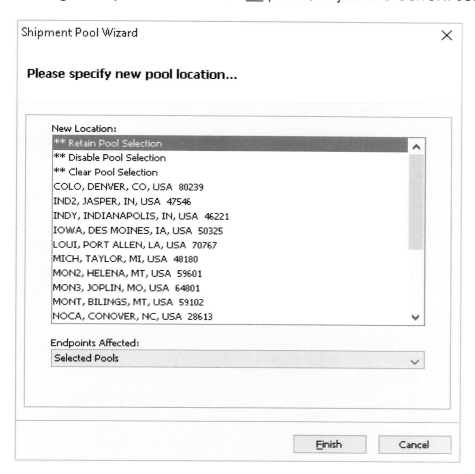

Fig. 7-11: Options for choosing a different pool point for the selected load(s).

We'll choose the location "INDY" and click "Finish". This will redirect any loads previous using Jasper as a pool point. Now we re-optimize and see that it worked – we now have only one pool point in Indiana (Fig. 7-12):

Fig. 7-12: We have successfully used 'Modify Shipment Pools' to eliminate one pool point and redirect loads through another.

Now we can answer the question: What difference did this make? Here are the "before" and "after" optimization results:

Load Count:	643		**Load Count:**	565
Optimized CO$_2$:	321 tons		**Optimized CO$_2$:**	278 tons
Optimized Distance:	145,002 mi		**Optimized Distance:**	125,590 mi
Optimized Cost:	$41,174.84		**Optimized Cost:**	$40,793.44

It looks like the optimizer was able to use fewer trucks and routes overall, presumably because we're filling them up in Indianapolis more efficiently and asking each route to do more. The transportation cost savings are minimal, however, at least in this analysis.

Load/Event Time Tables

Understanding the operational feasibility of the resulting run is critical to understanding the validity of what the optimizer produced. Instead of waiting to see what happens during actual execution, the modern transportation optimizer shows the user how likely the load plan is to be executed successfully. Additional insight into what's happening in our optimization plan can be seen with the timetable graphs located under the "Analysis" window in the right-hand commands in Mojo (Fig. 7-13):

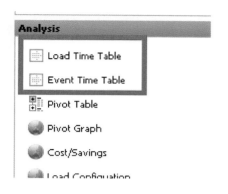

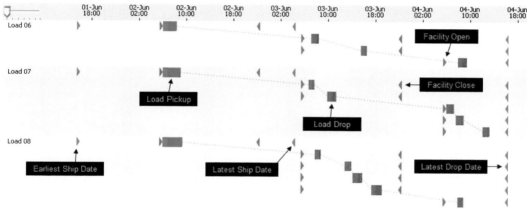

Fig. 7-13: Options for viewing optimization results graphically, including load and event timetable chars.

The blue inward-facing carets indicate earliest ship date and latest drop date. The pink inward-facing carets indicate facility opening and closing.

Light-shaded areas represent the service time base, as specified in the wizard parameters. Dark areas represent additional service times. The key thing to look at is where in the time range the events occur. If a lot of the events are pushing up against the time window, then it is an indication that the optimizer-suggested load will be difficult to achieve if there are any glitches in the process.

Pool locations are indicated by and horizontal orange band.

Take a look at Fig. 7-14, showing unusually long pickup and delivery times:

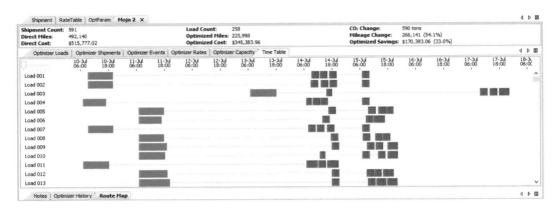

Fig. 7-14: This timetable suggests unusually long time allowances for pickup and delivery. Is there something about our constraints, versus the nature of our freight?

This chart suggests that the per-xxx time settings in the wizard in this case are unrealistic – in fact, this chart was generated by a model with a lot of small individual shipments but specifying 15 minutes of additional time per shipment – no wonder it's taking so long to load and unload!

Looping Improvement Options

The last screen of the optimizer wizard includes options for "looping improvements". Today's transportation optimizer can run repeated iterations, changing the value of selected parameters and reporting which combination produced the best results. The optimizer can also be told how many runs deep to calculate results for differing scenarios.

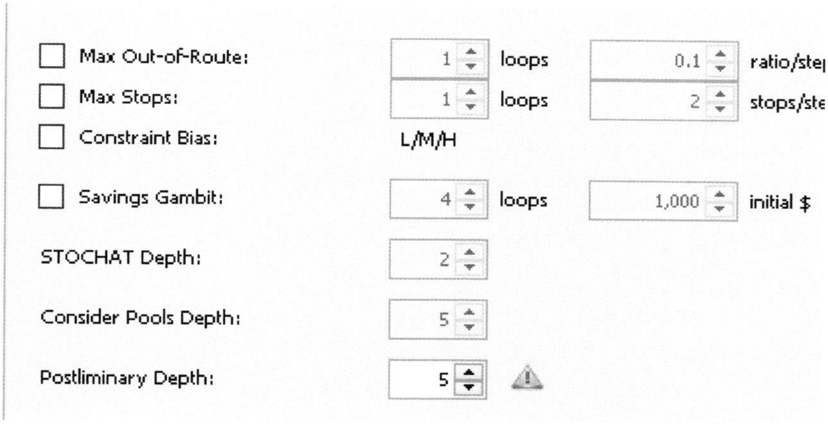

Fig. 7-15: Looping improvement options & search depths on final screen of optimizer wizard settings.

Here's a discussion of these options:

Max Out-of-Route: The first looping improvement option tells Mojo to run multiple M-OOR scenarios with the specified number of loops and the increment to use in each loop. Example: the Max Out-of-Route parameter on the second wizard screen is set to 1.4, then on this screen the settings are 3 additional loops with an increment of 0.1. Mojo runs loops at values of 1.4, 1.3, 1.2 and 1.1. The best option will be listed in the "Notes" tab of Mojo results.

Max Stops: Tells Mojo how many times to consider a new maximum-stop value and how much to increase that value on each loops.

Constraint Bias: Conduct multiple runs with each possible constraint bias, low, medium and high.

Savings Gambit: Potentially finds fewer loads but an overall savings is not guaranteed. At initial settings of 4 loops and initial value of $1,000, Mojo finds loads that each save a minimum of $1,000, then $667, then $333, then finally all remaining loads with any savings.

STOCHAT Depth: Sets Mojo's depth when using the "STOCHAT" strategy. Valid range is 1-4 with default of 2.

Consider Pools Depth: How deep to search in pooling scenarios. Possible values are 1-10 with a default of 5. At a setting of 2, Mojo considers only two runs, all shipments forced through a pool and none forced through a pool. Intermediate settings reflect additional combinations of pooled and non-pooled shipments.

Postliminary Depth: How deep to look overall. Possible values range from 0 to 100. A value of 0 performs no adjustments to Mojo's original solution. Values between 10 and 20 usually provide the best compromise between optimizer time and overall savings. Large datasets (>5000 shipments) will most likely perform unacceptably with values above 5.

In the next section, we'll see a way to tell whether these looping improvements and changes to our depths are worth the extra time.

Cost/Savings Analysis

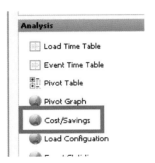

Optimizers can now display detailed savings information to the user for quicker analysis. In Mojo, the "Cost/Savings" option adds three new tabs to the results window labeled "Run Savings" (savings versus time of the optimization run), "Freight Spend" (spending for each optimized carrier) and "Load Savings" (loads grouped by the percentage of savings).

The "Run Savings" chart tells you how much "bang for the buck" the optimizer got from its processing time. This can be useful in determining whether the looping and search-depth options that you have chosen in the optimization wizard are worthwhile, especially on larger runs.

Fig. 7-16 shows two such charts with a striking difference over the length of the run.

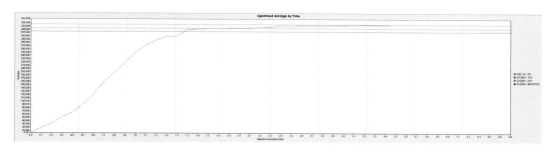

Fig. 7-16: Two run-savings graphs for the same data. The first achieves an optimizing savings of 50.4% in 4.6 seconds, using a postliminary depth of 20. The second achieves 52.4% in 108.9 seconds using a depth of 100. Is two minutes of extra optimizer time worth 2 percentage points?

Why Did the Optimizer Do THAT?

One of the most common questions about optimization is: Why did the optimizer build loads THAT way? Why did it run three different trucks to deliver three shipments that could have been consolidated? Why send shipments across the country to Tacoma, WA, in separate loads on the same day?

The answer is almost always (1) because it was least-cost or (2) because of constraints in the rate table or the settings in the optimization wizard.

Our analysis tools, especially the Load Preferences commands, allow us to dig into the optimizer's decision-making, run new scenarios and even override the optimizer.

Case Study: Tacoma, WA

In this scenario, which we used as an illustration in the first chapter, shipments bound for Tacoma, WA were optimized into two separate loads using the same carrier. We want to know why.

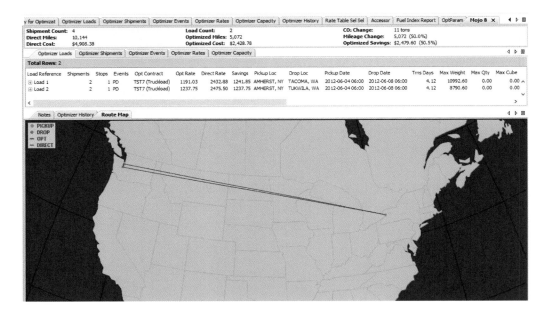

Fig. 7-17: Why send two trucks across the country on the same day, at the same time, when the shipments could have fit on the same truck?

Users can force the optimizer to put the shipments together with the "Propose Load Preference" command. The user may select the two loads, and then choose the "Propose Load Preference" command:

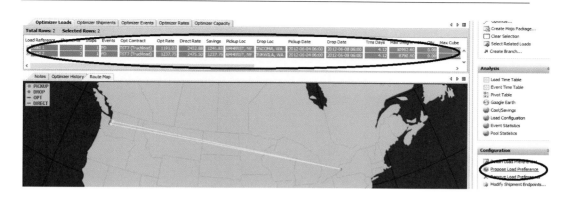

Fig. 7-18: Selecting the loads you want and choosing "Propose Load Preference" assigns these two loads the same "preference" value to use for the next run.

Now when we re-optimize we will choose to enforce the load preference (the default setting was no enforcement):

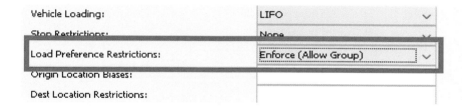

Fig. 7-19: We tell the optimizer to respect the settings that we have created for load preference.

The optimizer obeys us (as it should!) and dutifully puts all shipments on the same load. However, comparing the new load to the old two-load solution, the total cost is now higher. Doing it our way in this example cost $3,587 for one load, versus the original cost of $2,428 for two loads!

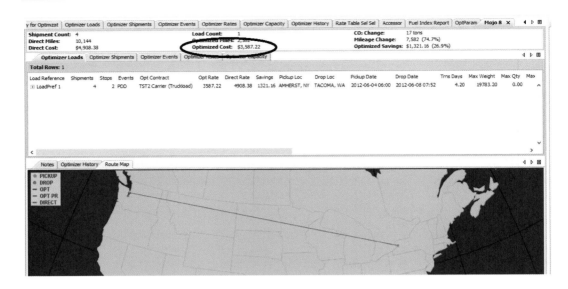

Fig. 7-20: Result of forcing our Tacoma-bound shipments into a single load, using the "Propose Load Preference" command – at a higher cost.

Why? Notice that for the single load, a different carrier was used than for the two separate loads, at a higher rate overall. This suggests we look at the rate table, where we find the answer. The first available carrier has a "Max Stops" value of exactly 1 – so we can't use that carrier for all the shipments. We can have a single load if we insist, but we'll have to use a more expensive carrier to do it.

Fig. 7-21: A look at the rate table explains why Mojo originally broke the shipments into two separate loads to Tacoma – the least-cost carrier has a Max Stops value of 1.

Load Preferences are a useful tool for analyzing Mojo's results and considering alternative scenarios. In this example we used "Propose Load Preference" to force a grouping upon shipments. In the next example, we'll use "Retain Load Preference" to remember our groupings and use them.

Case Study: Rome, GA

In this scenario we have 90 small shipments bound for various destinations in the southeastern U.S. Of these, 32 are bound for a customer facility in Rome, Georgia. We run a Mojo optimization...

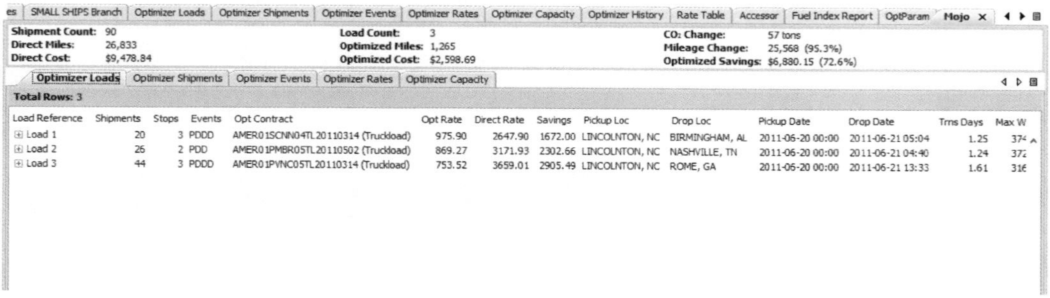

Fig. 7-22: First-pass results at optimizing our 90 small shipments.

... and see that Mojo has built three loads from our shipments, for a total optimized cost of $2,598, representing a cost savings of 73 percent over direct cost and a mileage savings of 95 percent. Nice!

But interestingly, we also can see from the "Optimizer Shipments" tab that Mojo has spread the Rome-bound shipments across all three loads. What if that's not something that our customer wants, or something the receiving crew in Rome can handle?

Shipment Count:	90		Load Count:	3		CO: Change:	57 tons	
Direct Miles:	26,833		Optimized Miles:	1,265		Mileage Change:	25,568 (95.3%)	
Direct Cost:	$9,478.84		Optimized Cost:	$2,598.69		Optimized Savings:	$6,880.15 (72.6%)	

Total Rows: 90 Selected Rows: 1

Primary Reference	Notes	Load Reference	Optimized	Pickup Window	Delivery Window	Direct Rate	Direct Contract	Direct Days	Direct Zone	Pickup Event	Delivery Event	Origin Code	Origin Nar
100		Load 1	true	0.00	0.00	60.00	ATD LTL	3	1		2	AMERICA	AMERICA
101		Load 3	true	0.00	0.57	62.84	ATD LTL	3	1		4		AMERICA
102		Load 1	true	0.00	0.00	60.00	ATD LTL	3	1		2		AMERICA
103		Load 1	true	0.00	0.00	60.00	ATD LTL	3	1		2		AMERICA
104		Load 2	true	0.00	0.00	60.00	ATD LTL	3	1		2		AMERICA
105		Load 1	true	0.00	0.00	60.00	ATD LTL	3	1		2		AMERICA
106		Load 1	true	0.00	0.00	60.00	ATD LTL	3	1		2		AMERICA
107		Load 3	true	0.00	0.57	94.27	ATD LTL	3	1		4		AMERICA
108		Load 3	true	0.00	0.57	102.19	ATD LTL	3	1		4		AMERICA
109		Load 3	true	0.00	0.57	120.10	ATD LTL	3	1		4		AMERICA
110		Load 2	true	0.00	0.00	60.00	ATD LTL	3	1		2		AMERICA
111		Load 3	true	0.00	0.57	125.67	ATD LTL	3	1		4		AMERICA
112		Load 3	true	0.00	0.57	62.84	ATD LTL	3	1		4		AMERICA
113		Load 3	true	0.00	0.57	62.02	ATD LTL	3	1		4		AMERICA

Fig. 7-23: Our 32 shipments with the same destination are spread across all three loads. Why send all three trucks to the same place?

We can force Mojo to send only one truck to that destination. We do this by installing a Load Preference in our original shipment report. Click the "Optimize" command (from the Mojo tab, not the "Route optimizer... command from the Shipment report), and this time when the wizard runs, set the "Truckload Max Stops" parameter on the second screen to 1.

Vehicle Max Quantity:	10,000
Vehicle Max Cube:	
Truckload Max Stops:	1
Vehicle Loading:	
Stop Restrictions:	No Multi-Pick

Fig. 7-24: As our first step in overriding Mojo, we're telling each truck it can only make one stop. Now we will get at least one truck that does nothing except go to Georgia, which is what we want.

A new set of Mojo results appears. The net effect of Max Stops = 1 is that each load now contains only shipments for that load's lone destination. Now we click the "Retain Load Preferences" command in the right-hand Task Window. A "Load Preference" column will be added to the shipment report, reflecting the existing groupings of shipment by load:

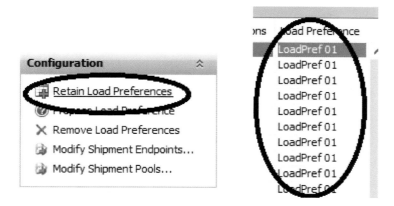

Fig. 7-25. Now that we have set Max Stops = 1, which forces all shipments from the same destination onto the same load, choosing "Retain Load Preferences" creates a column in the original shipment report that reflects the grouping we have created.

Now we run the wizard again. Set Max Stops = 3 (back to the original value), so that we're not sending a bunch of other separate trucks all over the place. All we care is that we now have all our Rome shipments on the same truck. In the wizard, change the "Load Preference Restriction" parameter to the value "Enforce (Allow Groups)."

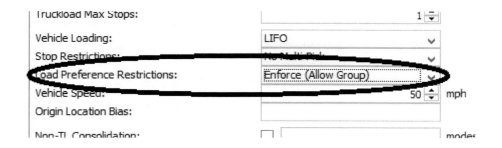

Fig. 7-26: We're enforcing load preferences how, so all our Georgia shipments with the same load preference are put together.

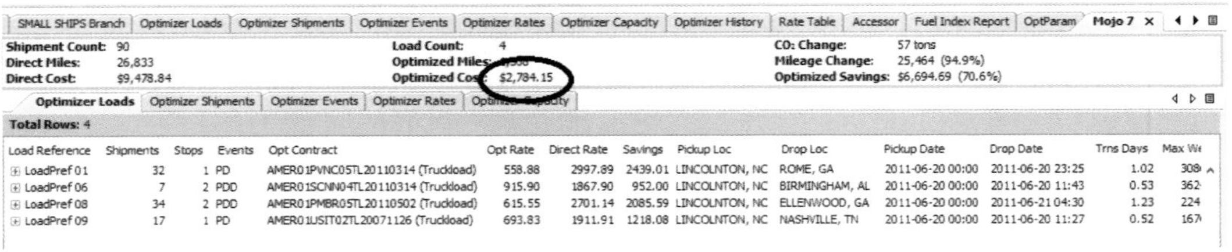

Fig. 7-27: Results of creating a Load Preference, then using "Enforce (Allow Groups)."

So we got what we wanted. By using and enforcing Load Preference, we forced all our Rome-bound shipments onto the same load.

However, notice that the optimizer had to create <u>four</u> loads instead of three. And the total cost is just shy of $200 more than the original solution. It's up to the customer, of course, to decide whether the extra $200 is worth not having three different trucks show up in Georgia.

Both of the above examples demonstrate the use of Load Preference as a tool for analyzing optimization results. The reason that the optimizer builds its loads in certain ways usually is a matter of least cost, or it reflects a constraint in the rate table or a setting in the Mojo Optimization Wizard.

Discussion Questions

1. The theme of this chapter is tuning our optimization results. Why should we have to tune them in the first place – isn't that the job of the optimizer? What tools help the user to tune and understand the impact of the different models/runs?

2. What does it mean to say we are adjusting the "inner time windows" of a proposed load? Why would we do this and what would we gain from it? When couldn't we do it?

3. The chapter deals with examples of an optimizer sending shipments on different trucks to the same general area, or splitting up dozens of shipments bound for the same dock onto multiple docks. Why did the optimizer produce these "strange" results, and should we try to "correct" them?

###

Chapter 8: Maximizing Carrier Capacity

We'll use the term "carrier capacity" to describe the <u>overall availability</u> of trucks (or planes, trains, ships or rail cars) from our carriers.[1]

Carrier capacity is a common concern in the real world. In planning our routes and building our loads we cannot assume there will always be as many trucks as we need, nor that they are available exactly when and where we need them.

Our contracts with carriers spell out available lanes, and the rates that apply to them. But a contract is not a guarantee of unlimited capacity on demand. (This is why having "the lowest possible rate" is not always possible. What good is a rate without a truck?)

The extent to which capacity is an issue depends on the nature of your business and, to an extent, the carrier mode you are employing. Let's put it this way – when you mail a letter, you never worry whether there are enough mail trucks that day! In a similar vein, we're least likely to have to count trucks when dealing with low or average volume of parcel movements.

Even a lot of less-than-truckload (LTL) carrier contracts involve the automatic acceptance of a load tender, which is pretty close to getting capacity on demand. However, systematic or high-volume LTL operations might need to nail down capacity expectations in their contracts.

---

[1] In this context "capacity" refers to capacity available for hire from our third party common carriers, as opposed to private fleet assets. We'll talk about optimization of private fleet assets in a later chapter.

As you might have guessed, capacity is most commonly a concern in truckload modes and modes that use containers. For this chapter we will focus on truckload moves.

Truckload capacity can fluctuate by season (for example, harvest time in agricultural areas). Capacity can expand and contract with the economy. And some capacity crunches are acute, caused by short-term factors such as weather or disasters, and are harder to predict.

Capacity and Optimization

Today's optimizer must consider capacity to produce reasonable executable runs. We'll see examples where, without having to respect a reasonable capacity constraint, the optimizer simply assigns every single load to the same least-cost carrier! Capacity matters if we are optimizing to develop an accurate model for identifying our network needs.

Examples of not using capacity in optimization would be when our main concern is simply building routes, and letting capacity take care of itself later. In that case we might be assigning carriers with a static route guide, or we might be letting carriers set their own "constraint" on capacity by rejecting our tenders.

When it comes to applying capacity considerations to optimization, we'll look at three levels of strategy:

(1) None – we'll assume there are no practical limits, and let the optimizer build loads accordingly. Again, if our business is mostly relying on-demand parcel or small LTL, this works just fine.

(2) Global limits – we'll set some overall assumptions on capacity to use in developing optimization models.

(3) Precise limits – we'll supply granular capacity limits in terms of number of trucks available, down to the level of individual carriers and contract lanes.

In all cases where we have applied capacity constraints, of course, we want to be able to drill into our results and to analyze how the results were affected by capacity considerations.

Applying Capacity in Mojo

The first decision in the Mojo wizard is whether to enforce carrier capacity at all, and if so, by what counting method.

Capacity settings are grouped in a section on the third screen of the four wizard screens. Let's look at the first setting, labeled "Carrier Capacity Strategy (Primary)":

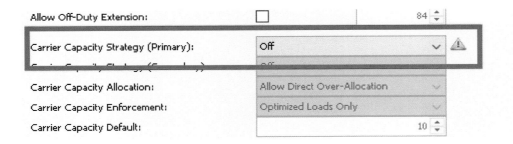

Fig. 8-1: Carrier capacity enforcement in the optimizer wizard. When this is set to "Off" we're choosing not to consider limits at all.

A setting of "off" means that if we have 500 loads, and the "best" contract every time is with Louie's Trucking, then the optimizer will propose to hire Louie all 500 times (no matter how many trucks Louie actually can give us).

Fig. 8-2 shows just that kind of result from a small Mojo run that resulted in 40 recommended loads. Louie always had the lowest rates in the rate table – so with no capacity being enforced, the optimizer simply assigned every load to that carrier.

Optimizer Loads	Optimizer Shipments	Optimizer Events	Optimizer Rates	Optimizer Capacity

Total Rows: 40

Load Reference	Shipments	Stops	Events	Opt Contract	Opt Rate	Direct Rate	Saving
⊞ Load 01	2	1	PD	Louie Truckload (Truckload)	713.10	1426.21	713.
⊞ Load 02	2	1	PD	Louie Truckload (Truckload)	713.10	1426.21	713.
⊞ Load 03	2	1	PD	Louie Truckload (Truckload)	713.10	1426.21	713.
⊞ Load 04	2	1	PD	Louie Truckload (Truckload)	713.10	1426.21	713.
⊞ Load 05	2	1	PD	Louie Truckload (Truckload)	713.10	1426.21	713.
⊞ Load 06	2	1	PD	Louie Truckload (Truckload)	713.10	1426.21	713.

Fig. 8-2: With no limit on carrier capacity, the same least-cost carrier was awarded every single load in this scenario. But is it realistic?

From the earlier chapter on reading optimization results, you might remember that Mojo results include a tab labeled "Optimizer Capacity". This tab tells us exactly how carrier capacity was employed in the last run. Fig. 8-3 shows this tab's contents for the optimizer run described just above:

Direct Cost: $52,540.61   **Optimi:**

Optimizer Loads	Optimizer Shipments	Optimizer Events	Optimizer Rates	Optimizer Capacity

Total Rows: 4

Date	Day	SCAC	Origin Code	Capacity Used
2016-07-12	Tue	LOTL	BUR	9
2016-07-12	Tue	LOTL	MSCC	8
2016-07-13	Wed	LOTL	BUR	12
2016-07-13	Wed	LOTL	MSCC	11

Fig. 8-3: No enforcement of carrier capacity. Over four days of planned execution, the optimizer uses the same carrier for all 40 loads created by the run.

Capacity Limits/Global Defaults

Clicking on the list of options for the setting "Carrier Capacity Enforcement" we see there are several more possibilities.

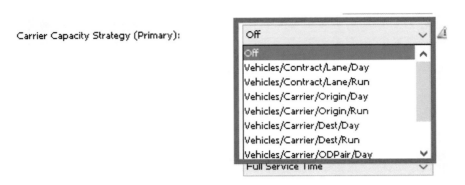

Fig. 8-4: More options in the optimization wizard for applying capacity limits.

We'll go through these options in detail in just a second. But they work together with another setting labeled "Carrier Capacity Default". This is a global limit on the number of trucks that will be allowed - according to the counting method chosen in the higher setting.

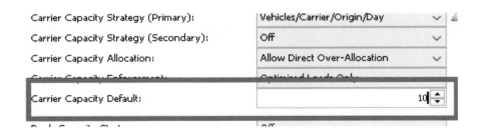

Fig. 8-5: Setting a global default on carrier capacity. This limit of 10 trucks will be applied according to the counting method chosen in the higher setting.

Now let's go back to the methods for counting trucks. At first glance the names might seem to run together in a list of confusing options but they are quickly figured out.

Notice that for each combination there are two versions, one that ends with "Day" and one that ends with "Run".

That means either the global limit should apply for each <u>day</u> of execution in your optimization results, or it should apply as an overall limit in this <u>run</u> of the optimizer.

Here are the options for counting capacity:

Vehicles/Contract/Lane

This setting applies a limit on the number of trucks that can be used from any one carrier <u>contract</u> on this lane.

Example: For a lane defined as North Carolina to Florida, and a global setting of 3, only three trucks per contract can be sent on that lane (Fig. 8-6).

Direct Cost:	$52,540.61				Optimi

Optimizer Loads	Optimizer Shipments	Optimizer Events	Optimizer Rates	Optimizer Capacity

Total Rows: 3

Contract	Lane	Capacity Used	Capacity Max	Capacity %
Android Truckload	NC,USA to FL,USA	3	3	100.00
Apple Truckload	NC,USA to FL,USA	3	3	100.00
Louie Truckload	NC,USA to FL,USA	3	3	100.00

Fig. 8-6: The optimizer is enforcing a per-lane limit for each contract.

Vehicles/Carrier/Origin

This sets a limit on carrier capacity from any given <u>origin</u> (defined by location code). Using the same data as in the previous example:

Optimizer Loads	Optimizer Shipments	Optimizer Events	Optimizer Rates	Optimizer Capacity

Total Rows: 8

... ∧ ↕	Origin Code	Capacity Used	Capacity Max	Capacity %
ANDY	BUR	3	3	100.00
ANDY	MSCC	3	3	100.00
ANDY	MSCC2	2	3	66.67
IMAC	BUR	3	3	100.00
IMAC	MSCC	3	3	100.00
LOTL	BUR	3	3	100.00
LOTL	MSCC	3	3	100.00
LOTL	MSCC2	3	3	100.00

Fig. 8-7: Same global default limit of three trucks, but this time applied per origin location code.

Vehicles/Carrier/Dest

This set a limit on carrier capacity to any given destination location code. Again, using the same data:

Fig. 8-8: *Same default limit of three trucks, but this time applied per destination location code.*

Vehicles/Carrier/ODPair

Regardless of lane definitions in the rate table, this limit is applied to the number of trucks available from any specific origin code paired with a specific destination code.

Fig. 8-9: *Capacity limit enforced against origin-destination pairs (location codes).*

Vehicles/Carrier

Lastly, this is a limit on the number of trucks available from the same carrier.

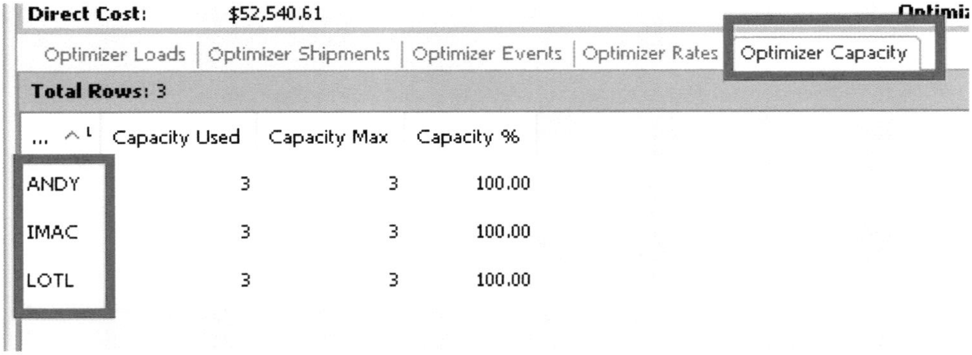

Direct Cost:	$52,540.61			Optimi:

Optimizer Loads	Optimizer Shipments	Optimizer Events	Optimizer Rates	Optimizer Capacity

Total Rows: 3

... ∧ ↓	Capacity Used	Capacity Max	Capacity %
ANDY	3	3	100.00
IMAC	3	3	100.00
LOTL	3	3	100.00

Fig. 8-10: Per-carrier limit enforced by the optimizer.

Remember that all the above limits can be calculated either by day, applying separately to each day of execution in the optimization results, or as a single limit applied to the overall run of the optimizer.

Lane-Level Capacity Limits

As we just saw, the wizard setting "Carrier Capacity Default" sets a global or generic capacity limit that applies according to the specified calculation method.

However, for precise and granular control over carrier capacity, we can specify individual limits in the rate table. That means for each carrier, and each line of the rate table, we can declare individual capacity limits. These lane-level limits, if declared, will override the global default for that lane.

A column in the rate table titled "Capacity" (like all rate table column headers, that exact name is required) is used to declare the capacity limit.

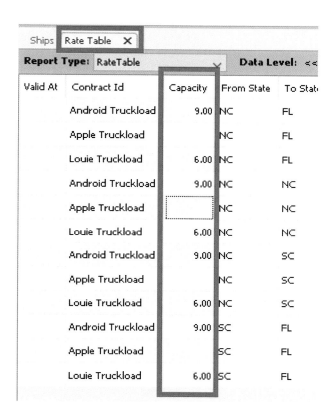

Fig. 8-11: A 'Capacity' column in the rate table will override the global default, and will limit available capacity by individual lane.

In Fig. 8-11 the carriers 'Android' and 'Louie' have specified limits on the listed interstate lanes. The carrier 'Apple' does not, so it will respect the global default value of 3.

Applying a limit per carrier to our run, here is the result using the above rate table:

Direct Cost:	$52,540.61			Optim

Optimizer Loads | Optimizer Shipments | Optimizer Events | Optimizer Rates | Optimizer Capacity

Total Rows: 3

... ^↓	Capacity Used	Capacity Max	Capacity %
ANDY	9	9	100.00
IMAC	3	3	100.00
LOTL	6	6	100.00

Fig. 8-12: The capacity limits that were specified in the rate table are used for carriers Android ('ANDY') and Louie ('LOTL'). The global default was applied to carrier Apple ('IMAC').

'Secondary' Capacity Strategy

The following wizard setting in the carrier-capacity section is labeled "Carrier Capacity Strategy (Secondary)". If a primary strategy is being used, this setting is enabled and it allows the user to apply a <u>second</u> layer of capacity limits, with the same options:

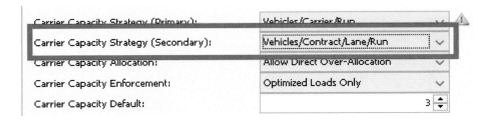

Carrier Capacity Strategy (Primary):	Vehicles/Carrier/Run
Carrier Capacity Strategy (Secondary):	Vehicles/Contract/Lane/Run
Carrier Capacity Allocation:	Allow Direct Over-Allocation
Carrier Capacity Enforcement:	Optimized Loads Only
Carrier Capacity Default:	3

Fig. 8-13: Enforcing a second layer of capacity limits in the optimization wizard settings.

The settings applied in the "secondary" strategy are applied along with those of the first, with the most restrictive limit taking effect.

Besides the global default, we can again set lane-level limits for our secondary strategy with another column in the rate table,

"Capacity 2". This again gives us lots of flexibility in the way we use capacity.

For example, let's say that we use the "Capacity" column in the rate table to declare a limit per carrier – but "Capacity 2" to limit the number of trucks <u>per origin</u>. This is a real-world example – a carrier is willing to give us up to X trucks a day, but does not want us pulling too many from the same place.

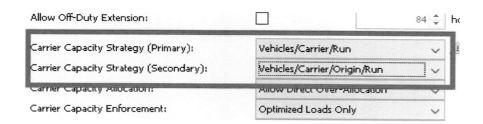

Fig. 8-14: Our primary strategy is set to limit total trucks from any given carrier for this run. Our secondary strategy further limits us to a smaller number of trucks from any given origin.

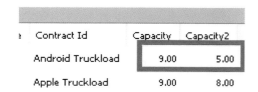

Fig. 8-15: The rate table for carrier 'Android' allows us up to 9 trucks overall (the 'Capacity' column to be is used with the primary strategy) but only 5 trucks from any one origin (the 'Capacity 2' column that is used with the secondary strategy).

Direct Distance: 53,071 mi
Direct Cost: $52,540.61

Optimized Distance: 36,506 mi
Optimized Cost: $37,514.23

Optimizer Loads | Optimizer Shipments | Optimizer Events | Optimizer Rates | Optimizer Capacity | Optimizer Capacity 2

Total Rows: 6

... ∧ ∟ Origin Code		Capacity Used	Capacity Max	Capacity %
ANDY	BUR	5	5	100.00
ANDY	MSCC	4	5	80.00
IMAC	BUR	8	8	100.00
IMAC	MSCC2	1	8	12.50
LOTL	BUR	5	5	100.00
LOTL	MSCC	1	5	20.00

Fig. 8-16: Results of applying the settings in Fig. 8-14 and 8-15. Our primary strategy said we were entitled to 9 trucks a day from carrier ANDY, but our secondary strategy limited us to only 5 from any one point of origin.

Capacity Limits & Non-Optimized Shipments

One possible outcome from enforcing capacity limits in an optimization is an increase in the number of shipments that could not be optimized, given the supplied constraints.

This is, presumably, a good thing, because it shows us where we would run into trouble in actual execution, or where in an analysis we need to think about acquiring more capacity.

In the earlier chapter about reading results, we saw that we can look at the "Optimizer Shipments" tab, then the column labeled "Optimized", and you'll see a true or false result for each shipment. (Remember also to click on the column header to sort in ascending or descending order, to group all the "false" results.)

Let's go back to the earlier example in which we had 40 loads to move over two days, but tight capacity limits (3 trucks per carrier).

The result is that the optimizer tells us that <u>it cannot optimize all our shipments</u> within the given constraints. The "Optimized" column value for several of our shipments is set to "false".

Optimizer Loads	Optimizer Shipments	Optimizer Events	Optimizer Rates	Optimizer Capacity

Total Rows: 80

Primary Reference	Notes	Load Reference	Optimized	^ ↓	Pickup Window	Delivery Window	Direct Rate	Dire
⊞ Shipment 17		Load 28	false		0.00	0.00	616.72	Lou
⊞ Shipment 18		Load 29	false		0.00	0.00	616.72	Lou
⊞ Shipment 19		Load 30	false		0.00	0.00	616.72	Lou
⊞ Shipment 20		Load 31	false		0.00	0.00	616.72	Lou
⊞ Shipment 41		Load 32	false		0.00	0.00	601.23	Lou
⊞ Shipment 42		Load 33	false		0.00	0.00	601.23	Lou
⊞ Shipment 43		Load 34	false		0.00	0.00	601.23	Lou

Fig. 8-17: Some shipments could not be optimized under the constraints.

Remember also (from the chapter on reading results) that we can look under the "Notes" tab of optimizer results to see the most common reasons that shipments could not be optimized (Fig. 8-18):

```
Limiting Constraints
   Max Out-of-Route          :  0
   Truckload Max Stops       :  0
   Shipment Type             :  0
   Temperature Range         :  0
   Vehicle Loading (LIFO)    :  200
   Vehicle Max Weight        :  1,200
   Vehicle Max Quantity      :  0
   Vehicle Max Cube          :  0
   Loading Priority          :  0
   Time Window/Loc Hours     :  954
   Optimized Rate            :  0
   Carrier Capacity          :  918
   Pickup/Drop Clustering    :  0
```

Fig. 8-18: List of the most common reasons our capacity-constrained shipments could not be optimized.

Notice in Fig. 8-18 that the most common constraint is vehicle weight – nothing to do about with that, since we can't make our trucks bigger. But next after that, the two biggest constraints were "Time Window/Loc Hours" and "Carrier Capacity".

In other words, under the given limits on available trucks, we couldn't get enough trucks to deliver everything that needed delivering within the specified time windows.

So we either need more trucks from our existing carriers, trucks from other carriers or external sources (such as public load boards), or to be able to tweak our constraints to see if we can fit the given shipments onto trucks a different way. Let's look at a simple example next.

Gaining Capacity with Time Windows

Stretching our allowed time windows, especially the "inner" windows for late-late pickup or early-early delivery, is a common tactic used to get around capacity restrictions. The additional flexibility lets the optimizer build more loads than it might have been able before.

Here's an example in which loads are supposed to be picked up one day, but the specified delivery window does not start until the next day. Coupled with a tight per-day restriction on carrier capacity, the optimizer cannot find a way to create an entirely optimized result (Fig. 8-19):

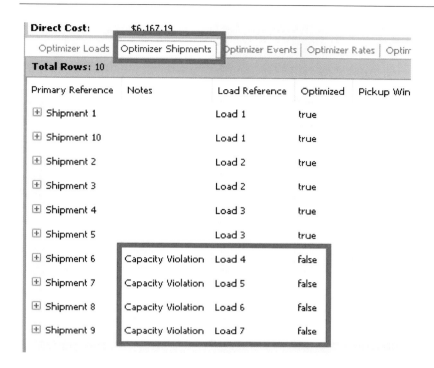

Fig. 8-19: With tight restrictions on carrier capacity, the optimizer reports that it has failed to optimize these loads under the given constraints.

e	Dest Zip	Dest Ctry	Dest Geo	Target Ship (Early)	Actual Ship	Target Ship (Late)	Target Delivery (Early)	Actual Deli
	33710	USA	27.789703,-82.728149	2016-07-12 06:00	2016-07-12 06:00	2016-07-12 18:00	2016-07-13 06:00	2016-07-1:
	33710	USA	27.789703,-82.728149	2016-07-12 06:00	2016-07-12 06:00	2016-07-12 18:00	2016-07-13 06:00	2016-07-1:
	33710	USA	27.789703,-82.728149	2016-07-12 06:00	2016-07-12 06:00	2016-07-12 18:00	2016-07-13 06:00	2016-07-1:

Direct Distance: 6,229 mi   **Direct Cost:** $6,167.19   **Optimized Distance:** 4,361 mi   **Optimized Cost:** $4,317.03

Optimizer Loads | Optimizer Shipments | Optimizer Events | Optimizer Rates | Optimizer Capacity

Total Rows: 10

Fig. 8-20: Notice that the shipment time windows specify a pickup on one day, and assume the delivery cannot be made until the start of the next day at the earliest.

So this seems like an excellent time to try to widen delivery time windows, especially the inner windows allowing later pickups and earlier deliveries. If we can stretch our pickups to be later, or our deliveries to be earlier, can we do better?

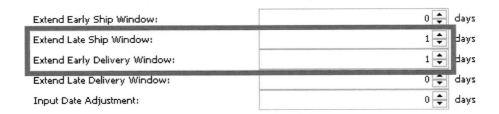

Extend Early Ship Window:	0	days
Extend Late Ship Window:	1	days
Extend Early Delivery Window:	1	days
Extend Late Delivery Window:	0	days
Input Date Adjustment:	0	days

Fig. 8-21: Attempting to stretch late-pickup and early-delivery times looking for more flexible use of carrier capacity.

Yes! In fact the optimizer now is able to push its latest pickups into the second day, still making deliveries on time – but getting the advantage of a new day's worth of trucks.

Direct Cost:	$910.35					Optimized Cost:	$455.18			

Optimizer Loads | Optimizer Shipments | Optimizer Events | Optimizer Rates | Optimizer Capacity

Total Rows: 5

Load Reference	Shi...	Stops	Events	Opt Contract	Opt Rate	Direct Rate	Savings	Pickup Loc	Drop Loc	Pickup Date	Leev
⊞ Load 1		2	1 PD	Louie Truckload (Truckload)	91.04	182.07	91.04	Charlotte, NC	Columbia, SC	2016-07-12 06:00	
⊞ Load 2		2	1 PD	Louie Truckload (Truckload)	91.04	182.07	91.04	Charlotte, NC	Columbia, SC	2016-07-12 06:00	
⊞ Load 3		2	1 PD	Louie Truckload (Truckload)	91.04	182.07	91.04	Charlotte, NC	Columbia, SC	2016-07-12 06:00	
⊞ Load 4		2	1 PD	Louie Truckload (Truckload)	91.04	182.07	91.04	Charlotte, NC	Columbia, SC	2016-07-13 06:00	
⊞ Load 5		2	1 PD	Louie Truckload (Truckload)	91.04	182.07	91.04	Charlotte, NC	Columbia, SC	2016-07-13 06:00	

Fig. 8-22: Success. By allowing pickups stretching into the second day, we gained a new day's worth of carrier capacity. All our shipments are optimized, and all our deliveries are still on time.

More about Non-Optimized Shipments

In the wizard settings, notice there are other settings under the capacity section labeled "Carrier Capacity Allocation" and "Carrier Capacity Enforcement". These settings relate to the optimizer's initial treatment of non-optimized shipments.

Looking first at "Carrier Capacity Enforcement", we see that the options are "Optimized Loads Only" and "All Loads" (Fig. 8-23).

Fig. 8-23: How to enforce carrier capacity – should we enforce it even on non-optimized loads?

If the setting is "Optimized Loads Only" then any non-optimized loads will simply be assigned a direct-cost carrier rate <u>regardless</u> of carrier capacity limits. The loads will be flagged for any capacity violations.

If the setting is "All Loads", then the optimizer can try to respect capacity limits even on the shipments it could not optimize. Exactly how that works is controlled by the other setting, labeled "Carrier Capacity Allocation" (Fig. 8-24):

Fig. 8-24: 'Carrier Capacity Allocation' options for non-optimized shipments.

The settings here are "Allow Direct Over-Allocation" and "No Over-Allocation."

If the setting is "Allow", then the optimizer will allow the shipment to be assigned a direct rate outside of capacity limits – and will flag the load as a violation of the constraint under the load's "Flags" column in the Optimizer Loads tab.

If the setting is "No Over-Allocation", then the optimizer will try to find a rate for the load that obeys capacity limits, until it runs out of options and has to flag the load for a violation.

Interestingly, if this last setting is used, it might require the optimizer to keep going until it finds a rate with "negative" savings, which is a way of saying that our optimization cost is going up instead of down! But that is the "price tag" for enforcing carrier capacity limits no matter what the result.

Fig. 8-25: We're trying to apply capacity limits on all loads, and flagging any direct-ship loads that violate those limits. The setting 'Carrier Capacity Enforcement' is set to 'All Loads' and the setting 'Carrier Capacity Allocation' is set to 'Allow Direct Over-Allocation'.

Conclusion

The importance of carrier capacity can vary in optimization scenarios, both by mode and by the nature of our business.

We might worry less about capacity when it comes to low- or medium-volume use of parcel and even in auto-accept LTL scenarios. However, in higher-volume LTL scenarios, and in many truckload, ocean, rail, and intermodal scenarios, the actual capacity available to use becomes a matter of critical importance, whether in optimizing for actual execution, or for modeling and analysis of our network needs.

When we optimize, we can choose not to enforce carrier capacity at all, or by a simple "global" or default capacity limit that we can enforce in a variety of ways. This allows us to consider at least some global limit in our optimization models.

At a more precise and granular level, however, we can supply capacity information on individual lines of the rate tables used in optimization. We also can apply both a "primary" and "secondary" strategy to apply capacity limits in two ways.

Lastly, we have options for how to handle those shipments that could <u>not</u> be optimized. If we place them on non-optimized loads, should we force those loads to respect our declared capacity limits anyway - even if it results in "negative savings"?

By adding the ability to apply carrier capacity considerations to the field of optimization, we have taken a giant step toward a tool that works for us in any real-world scenario.

In the next chapter we'll next apply similar real-world considerations to our <u>network</u> – the physical places to which our trucks, trains, planes and boats actually <u>go</u>.

Discussion Questions

1. What does the term "carrier capacity" mean in the logistics business? Why aren't capacity concerns taken care of by the contracts between logistics providers and their carriers? Under what circumstances is capacity more likely or less likely to be a worry?

2. Why do we care about carrier capacity when we are building loads through optimization? What are the optimization risks of not considering capacity? What are some of our options for applying capacity constraints in optimization?

3. If we are applying capacity limits in optimization, how do we know whether all our shipments were successfully optimized? If shipments could not be optimized because of capacity constraints, what are some of the ways we can handle it?

###

Chapter 9: Controlling Facility Capacity

The previous chapter dealt with taking practical limits on carrier capacity into account in our optimizations. In this chapter, we'll see today's optimizers can also consider constraints on the <u>physical locations</u> where we're picking up, delivering, or passing through on the route.

Such considerations include:

- Hours of operation.
- Dock capacities.
- Load/unload service times.
- Restrictions by mode or carrier.

Just as you might not need to count trucks, depending on the nature of your business, you might not need to consider these facility constraints.

But facility capacity is as common a constraint as carrier capacity – <u>most</u> origins, <u>many</u> destinations and <u>all</u> intermediate facilities are going to have some number of docks or finite capacity for what they can handle at one time.

For coordinated, relatively high-volume optimization and execution across standing networks, facility considerations become more important. In those scenarios, we cannot afford to assume that we always have all the capacity we need, on demand.

In short, facility constraints can prevent route optimization! We'll see some things we can do about it, in the "Results and Improvements" section at the end of this chapter.

Facility Service Times

When it comes to settings for facility load/unload service times and operating hours, our optimizer gives us the same kind of options that we had in the previous chapter on carrier capacity:

(1) We can use global, default assumptions in our model. We can tell the optimizer to assume that every location is open from XX am to XX pm, everybody takes this long to load/unload, and everybody has this many docks. This is not precise, but it at least recognizes the real-world impact of such limitations. These global settings allow us to set basic parameters that can then be overridden in specific instances allowing for an 80/20 type of control.

(2) Or we can supply exact values for hours of operation and service times <u>by individual facility</u> for precise calculations.

The settings for facility service times and hours of operation are found in a group on the second page of the optimization wizard (Fig. 9-1).

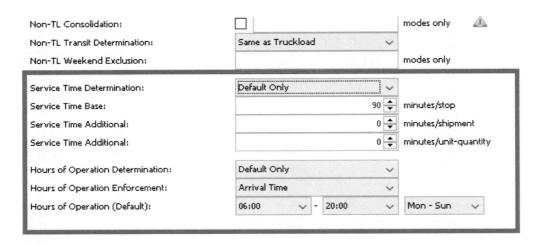

Fig. 9-1: Location-related settings on the second screen of the optimization wizard.

Notice the first setting labeled "Service Time Determination" (Fig. 9-2). The possible values for this setting are "Default Only" or the names of any open reports of type "Location".

Fig. 9-2: We can tell the optimizer to use global defaults for service times and hours of operation, or we can tell it to use specific values that come from an open 'location' report.

Specifying Service Times by Facility

Until now we have dealt mostly with spreadsheets of type "Shipment" or "RateTable". Now we'll add a new type called "Location".

A Location report includes a list of location codes and details about them. A list of possible columns and values in Location reports is found in the appendix, but at a minimum they must include a location code, and a geocode for that entry.

(If geocodes are missing, remember the application can add them with the "Add GeoData" command, if there are city-state and/or postal code columns.)

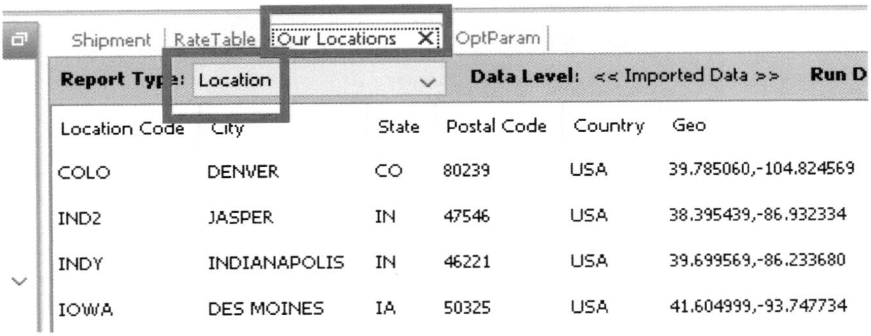

Fig. 9-3: An open report of type "Location".

If only one location report is open, that name will be the only choice besides "Default Only" in the "Service Time Determination" setting. If more than one is open, the user can choose which Location report to use.

If we're using a Location report to provide specific service times, instead of global defaults, the optimizer will look for additional columns in the list to supply those values. The columns are named:

Service Time Base
Service Time per Shipment
Service Time per Quantity
Delivery Idle Time

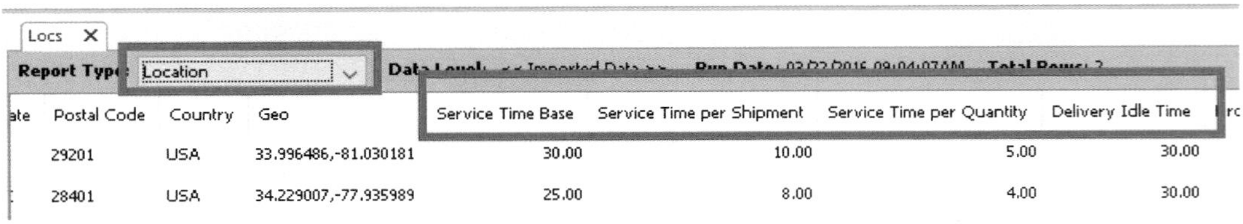

Fig. 9-4: Service time column information for each facility listed in a Location report.

"Service Time Base" is a standard time allowance for arrival, load/unload and departure. A stop scheduled by the optimizer will always be allowed this much time. (This setting also is the best way to allow for urban congestion associated with a location.)

The two "Additional" values can be used to add extra time allowance at a stop either per shipment count, or per unit of quantity (the "Quantity" value mapped for each shipment).

The purpose of these "Additional" settings is to take into consideration cargo types that might require special handling time. A word of warning, though: These settings can throw off time calculations if misused. Take another look at this service time chart we first saw in Chapter 7, showing unusually long allowances:

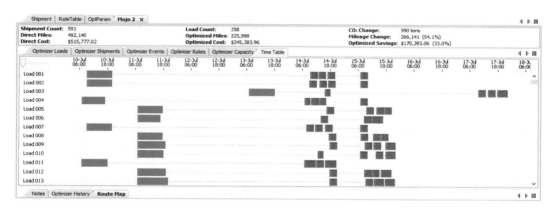

Fig. 9-5: The dark portion of each loading (green) time shows an unusually long load time. The diagnosis in this case was that the wizard had been set to allow 15 extra minutes per shipment for loads consisting of numerous shipments.

"Delivery Idle Time" is an allowed waiting period specific to this location. If a truck shows up and all docks are full, it can wait for up to the allowed time. The less wait time allowed, the tighter the schedule, and the fewer options the optimizer has for building loads. (For global defaults, idle time is built into the base stop time.)

Global Defaults

The next three wizard settings after "Service Time Determination" are used to set global service time defaults. That means they'll be used (1) always, when the "determination" setting is "Default Only" or (2) as a fallback when no information is available for a specific location.

Service Time Base:	90	minutes/stop
Service Time Additional:	0	minutes/shipment
Service Time Additional:	0	minutes/unit-quantity

Fig. 9-6: Wizard settings for global defaults for a base per-time stop, along with an additional time allowance for each shipment and/or unit of quantity on the load.

Mode and SCAC Restrictions

We also can have columns in a Location report to restrict a pool location by mode and carrier SCAC, on the pickup or drop side or both. And we can specify an individual max <u>hold</u> time at this location – how long a shipment can wait before being put on an outbound load. Here are those columns:

Drop Modes	String
Drop SCACs	String
Pickup Modes	String
Pickup SCACs	String
Max Pool Hold Time	Numeric

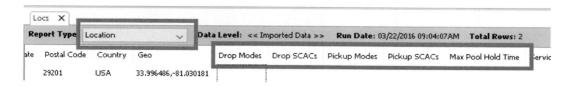

Fig. 9-7: Columns in a Location report for restricting the location by pickup and drop modes or SCACs and setting a max pool hold time.

Hours of Operation

The same overall options apply to our treatment of facility operating hours – we can set global defaults, or use a location list to supply specific hours by individual facility.

Fig. 9-8: Optimizer settings for operating hours. We can use global defaults, or use an open location report to set hours by facility.

As with service times, the "determination" setting can be "Default Only" or the name of an open Location report. Another option here for this setting, "Use Shipment Hours", uses the shipment's "early" and "late" target dates for pickup or delivery as the operating hours.

The "enforcement" setting can be "Arrival Time", or "Arrival/Departure". The first value means the optimizer just needs to get the truck to the facility before closing time. The second setting means there must be enough time to complete the load/unload and depart before closing time.

The third setting, "Hours of Operation", provides global defaults to use for operating hours. These values will be used for all locations if the determination setting is "Default Only," or will be used as a fallback if information for a location is not available.

The related columns in a Location report are:

Location Code
Days
Hours

Example formats for location hours:

Mon-Fri, Mon-Sat, Mon-Sun
Mon,Tue,Wed,Thu,Fri,Sat,Sun
Date: 12-25
Date: 2012-11-22

Location Code	Name	City	State	Postal Code	Country	Geo	Days	Hours
CPS	Columbia	Columbia	SC	29201	USA	33.996486,-81.030181	Mon-Fri	07:00-15:00
WIL	Wilmington	Wilmington	NC	28401	USA	34.229007,-77.935989	Mon-Fri	07:00-16:30

Report Type: Location   Data Level: << Imported Data >>   Run Date: 03/22/2016 09:04:07AM

Fig. 9-9: Columns in a Location report for setting operating hours.

Specific dates are considered before recurring dates; weekly or day-of-week after that. Hence a location might be open Mon-Fri except on Dec. 25. Location codes also may include *DEFAULT* (with asterisks) for all locations not listed in the report, or *GLOBAL* applying to all locations if not overridden.

Dock Capacity

Finally, we also must consider the number of docks available at each facility. By now our options are familiar: We can use global assumptions for each location, or we can use columns in a Location report to supply figures by individual location.

Dock capacity settings are found on the third wizard screen, just beneath the carrier capacity settings:

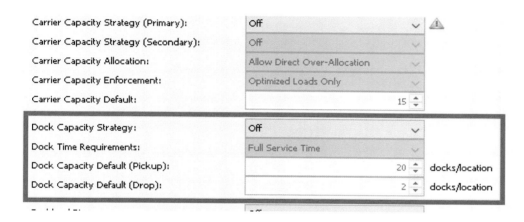

Fig. 9-10: Dock capacity settings on third wizard screen.

The "strategy" setting can be "Off", "On" or set to the name of an open Location report.

If "Off", the optimizer does not consider dock limitations at all, starting pickups as early in the day as possible. If the strategy is "On", the optimizer uses defaults as determined in the following settings.

If using a Location report, the optimizer will look, for each location code specified, for these columns:

Pickup Docks   (a number)
Drop Docks   (a number)

Report Type:	Location			Data Level: << Imported Data >>		Run Date: 03/22/2016 09:04:07AM		Total Rows
Location Code	Name	City	State	Postal Code	Country	Geo	Pickup Docks	Drop Docks	Day
CPS	Columbia	Columbia	SC	29201	USA	33.996486,-81.030181	5.00	5.00	Mor
WIL	Wilmington	Wilmington	NC	28401	USA	34.229007,-77.935989	3.00	3.00	Mor

Fig. 9-11: Columns in a Location report to specify dock capacity for each individual facility.

The next wizard setting, "Dock Time Requirements", gives us an option for how to calculate stop times. The settings are "full Service Time" (use the base stop time, plus any per-shipment and per-unit allowance), and "Shipment Service Time" (use only the per-shipment and per-unit allowance). Using the second setting means that our service time depends entirely on the variable number of shipments/quantity, without a fixed base.

Dock Time Requirements:

Full Service Time
Full Service Time
Shipment Service Time

Fig. 9-12: Option to calculate service time at a dock including a base allowance, or entirely according to number of shipments/quantity on the load.

Finally, the last two dock settings set global defaults for the number of inbound and outbound docks available by location.

Other Location-Related Parameters

This seems like a good place to mention three other options in the optimization wizard for the way we want to treat locations: origin bias, destination restrictions, and clustering.

Fig. 9-13: Parameters on the second wizard screen for origin- and destination-related settings.

The setting labeled "Origin Location Biases" allows you to enter a list of location codes, separated by commas, to use to suggest a priority when multiple pickup locations are possible.

An example would be multiple warehouse pickups in the same city. The setting is labeled "bias" because it suggests an event order to the optimizer, but does not force it.

The setting labeled "Dest Location Restrictions" allows you to enter a list of location codes, separated by commas, which must be scheduled as the last stop on their route. However, if you force two such designated locations onto the same route, the resulting load will be flagged for a violation as "DestRestriction-constrained".

Clustering

Settings on the final wizard screen allow you to require clustering within a certain radius for all drops or pickups on a route. For each event type (pickup or drop), you can enter a comma-separated list of modes or carrier SCACs to which the radius applies. Using the setting without a list will apply to all modes or all SCACs.

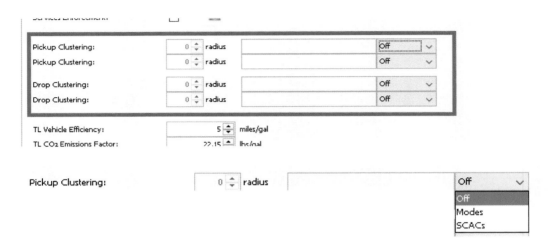

Fig. 9-14: Ability to require clustering of pickup or drop events, for specified modes or SCACs if desired or for all loads.

Results & Improvements

(1) Optimizer Events Tab

In the optimizer results, detailed information is attached to each scheduled event under the "Optimizer Events" tab. Note that each event include information about service time, operating hours, and dock usage.

City	State	Zip	Ctry	Geo	Actual Day	Actual Date	Service Time	Loc Hours	Docks Used	Dock Capacity	Dock Arrival	Dock Departure	SCAC	Mo
Burlington	NC	27215	USA	36.033420,-79.490882	Tue	2016-07-12 06:00	75	06:00 - 22:00	3	3	2016-07-12 06:00	2016-07-12 07:15	LOTL	Tru
Wilmington	NC	28401	USA	34.229007,-77.935989	Tue	2016-07-12 10:54	41	07:00 - 16:30	3	3	2016-07-12 10:54	2016-07-12 11:35	LOTL	Tru
Burlington	NC	27215	USA	36.033420,-79.490882	Tue	2016-07-12 06:00	75	06:00 - 22:00	3	3	2016-07-12 06:00	2016-07-12 07:15	LOTL	Tru

Row above table: No Pools: $52,540.61 — Optimized Cost: $28,926.20 — Optimized Savings: $27,360.81 (48.6%) No Pools: $23,614.41 (

Tabs: ...ments | Optimizer Events | Optimizer Rates | Optimizer Capacity |

Fig. 9-15: Location-related information for each event in the optimization, under the 'Optimizer Events' tab.

For each event listed in the Optimizer Events tab, clicking its expandable icon opens "drill-down" details. One of these, "Related Docks", shows the loads being processed at the related docks of this facility at the same time.

| Direct Distance: | 56,656 mi | | | | | Optimized Distance: | | 23,218 mi | |
| **Direct Cost:** | $56,287.01 | **No Pools:** $52,540.61 | | | | **Optimized Cost:** | | $28,926.2 | |

Optimizer Loads | Optimizer Shipments | **Optimizer Events** | Optimizer Rates | Optimizer Capacity

Total Rows: 168

Load Reference	Type	Seq Num	Distance	Weight	Quantity	Cube	User Num 1	User Num 2	Code	Name
⊟ Load 01	Pickup	1	0.00	44000.00	0.00	0.00			BUR	CNC Puppy Ir

    ⌐ Detail

       ⊞ Hours of Operation

       ⊞ Shipments

       ⊟ Related Docks

Load Reference	Contract	# Ships	Service Time	Dock Time	Arrival	Departure
Load 01	Louie Truckload	2	75	75	2016-07-12 06:00 (Tue)	2016-07-12 07:15 (Tue)
Load 02	Louie Truckload	2	75	75	2016-07-12 06:00 (Tue)	2016-07-12 07:15 (Tue)
Load 03	Louie Truckload	2	75	75	2016-07-12 06:00 (Tue)	2016-07-12 07:15 (Tue)

Fig. 9-16: 'Related Docks' information about other loads being processed at this facility at the same time.

(2) Adjustable Parameters

Just as we can't magically change the size of a truck, or the carrier capacity that we have, we can't change operating hours or the physical number of docks available at a location.

However, we do have flexibility in the way we schedule our drivers. On the third wizard screen, a setting labeled "Allow Off-Duty Extension" is commonly used to reflect the reality that drivers often do not depart and return on the same day, but must overnight. The setting allows the optimizer to consider arrivals that otherwise would occur before operating hours.

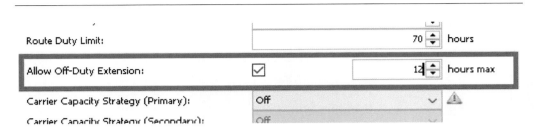

Route Duty Limit:		70 ⇕	hours
Allow Off-Duty Extension:	☑	12 ⇕	hours max
Carrier Capacity Strategy (Primary):	Off	⌄	⚠
Carrier Capacity Strategy (Secondary):	Off	⌄	

Fig. 9-17: 'Allow Off-Duty Extension' parameter allows the optimizer to assume the driver has arrived and is spending the night and is available for the next operating hours.

Another setting that can be adjusted to reflect real-world conditions is the "Delivery Idle Time" value that we can specify in a Location report. In practice, drivers often must wait for an available dock; not allowing enough flexibility here can prevent the optimizer from considering certain combinations. (On the other hand, part of the point of optimization is to schedule time more efficiently.)

Ships	Rate Table	**Locs** ✕	Mojo 2							
Report Type: Location ⌄				**Data Level:** << Imported Data >>			**Run Date:** 03/22/2016 10:09:29AM	**Tota**		
Location Code	Name	City	State	Postal Code	Country	Geo		**Delivery Idle Time**		
CPS	Columbia	Columbia	SC	29201	USA	33.996486,-81.030181		30.00	
WIL	Wilmington	Wilmington	NC	28401	USA	34.229007,-77.935989		30.00	

Fig. 9-18: Location report column allows flexibility in allowed wait time at a dock location.

In conclusion, the necessity of considering facility constraints – hours of operation, service times and dock capacity – depend somehow on the nature of our business. But for accurate modeling of scheduled loads moving across a network of facilities, the modern transportation optimizer must give us the ability to consider such limitations, either as global assumptions, or by specific facility.

Discussion Questions

1. To achieve an optimized result that works in the real world, what are some of the factors we should take into consideration about our network facilities?

2. What kinds of businesses might not need to consider facility constraints, and what kinds might be more likely to need to consider them?

3. Why would it be better at least to use global "default" settings for facility constraints, instead of using none at all?

###

Chapter 10: Leveraging Pooling & Cross-Dock Scenarios

When considering cross-docking or pooling the modern optimizer must allow the ability to force use or to use pools optionally. Consideration of pools is one of the most time-intensive operations that can be performed. The number of alternatives increases exponentially as more pools are considered for a shipment. Therefore the astute planner will limit the number of options the optimizer tries to consider for a given pooling scenario.

A <u>pool point</u> is an intermediate location between a shipment's origin and destination at which the shipment might be:

- o <u>Consolidated</u> on a new leg with other shipments heading in the same direction, or
- o <u>Cross-docked</u> and/or <u>re-consolidated</u> for a new leg, or
- o <u>Deconsolidated</u> to be put on its final delivery leg.

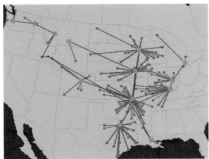

Fig. 10 -1: Example of a pooling strategy. Final delivery legs originate from pool points.

A pool point can be a warehouse, a distribution center, a loading dock or cross-docking facility.

A pool point might be part of the shipper's own network of facilities, or it might be owned and operated by a third party, including carriers.

Pool points can be restricted to certain modes or carriers.

Types of Pooling

The term <u>consolidation pooling</u> describes the practice of building consolidated loads toward the origin side, intended for long hauls toward the delivery side.

As an example, a food distributor in southern California brings together lettuce from one growing area, olives from another, nuts, pears, oranges, etc., and consolidates them on eastbound routes for truckload delivery to regional distribution centers.

<u>Distributive pooling</u> is the mirror philosophy of consolidation pooling – using pool points toward the destination with deconsolidation into LTL or parcel delivery legs.

As an example, a Midwestern manufacturer sends truckloads from its plants to regional distribution centers, where they are deconsolidated for distribution to retail outlets.

Fig. 10-2: Distributive pooling from a central point.

<u>Multi-pool</u> scenarios mean that the shipments involved might move through more than one pool point, involving perhaps both consolidation and deconsolidation along the way.

The necessity of pooling, and the benefits of a pooling strategy, are highly dependent on the nature of the business. A transportation <u>broker</u> often is just trying to find a carrier to move something from Point A to Point B for a client. In general, brokers are (usually) less likely to be relying on the same standing distribution network over and over.

On the other hand, <u>shippers</u> repetitively moving their own goods – bulk, manufactured or retail -- across a well-defined network of distribution centers and docks are excellent candidates for a pool strategy.

Third-party logistics providers, or 3PLs, operate on behalf of contracted clients and might be able to take advantage of network optimization. In ideal conditions, 3PLs might be able to optimize a network across multiple customers. That's also true for "4PLs", or "fourth-party" providers managing multiple 3PLs for clients.

Pooling Considerations in Optimization

When it comes to incorporating a pooling strategy in optimization, we start by asking two important questions:

(1) What existing pooling constraints must we include?

(2) What might we be able to do with a pooling strategy to get an improved result?

As examples in the "must" category, we might have to move through pre-assigned pool points.

Maybe we have to send all our widgets through Atlanta, and all our gizmos through Memphis, because that where our specialized widget-loading and gizmo-loading facilities are located.

Remember, too, that we might need to consider facility-related limitations that we covered in the last chapter, such as operating hours, load/unload service times, and dock capacity.

As examples in the "we might be able to do better" category: What if we are allowed to consider pooling, but only to use it when it produces the best result?

What if we could choose <u>which</u> pool points made the most sense, out of a list of possible locations in our network, instead of using a pre-assigned strategy of fixed pool points?

These are the kinds of questions we'll put to our optimization tool.

'Network' vs. 'Rate' Optimization

One overall warning about pooling strategies – the more front-end requirements that they include, such as preassigned pool points, the less likely they are to be our least-cost solution.

We'll sometimes see that when compared to direct-ship cost, our optimized savings when using pools actually is smaller than if we did not use pooling at all.

That's not surprising. If we have to move everything through Albuquerque, then that's just what we have to do. We'll have to get the best result with the requirements we've got.

Respecting pooling and facility constraints, while still arriving at the best scenario we can, is an example of pursuing the philosophy of <u>network optimization</u> we discussed in the first chapter.

Pooling in the Optimization Wizard

Let's turn to the nuts and bolts of setting up pooling in our optimization tool. There are four settings in the optimization wizard that work together.

<u>(1) Pool Strategy</u>

As with carrier capacity, our first decision is whether to consider pooling at all.

Most of the settings related to pools are found on the third wizard screen (Fig. 10-3). The first setting, "Pool Strategy", has a default setting of "Off", meaning the optimizer will not use pools.

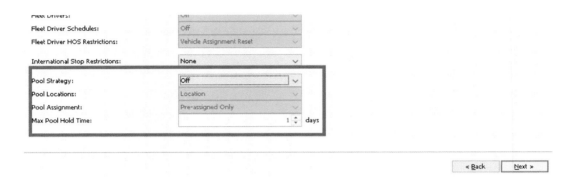

Fig. 10-3: Pool-related settings in the optimization wizard.

The other options for this setting are "Consider Pools", "Consider Hybrid" and "Force Pools".

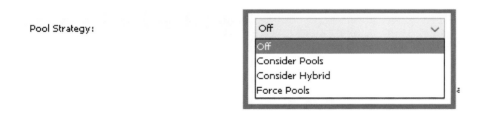

Fig. 10-4: Pool strategy options in the optimization wizard.

The "Force Pools" strategy instructs the optimizer to send each shipment through a pool point no matter what. We'll see examples of how this is used.

"Consider Pools" looks at a list of possible locations and decides which location, if any, would be the best choice for each shipment. Otherwise the optimizer might not assign one.

"Consider Hybrid" is a specialized option than deals with a deeper level of calculation and is not used in most cases.

(2) Pool Locations

If we're telling the optimizer to "consider" locations, we have to supply a list of locations to consider. Notice that the next setting in the wizard is named "Pool Locations":

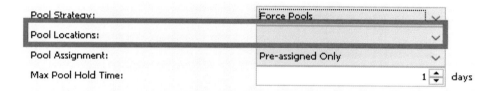

Fig. 10-5: The 'Pool Locations' setting is where we supply the name of a location report to use for possible pool points.

The value for this setting is the name of a report of type "Location" that has been opened.

We got our first look at Location reports in the last chapter. A list of possible columns and expected values in Location reports is found in the appendix.

Shipment	RateTable	Our Locations X	OptParam

Report Type: Location ▽   Data Level: << Imported Data >>   Run D

Location Code	City	State	Postal Code	Country	Geo
COLO	DENVER	CO	80239	USA	39.785060,-104.824569
IND2	JASPER	IN	47546	USA	38.395439,-86.932334
INDY	INDIANAPOLIS	IN	46221	USA	39.699569,-86.233680
IOWA	DES MOINES	IA	50325	USA	41.604999,-93.747734

Fig. 10-6: A list of possible pool points is opened. The report is of type 'Location'.

If only one location report is open, its name will be the only choice in the wizard setting. If more than one is open, the user can choose which Location report to use for pool points:

Pool Strategy: Force Pools ▽

Pool Locations: Our Locations ▽

Pool Assignment: Our Locations

Max Pool Hold Time: Location Hours   days

Fig. 10-7: If multiple Location reports are open, the user can choose which list will supply possible pool points to the optimizer.

In a Location report for pool points, the only required columns are "Location Code" and "Geo." (If you need to install geodata in your list, you also need columns for valid city-state combinations, zip and country.)

However, we also can add columns to restrict a pool location by mode and carrier SCAC, on the pickup or drop side or both. And we can specify an individual max <u>hold</u> time at this location – how long a shipment can wait before being put on an outbound load.

Drop Modes	String
Drop SCACs	String
Pickup Modes	String
Pickup SCACs	String
Max Pool Hold Time	Numeric

(3) Pool Assignment

So far we have seen settings for whether to "force" or merely to "consider" pool points, and how to supply a list of locations to "consider".

The next setting, "Pool Assignment", tells the optimizer <u>how</u> to make its decisions when selecting pool points.

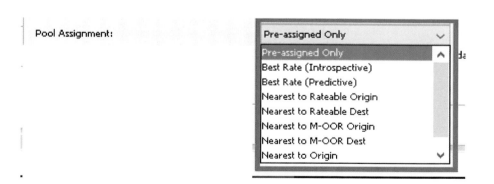

Fig. 10-8: Options for telling the optimizer how to assign pool points.

Pre-assigned Only	Use pre-assigned pool points from the shipment data. There must be a column from the Shipment report mapped in the 'Pool Locations' setting of the first wizard screen.
Best Rate	Choose the pool point from a Location list that produces the best rate. "Predictive" and "Introspective" describe search depth, with "Introspective" taking longer.
Nearest to Origin/Dest	Choose a pool point nearest to the shipment origin or destination
Nearest to Origin/Dest (Ratetable)	Choose the nearest pool point with a rate table origin or destination. (This ensures the leg in question can be rated.)
Nearest to Origin/Dest (MOOR)	Choose a pool point nearest to shipment origin or destination that falls within a max out of route limit.

Next we'll see examples of how these settings work together.

Examples & Results

Let's start with a straightforward pooling scenario. In this example our input data consists of 652 shipments. If we optimize without pooling, we get a consolidation into 82 execution loads and a savings of 78 percent against estimated direct-ship cost.

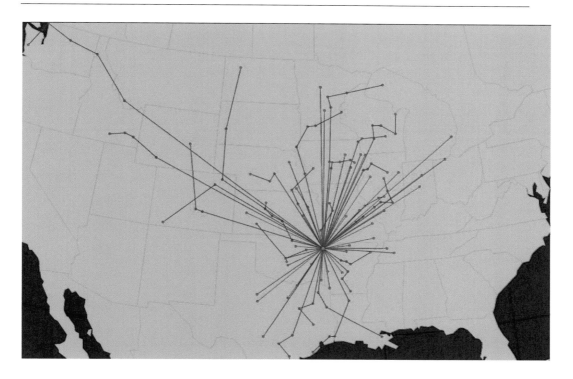

Fig. 10-9: Optimization without pooling.

Now we'll re-run the optimizer, this time telling the optimizer to use a column in the shipment data that contains pre-assigned pool points:

ry (Late)	Quantity	Weight	Max Freight Class	PoolPointID
. 23:59	3.00	151.00	60.00	MON3
. 23:59	4.00	199.00	60.00	MON3
. 23:59	4.00	199.00	60.00	MON3
. 23:59	3.00	166.00	60.00	MON3

Fig. 10-10: A column of pre-assigned pool points in our shipment data. Each shipment is telling us where it is supposed to go.

Remember that we use the first wizard screen to map columns from our shipment data. On that screen we'll tell the optimizer to use the column named "PoolPointID" to supply preassigned pools:

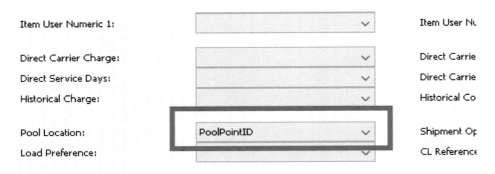

Fig. 10-11: Telling the optimizer to use this column in the shipment data to get our pre-assigned pool points.

Next we change the pooling settings on the third wizard screen. We'll use a strategy of "Force Pools", with an assignment of "Pre-Assigned Only". We're telling the optimizer that it must use the preassigned pool points from the shipment data.

Fig. 10-12: Telling the optimizer that it must assign a pool point for every shipment, and it must use the pre-assigned pool points from the shipment data.

The results in Fig. 10-13 are strikingly different from our first, non-pooled run. We have a lot more individual loads coming in and out of distinctive pool points – more than 600, nearly the number of our original shipments. But we do meet the requirements of our network, and in this example, even save a little money.

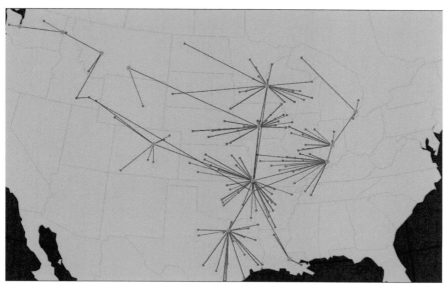

Fig. 10-13: The same shipments are now being forced through designated pool points.

Next we'll take the same shipment and use a "Consider Pools" strategy. Our data includes a Location report that has the same choices as the locations in the shipment data. We'll use an assignment method of "Nearest to Destination."

Pool Strategy:	Consider Pools	∨	
Pool Locations:	Our Locs	∨	
Pool Assignment:	Nearest to Destination	∨	
Max Pool Hold Time:		1 ⏶⏷	days

Fig. 10-14: Re-running the same data with different pool parameters.

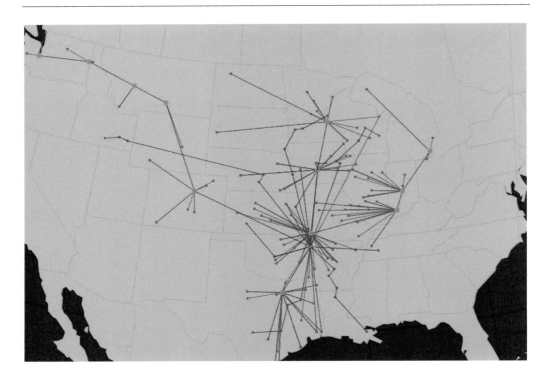

Fig. 10-15: Using a "consider pools" strategy allows more direct routes, but uses fewer legs overall.

The map in Fig. 10-15 is a little more "messy" than our first pooling result. There are non-pooled routes included in this result. However, the total number of <u>legs</u> in this "consider" strategy is fewer than half of the total legs required in the "force" strategy, at roughly the same savings! This approach seems to be a reasonable balance between the philosophies of "network", "route" and "rate" optimization.

Analyzing Pooling Results

In Chapters 6 and 7 we learned about reviewing the results of an optimization and looking for improvements. When we're using a pooling strategy, there's some additional information available to us.

Summary Statistics

The summary statistics now include estimated savings versus direct-cost estimates for both pooled and non-pooled scenarios.

Shipment Count:	652 Legs: 1283		Load Count:	643				
Direct CO₂:	935 tons		Optimized CO₂:	321 tons	CO₂ Change:	614 tons		
Direct Distance:	422,201 mi		Optimized Distance:	145,002 mi	Distance Change:	277,199 mi (65.7%)		
Direct Cost:	$477,183.01	No Pools: $201,197.98	Optimized Cost:	$41,174.84	Optimized Savings:	$436,008.17 (91.4%)	No Pools: $160,023.15 (79.5%)	

Fig. 10-16: Result statistics of a pooling scenario.

In Fig. 10-16, "Direct Cost" means the direct cost of the legs used in the pooling scenario. The "No Pools" value in the first column would be the direct cost of the shipments without using pools at all – notice how much lower it would cost to ship direct without pools!

The middle column shows the result of the optimization, and the third column calculates the savings between the first and second columns. "Optimized Savings" means we are comparing the optimized pooling result to the direct-ship cost of the pool legs. The "No Pools" value is the savings versus direct cost of never optimizing in the first place.

Optimizer Loads/Shipments Tabs

In the "Events" column of the Optimizer Loads tab, for the kind of events the optimizer has scheduled, the codes "I" and "O" (for inbound to a pool location, and outbound from a pool location) now join the "P" and "D" codes used for pickups and drops.

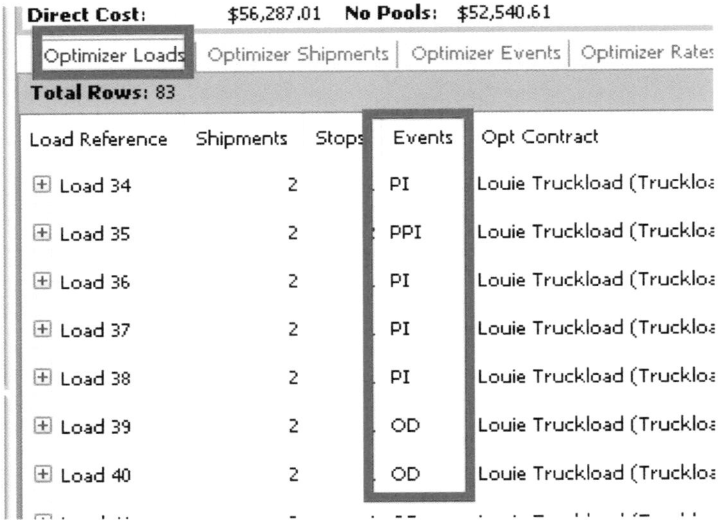

Fig. 10-17: Event sequences in pooling results – P for pickup, I for inbound to pool point, O for outbound from pool point, D for delivery.

In the Optimizer Shipments tab, pool point information is listed in columns for each shipment: Pool Direction, Pool Point, Pool Hold Time, Pool Zone (if used), Pool Direct Rate (rate on this leg before optimization).

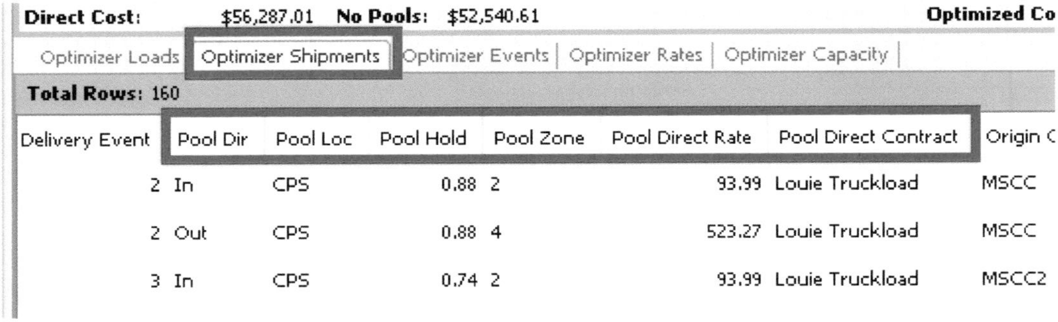

Fig. 10-18: Pool-related results reported in the Optimizer Shipments tab.

Optimizer Events Tab

As we saw in the last chapter, detailed information is attached to each scheduled event in the optimization under the "Optimizer Events" tab. Note that each event include information about service time, operating hours, and dock usage.

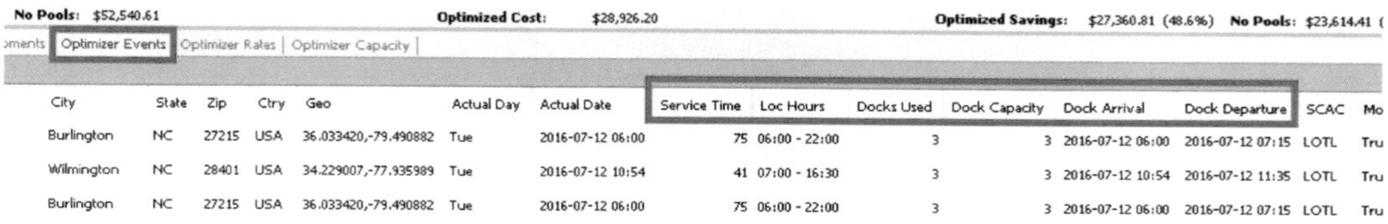

City	State	Zip	Ctry	Geo	Actual Day	Actual Date	Service Time	Loc Hours	Docks Used	Dock Capacity	Dock Arrival	Dock Departure	SCAC	Mo
Burlington	NC	27215	USA	36.033420,-79.490882	Tue	2016-07-12 06:00	75	06:00 - 22:00	3		3 2016-07-12 06:00	2016-07-12 07:15	LOTL	Tru
Wilmington	NC	28401	USA	34.229007,-77.935989	Tue	2016-07-12 10:54	41	07:00 - 16:30	3		3 2016-07-12 10:54	2016-07-12 11:35	LOTL	Tru
Burlington	NC	27215	USA	36.033420,-79.490882	Tue	2016-07-12 06:00	75	06:00 - 22:00	3		3 2016-07-12 06:00	2016-07-12 07:15	LOTL	Tru

Fig. 10-19: Location-related information for each event in the optimization, under the 'Optimizer Events' tab.

For each event listed in the Optimizer Events tab, clicking its expandable icon opens "drill-down" details. One of these, "Related Docks", shows the loads being processed at the related docks of this facility at the same time.

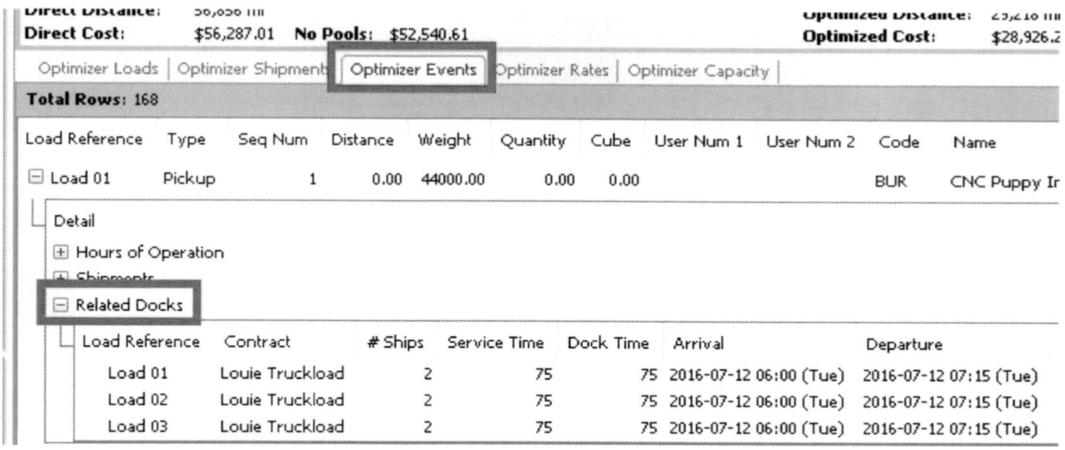

Fig. 10-20: 'Related Docks' information about other loads being processed at this facility at the same time.

Troubleshooting Tip

For first-time data, even if you just want the optimizer to "consider" pool points, it's a good idea to use a "Force Pools" strategy initially just to make sure there are no issues with your data or rates

The reason for this is that an error condition will appear if the optimizer could not assign a pool point to a shipment. For example, there might not be a valid outbound rate available from the designated pool point.

If we just start with a "consider pools" option, we'll miss such errors, since we can't tell whether a pool point was not assigned because of an error, or because the optimizer simply decided not to assign one.

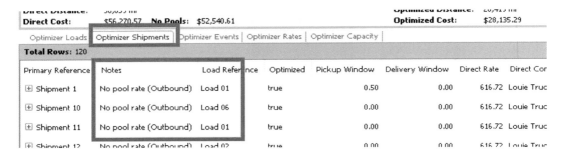

Fig. 10-21: We told the optimizer to use a pre-assigned pool point, but the rate table did not cover it. The error condition was revealed by using a 'Force Pools' strategy.

Multi-pooling

We also can tell the optimizer to use a <u>multi-pooling</u> scenario, in which two pool points are used in the course of moving a single shipment. A common application would be to model intermodal or multi-leg ocean moves.

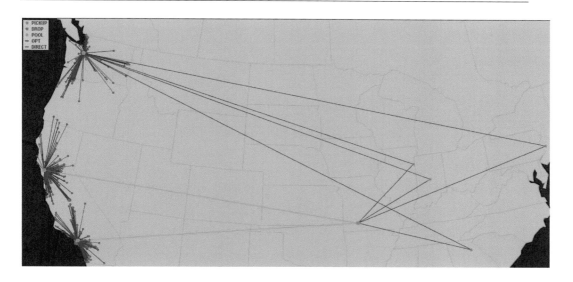

Fig. 10-22: Multipool scenario – pickup legs brought to consolidation pool points, deconsolidated at distribution pool points.

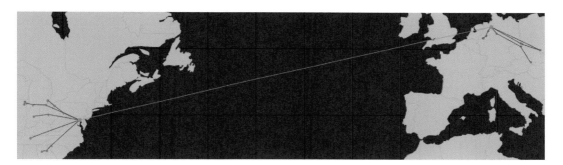

Fig. 10-23: Multipool international ocean movement.

Configuration of multipool movements requires:

(1) The Mojo option "multipool" installed in the application system preferences menu:

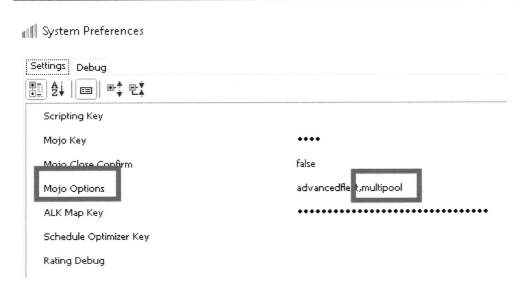

Fig. 10-24: Enabling multipool optimization in the System Preference window.

(2) A location report that uses the following syntax for multipool points with the characters "<" and ">":

For the inbound (first) pool point:

inbound location code<outboundlocationcode

For the second (outbound) pool point:

outboundlocationcode>inbound location code

To use the inbound and/or outbound pools as stand-alone pools (i.e. allowed to be used without chaining), you must also define the inbound and/or outbound pools using normal annotations.

Conclusion

Pooling is a powerful time- and cost-savings tool used by logistics personnel and the modern transportation optimizer makes complex usage possible. However, network considerations must be addressed to keep the problem manageable by the optimizer. We might be required to use certain facilities, for example in a preassigned-pool-point scenario where a shipment is bound for a mall and is distributed from a local cross-dock. We also should have the option to "consider" pool points when they make the most sense financially.

In general, many things may force us toward a network requirement in pooling that has the possibility of moving us away from a least-cost alternative. Nonetheless, our optimization must allow us to consider these constraints so we can still arrive at a realistic optimal solution that satisfies our pooling needs.

Discussion Questions

1. Is pooling a goal we should always strive for in optimization? Why or why not? Are certain kind of business scenarios more likely to support pooling?

2. What considerations might drive us to use pooling in our optimization even if it gives us something besides a least-cost solution?

3. To achieve an optimized pooling result that works in the real world, what are some of the factors we should take into consideration about our network facilities?

\#\#\#

Chapter 11: Making the Most of Private or Dedicated Fleet/Assets

The terms "private fleet", "private assets" or "dedicated assets" describe tractors, trailers, equipment and drivers that are under the ownership or control of the party doing the optimization.

In other words, we're talking about using optimization to decide whether and how to use <u>our own trucks</u>. The term "private" usually is distinct from "third-party carrier" or "common carrier". However, in some cases the common carrier has provided "dedicated" assets for the client's exclusive use.

An example of private fleet usage would be a large retail shipper using optimization to move its goods on its own trucks from its distribution centers to its retail locations.

Another example would be a produce shipper optimizing its own fleet of regional vehicles to supply its consolidation pool points, which are then served by common-carrier truckload.

Private-fleet assets can be worked into an optimization mix in a variety of ways:

- As the only carrier for all loads.
- As the required or preferred carrier for specific locations, geographic areas or load types (but see the warning just below).
- As a backup or last resort when other options are unavailable or undesirable.
- As an everyday alternative, "competing" with common carriers to be selected as the optimal solution.

Of the above options, the most flexible for the purpose of optimization is the last scenario, in which private assets "compete" alongside third-party carriers.

In fact, almost any other approach to allocating private assets – <u>especially</u> by an arbitrary geographic boundary – is a step away from an optimal result.

'Total Cost of Ownership'

Designing our decision-making about the right asset mix starts with a simple question:

How much does the private fleet really, <u>REALLY</u> cost to operate?

Many small- to mid-sized owners of private assets do not really know how much they cost to own and operate. The decision to use them instead is made on the basis of statements such as:

"We've already paid for them, so our only expenses are fuel and drivers." (This is <u>never</u> true.)

Or: "We invested in them, so it would be a waste not to use them." (This is not <u>necessarily</u> true.)

At the other extreme, large corporations will go to impressive lengths to construct a true cost model for their owned assets – and never think twice when there's a better option.

In some examples at the corporate level, teams of accountants are employed to develop models that capture expenses not immediately obvious. The purpose is to arrive at a figure known as "total cost of ownership."

The obvious expenses are the cost of the equipment itself, maintenance and drivers. But here are some other costs that might need to be considered:

- Insurance.
- Regulatory, permitting and licensing expense, including required training.
- Depreciation.
- Financing expense.
- Administrative costs.
- Allocation of common expenses.

Some cost models go even further and calculate the "opportunity cost" to the business of owning fleet assets in the first place. Would the business have been better off putting its money into building profits elsewhere, instead of into buying trucks?

These are difficult questions, which means that easy answers don't work. So the statement, "My only expenses are fuel and drivers" is untrue. And as for not wanting to "waste" assets that have been bought and paid for – think of the old saying about "throwing good money after bad."

Today's optimizer must help manage the equipment in a way that ensures proper use of both private and over-the-road carriers. . That decision should be made purely on business considerations. It is extremely critical to use the proper equipment on the move to ensure maximum transportation cost effectiveness.

Fleet Data for Optimization

When we optimize with common carriers we're not managing specific pieces of equipment. We're just saying, "We plan to hire X number of trucks from Carrier Z." It's up to Carrier Z to decide exactly which trucks to send us – we don't really care, except for equipment type.

In contrast, when we're building routes for <u>our</u> assets, we'll likely want to keep track by individual vehicle, and maybe even by individual driver. For that kind of route-building and precise scheduling we need to have information about:

- Exactly what equipment is available.
- Where it is now, and its home location (its "domicile").
- Available drivers and their schedules.

We'll supply those categories of information to our optimizer the same way that we supply shipment, rate and location data – using "reports" or spreadsheets that we open and then select in the optimizer wizard.

The Key Ingredient: Private Fleet Rates

Besides lists of equipment and drivers, the other data that the optimizer needs are the "rates" that we will "charge" for their use. The rates are listed in the rate table just like any common carrier – the private fleet is assigned its own, made-up SCAC.

The words "rates" and "charge" are in quote marks in that last paragraph because we're usually just talking about an estimated cost of operation that we will use to compare against real, outside carrier rates. (Unless a large organization uses an accounting scheme that actually charges transportation costs by department.)

Valid At	Contract Id	Contract Oid	Use Se...	Item Ra...	Effective Date	Expiration Date	Lane Calc	SCAC	Mo...	Service
HowardCo Sandbox	HowardCo LTL Customer	16227219700	true	false	2012-01-01 00:00	2020-12-31 23:59	CTRY-CTRY	HOWC	LTL	Standard
HowardCo Sandbox	HowardCo Private Fleet	21025322574	false	false	2015-01-01 00:00	2020-12-31 00:00	SC-SC	PFLT	TL	Standard
HowardCo Sandbox	HowardCo Private Fleet	21025322574	false	false	2015-01-01 00:00	2020-12-31 00:00	SC-SC	PFLT	TL	Standard
HowardCo Sandbox	HowardCo Private Fleet	21025322574	false	false	2015-01-01 00:00	2020-12-31 00:00	CTRY-CTRY	PFLT	TL	Standard
HowardCo Sandbox	KK TL Contract	20337017700	false	false	2014-09-05 00:00	2015-12-31 00:00	CTRY-CTRY	KKTK	TL	Standard
HowardCo Sandbox	LLTL Carrier Contract LTL	15338562500	true	false	2012-01-01 00:00	2020-12-31 23:59	CTRY-CTRY	LLTL	LTL	Standard
HowardCo Sandbox	LYND01 Carrier Contract	15338545900	false	false	2012-01-01 00:00	2015-12-31 00:00	CTRY-CTRY	LYND	TL	Standard
HowardCo Sandbox	Simone LTL Contract	16352290000	true	false	2012-01-01 00:00	2020-12-31 23:59	CTRY-CTRY	SIMO	LTL	Standard

Fig. 11-1: The private fleet's rates are included in the rate table where they compete against the rates of common carriers.

This is why it's so important to have an accurate cost model. If the true cost of using private assets is underestimated in the rate table, then the private fleet "looks too good" compared to other carriers, and the optimizer will wrongly favor it too often.

The simplest approach is to create a rate table using a cost-per-mile estimate derived from historical Total Cost of Ownership divided by historical mileage.

However, you also could create lanes that apply higher or lower rates by location code, city, state, or any other factor, to fine-tune the estimated cost.

Fixed vs. Variable Costs

Some asset owners refer to a "turn-on-the-truck" expense, meaning that it costs a certain amount just to set a truck in operation at all – before we begin to take into account variable costs such as fuel.

Fuel is a variable expense, obviously – the more we drive, the more it costs. But other expenses (licensing fees, an allocated share of administrative costs, etc.) do not necessarily vary according to miles or freight.

Can we model a flat or fixed "turn on the truck" cost in a rate table? Yes. We can assign a flat-rate <u>accessorial charge</u> to the appropriate lane or lanes in the rate table.

An "accessorial charge" is an additional charge on a lane for some kind of extra service, such as use of a lift gate, or two-man, indoor Saturday delivery. In practice there are dozens if not hundreds of categories of accessorial charges.

Accessorial charges can be variable – a charge calculated per stop, per mile, per pound, etc. – or they can be a flat rate attached to a load.

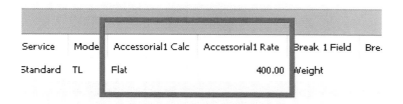

Service	Mode	Accessorial1 Calc	Accessorial1 Rate	Break 1 Field	Bre.
Standard	TL	Flat	400.00	Weight	

Fig. 11-2: A flat-rate accessorial charge assessed in a rate table. We can add a flat charge to our private fleet rates that represents a 'turn on the truck' fixed charge.

Here's a final word on private fleet rates:

As you might have surmised, accurate cost modeling is both science and art, and experts spend a lot of time trying to do it well. The critical point is that if the private fleet is to be represented fairly in the rate table, then the rates reflected there should be as realistic as we can make them.

About 'Domiciles'

In the fleet optimizations we're about to see, vehicles are assigned to a "domicile" or home location. By necessity, our optimization models must contemplate both the outbound movement of equipment from the domicile to first pickup, and a return leg to the domicile after the last drop.

We don't <u>have</u> to assign specific domiciles – but we do have to do <u>something</u> with our trucks when we're done with a route. So if we do not assign a domicile, the optimizer will return the truck to the origin of its load. (In any case, a truck cannot be re-used until it is returned.)

This is one of the big distinctions of managing our own assets. When we hire a truckload or LTL carrier's truck, we don't care what happens after the last drop. As far as we're concerned, that truck disappears magically into thin air.

But <u>our</u> trucks do <u>not</u> disappear by magic. Our returns require time, mileage, drivers and money, and we have to consider all those factors in our model. (As for third-party carriers – rest assured, they've already figured those costs into the rates they're charging us.)

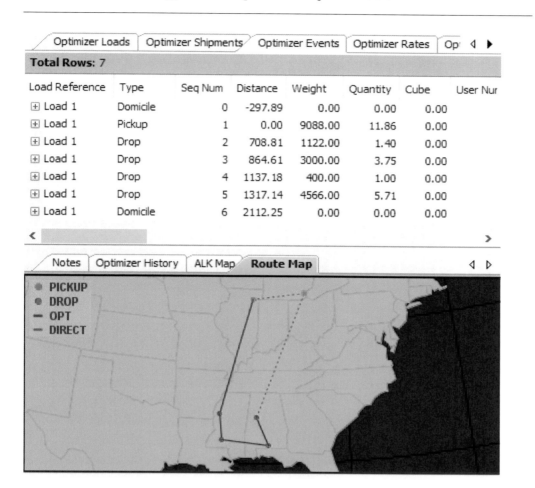

Fig. 11-3: An event list and associated route map from a private fleet optimization. The dotted lines show travel from and return to the domicile location.

Fleet Optimization Results

Let's jump to the end of an optimization run and see what we're aiming for – a result that considers private assets in the mix with common carriers.

Besides lists of shipments and rates, our input data also might include lists of domicile locations, vehicles, drivers and driver schedules. We'll see how each of these works in just a bit.

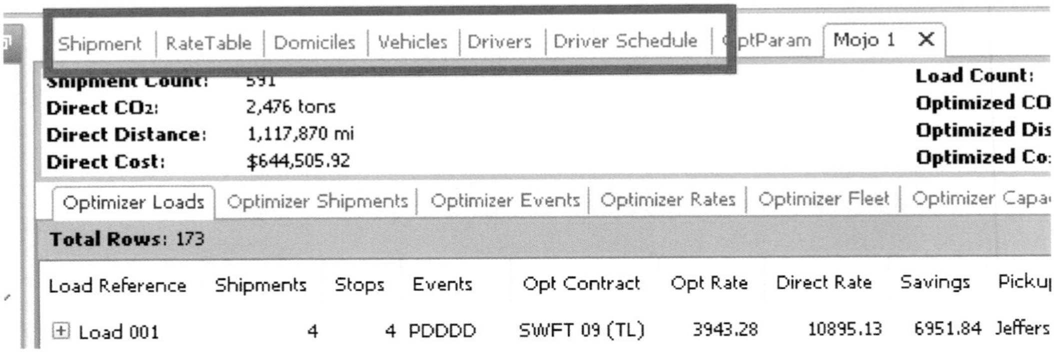

Fig. 11-4: Optimizing with private assets can involve the use of other kinds of data, such as lists of vehicles, drivers and driver schedules.

The results screen has some new features. For starters, there are new symbols in the sequence of characters that describe the events on a load. A "<" symbol represents the equipment outbound from its domicile location, and a ">" symbol represents the equipment return to its domicile (Fig. 11-5).

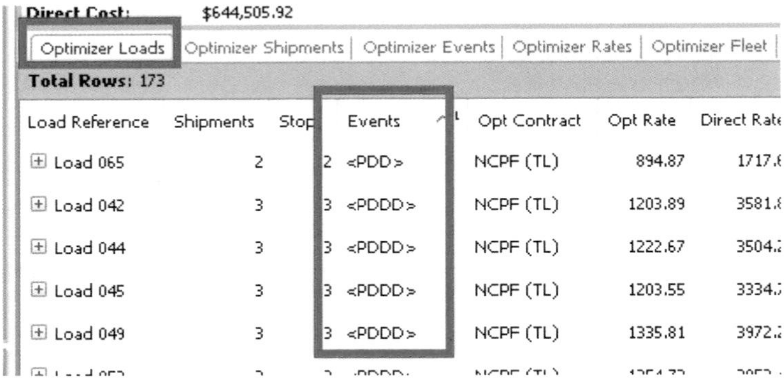

Fig. 11-5: When we assign a truck to a 'domicile' location, its outbound leg to the first pickup and its return to the domicile after the last drop are indicated with '<' and '>' symbols.

The expandable "Events" list in a load detail shows the truck's travel from, and return to, its assigned domicile location if any:

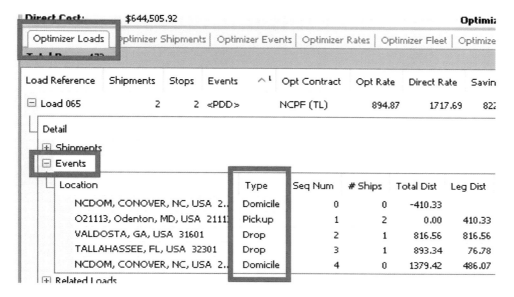

Fig. 11-6: Outbound and return legs of type 'Domicile' in a load's event sequence. Notice the outbound event is #0 in the sequence, and the distance to first pickup is reflected as a negative value.

The "Optimizer Events" results tab includes Domicile events in the list:

Load Reference	Type	Seq Num	Distance	Weight	Quantity	Cu
⊞ Load 049	Domicile	5	2311.53	0.00	0.00	
⊞ Load 050	Domicile	0	-410.33	0.00	0.00	
⊞ Load 050	Pickup	1	0.00	7460.00	36.00	

Total Rows: 790

Fig. 11-7: Outbound and return domicile events displayed in 'Optimizer Events' results tab.

A new tab of results labeled "Optimizer Fleet" shows us utilization by vehicle and driver:

Optimizer Loads	Optimizer Shipments	Optimizer Events	Optimizer Rates	**Optimizer Fleet**	Optimizer Capacity

Total Rows: 12

Vehicle Id	Driver Id	Load Reference	Location Code	Driver Week	Duty Hours	Start Duty	End Duty
NCV01	D03	Load 042	NCDOM	2008-06-30 00:00	53.41	2008-06-30 15:03	2008-07-04 13:12
NCV01	D03	Load 044	NCDOM	2008-07-07 00:00	54.16	2008-07-07 00:01	2008-07-10 22:56
NCV01	D03	Load 045	NCDOM	2008-07-14 00:00	53.39	2008-07-14 00:01	2008-07-17 22:10
NCV01	D03	Load 046	NCDOM	2008-07-21 00:00	52.93	2008-07-21 00:01	2008-07-24 21:42

Fig. 11-8: Utilization of private fleet assets, by vehicle, reported in the 'Optimizer Fleet' results tab.

Lastly, vehicle and driver utilization are noted in the load and event timetable charts available from optimization results, and can be analyzed in the result pivot table.

Fig. 11-9 is a simple pivot table showing breakdown between private and common-carrier assets by spend, shipment and load count. "NCPF" is the SCAC assigned to our own assets:

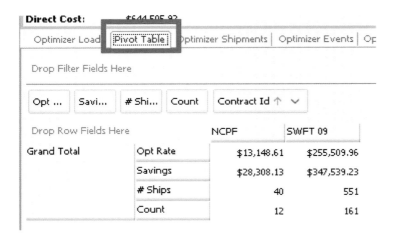

Fig. 11-9: Pivot-table analysis of utilization of private assets vs common carrier in an optimization.

Optimization Wizard Settings

Let's turn now to the nuts and bolts of setting up a private fleet scenario in the optimizer wizard. We'll need to supply the wizard with some or all of the following information:

1. Whether to use individual vehicle assignments at all.
2. A setting regarding fleet capacity limits for non-optimized shipments.
3. A location list to use for vehicle "domiciles".
4. A list of vehicles available for assignment.
5. A list of drivers available to operate those vehicles.
6. A list of schedules that control driver duty.
7. A setting for how to calculate driver rest time.

All fleet-related settings are grouped on the third wizard screen, just above the pool-related settings that we explored in the last chapter:

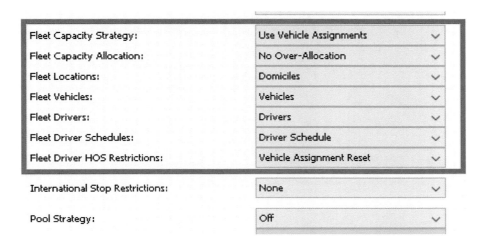

Fleet Capacity Strategy:	Use Vehicle Assignments
Fleet Capacity Allocation:	No Over-Allocation
Fleet Locations:	Domiciles
Fleet Vehicles:	Vehicles
Fleet Drivers:	Drivers
Fleet Driver Schedules:	Driver Schedule
Fleet Driver HOS Restrictions:	Vehicle Assignment Reset
International Stop Restrictions:	None
Pool Strategy:	Off

Fig. 11-10: Fleet-related settings in the optimization wizard.

The first setting, labeled "Fleet Capacity Strategy", is where we tell the optimizer whether we'll be assigning and tracking our own trucks. This setting has two possible values: "Same as Non-Fleet" and "Use Vehicle Assignments".

Fig. 11-11: Possible values for 'Fleet Capacity Strategy' parameter.

If this value is "Same as Non-Fleet" then fleet assets are assigned from the rate table just like any common carrier, according to the settings that we previously covered in the chapter on carrier capacity.

If this value instead is "Use Vehicle Assignments", then we'll be assigning and tracking individual vehicles in a private fleet scenario. We'll learn more about how to do this in a minute.

The next setting, "Fleet Capacity Allocation", tells the optimizer what to do with non-optimized shipments. The first setting looks for a direct rate that still respects carrier capacity. The second setting simply assigns a direct rate without regard for capacity limits.

Fig. 11-12: The 'Fleet Capacity Allocation' setting controls how direct rates are assigned to non-optimized shipments.

Next comes a setting labeled "Fleet Locations". This is the name of a Location report that includes a list of locations to be used for the assignment of vehicles to domiciles. The minimum columns required are a location code and a geocode.

Fig. 11-13: A location report named 'Domiciles' will be used to locate the domiciles of listed equipment. 'Domiciles' is the name of one of the Location reports currently open.

The setting "Fleet Vehicles" can be set to "Off", or it can be set to use a new report type, "Vehicle". A "Vehicle" report is a list of the actual equipment in our fleet. Its columns are:

Vehicle Id	A unique vehicle identifier
Location Code	Valid fleet location code to use as vehicle's domicile. If blank, the vehicle is returned to the load origin instead.
Contract Id	Valid rating contract to use for this fleet vehicle. A contract may be assigned only one domicile, so you may need to duplicate contracts for fleets that use more than one domicile.
Availability Start	Optional date/time indicating vehicle available. Can be used to remove vehicles from service for scheduled maintenance periods.
Availability End	Optional column that works with 'Availability Start'.

In optimizing private assets, we also can decide whether to assign and track individual drivers (or pools or teams of available drivers). If so, the setting labeled "Fleet Drivers" allows us to choose a report type of "Driver" that contains such a list.

Fleet Drivers:

Fig. 11-14: The 'Fleet Drivers' setting lets us supply a list of drivers to use in the optimization.

A report of type "Driver" contains these columns:

Driver Id	Unique driver identifier
Location Code	Valid fleet location code. Driver will be assigned to vehicles domiciled at this location. (This means drivers cannot be assigned to vehicles without domiciles.)
Max Weekly Duty	(Optional) A numerical value, typically 60 for U.S. drivers
First DOW	(Optional) Sun, Mon, Tue, etc. – first day of work week. To enforce a rest period before the first DOW, use a "Driver Schedules" report – described below
Schedule Id	(Optional) Use a driver schedule (described below) that has this Id for this driver – if this column is not specified, the optimizer uses the Driver Id to look for a schedule

Just two more settings to go.

If we're using a Driver report, we also have the option to use a Driver Schedule report (type "DriverSch"). This allows us to spell out exact schedule limitations.

A single Driver Schedule report can hold multiple schedules, since each line includes the name of the individual schedule to which it belongs. The columns are:

- Schedule Id
- Days
- Hours

"Schedule Id" is the name of the schedule to which this line belongs. The value corresponds to the "Schedule Id" in a Driver report – the optimizer will apply any matching schedule to that driver.

The formats for setting days and hours are like those used in hours of operation, discussed in the chapter on facility capacity. To review, the allowed formats are:

For days: MON,TUE,WED, or Date:12-25
For hours: 0900-1800,2100-2400

A schedule might apply to an individual driver, or to a group of drivers. The schedule limits the dates/times that a driver is assigned to a load and away from the domicile.

The driver schedule therefore is one way to enforce driver duty limits. For example, if the Driver report has a weekly limit of 70 hours and a Monday week start, we can use a driver schedule to guarantee an off-duty period before the week start (i.e., no schedule on Sunday or Monday morning).

The last fleet-related setting is labeled "Fleet Driver HOS Restrictions" and it gives us flexibility in enforcing required driver rest. There are two settings, "Vehicle Assignment Reset" and "Require Rest Reset".

Fleet Driver HOS Restrictions:

Fig. 11-15: Options for enforcing driver hour restrictions.

If this setting is "Vehicle Assignment Reset", then the driver is assigned for a new duty period regardless of any prior rest period. This scenario might be used for assignment to a named driver group, with the assumption that any individual driver is property rested.

The other setting, "Require Rest Reset", enforces the driver rest requirement set in the earlier wizard setting labeled "Driver Off-Duty Rest" (a default value of 10 hours).

Requiring Asset Use

We can use wizard parameters to make sure that private fleet equipment is used in a specific way desired by the client. Let's say we want to make sure only private assets are used for refrigerated loads. This is a simple enforcement of equipment types in the wizard. The equipment is requested in the shipment data:

Mojo Shipments ✕								
Report Type: Shipment ⌄		**Data Level:** HCS Logistics Inc.	**Run Date:** 06/24/2015 02:35:23PM		**Total Rows:** 58			
Owner	Primary Reference	Equipment	Origin Code	Origin Name		Origin City	Origin State	Orig
HCS Logistics Inc.	S-0013 (BOL)	48 Ft Reefer (48R)	MSSC	Main Street Shipping Co		Saluda	NC	287
Wilson Plastics Co.	S-0037 (BOL)		WILS	Wilson Plastics Co.		Charlotte	NC	282

Fig. 11-16: Equipment requested in shipment data.

Meanwhile our private fleet's rate table should include a "Carrier Equipment" column (the column name must be exact) that states that this carrier does indeed provide the equipment type:

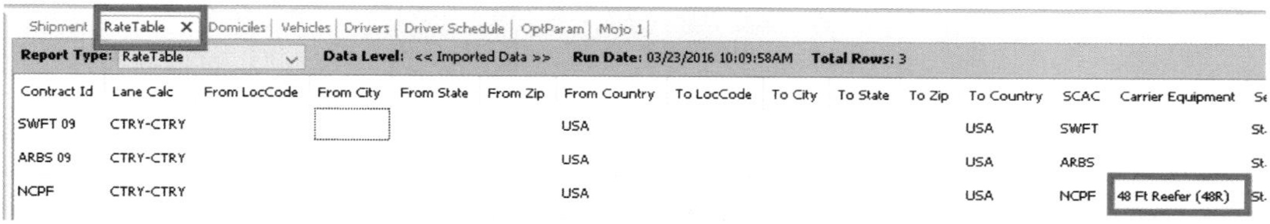

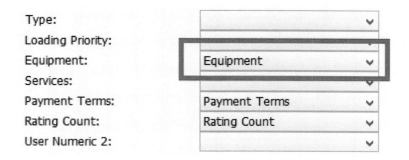

Fig. 11-17: Rate table entries that supply the requested equipment.

The final piece of the puzzle is turning on equipment enforcement in the optimization wizard. On the first wizard screen make sure that the shipment report's "Equipment" column is properly mapped. At the top of the fourth screen, make sure we actually are enforcing the equipment requirement.

Type:	⌄
Loading Priority:	
Equipment:	Equipment ⌄
Services:	⌄
Payment Terms:	Payment Terms ⌄
Rating Count:	Rating Count ⌄
User Numeric 2:	⌄

Fig. 11-18: Mapping equipment column from the shipment data on the first wizard screen.

Mojo Optimization Wizard

Mojo Optimization Params (Page 3)

Select your optimization options.

Equipment Enforcement: ☑ ⚠

Services Enforcement: ☐ ⚠

Pickup Clustering: 0 ⬍ radius

Pickup Clustering: 0 ⬍ radius

Fig. 11-19: Instucting the optimzer to enforce the equipment requirements of the shipment data against the equipment types available in the rate table.

Upon optimization, Mojo obeys the constraint and assigns refrigerated shipments to the private-fleet carrier that provides that equipment:

Load 21	1	1	PD	Simone LTL Contract (LTL)	445.90	445.90	0.00		St. Petersburg, FL
Load 22	1	1	PD	HowardCo Private Fleet (TL)	2698.56	2698.56	0.00	48 Ft Reefer (48R)	Saluda, NC

Notes Optimizer History Route Map

Fig. 11-20: The optimizer assigns refrigerated shipments only to the private fleet lanes in the rate table that supply the necessary equipment.

Instead of equipment, we could just as easily require services that only the private fleet provides. We could use all-purpose, user-defined fields in shipment reports to match them with rate tables. We could create customized names to avoid confusion with values in common carrier rate tables as well.

Technical Footnote

Enabling the optimizer's fleet capability discussed in this chapter requires the option "advancedfleet" to be added to the "Mojo Options" setting in the application's System Preferences. For more information see the "Mojo Options" topic in the appendix.

Chapter Discussion

1. What do many small or mid-sized owners of private fleet assets often get wrong?

2. What is the biggest challenge to setting up an optimization in which private assets "compete" fairly against third-party carriers in the mix?

###

Chapter 12: Studying Optimization Scenarios

The modern transportation optimizer must allow the user to consider all types of transportation challenges in a single model. Large savings can be achieved by performing backhauls for inbound moves while also looking at cross-docking, as one example.

In this chapter we'll study a few widely different strategies for optimization. Besides the fact that each is interesting in its own right, we'll see more examples of how to design the optimizer's settings to move it toward the business problem we're trying to address, and better yet, maximize savings and efficiencies by solving several problems at the same time.

Consider:

- <u>Continuous optimization</u>, in which a steady stream of incoming shipments justifies frequent optimization runs, and possibly even re-optimization of the previous shipment pool.

- <u>Continuous moves</u>, in which we ask the optimizer to design runs with many interleaved pickups and drops along the way – akin to a delivery route or "milk run".

- <u>Backhaul </u>strategies in which we instruct the optimizer to permit more routes that include a leg bending back toward the origin, to reduce deadhead miles.

- A <u>zone-skipping</u> strategy used to avoid parcel multi-zone rates by consolidating on long cross-country hauls to designated pool points.

- Optimization of <u>inbound</u> freight coming to shippers from their vendors and suppliers.

Continuous Optimization

The term "continuous optimization" describes the practice of frequent re-optimization of shipment data to add additional freight to existing loads. How often this is done depends on the business need – daily, more than once a day, even every few hours.

We'll talk about two styles of continuous optimization:

(1) Deliberately holding back shipments from the current solution in hopes of finding an improvement in the next run. Naturally, the tradeoff is the risk of making something late.

(2) Re-optimizing to add new shipments to loads "in progress" that are being assembled on docks during the day. The trick to this approach is preserving existing load assignments – we're not going to re-shuffle what's already on the loading dock.

<u>'Back in the Pool'</u>

The deliberate delay of a freight movement runs against our natural grain. It makes sense only when (1) there's still time to get it there and (2) there's some other potential advantage to waiting.

You might remember that in the "Optimizer Loads" tab of results, there's a column titled "Leeway". This column contains a figure representing how many fractional days the optimizer estimates the load could be delayed and still achieve an on-time delivery. (This is not a guarantee – only the optimizer's estimate.)

Load Reference	Shipments	Stops	Events	Opt Contract	Opt Rate	Direct Rate	Savings	Pickup Loc	Drop Loc	Pickup Date	Leeway	Drop Date
⊞ Load 001	4	4	PDDDD	SWFT 09 (TL)	3943.28	4476.00	532.72	Jeffersonville, IN	SANTA ROSA, CA	2008-07-10 07:00	3.45	2008-07-14
⊞ Load 002	4	4	PDDDD	SWFT 09 (TL)	3918.74	4476.00	557.26	Jeffersonville, IN	CONCORD, CA	2008-07-10 07:00	3.45	2008-07-14
⊞ Load 003	4	4	PDDDD	SWFT 09 (TL)	4098.45	4476.00	377.55	Jeffersonville, IN	SALEM, OR	2008-07-10 07:00	3.45	2008-07-14
⊞ Load 004	4	4	PDDDD	SWFT 09 (TL)	4105.88	4476.00	370.12	Jeffersonville, IN	MEDFORD, OR	2008-07-11 07:00	2.37	2008-07-15
⊞ Load 005	3	3	PDDD	SWFT 09 (TL)	3787.94	4047.00	259.06	Jeffersonville, IN	SAN JOSE, CA	2008-07-10 07:00	3.45	2008-07-14
⊞ Load 006	4	4	PDDDD	SWFT 09 (TL)	3945.83	4062.00	116.17	Jeffersonville, IN	PORTLAND, OR	2008-07-10 07:00	3.45	2008-07-14

Fig. 12-1: 'Leeway' column in optimization results.

Leeway calculations lend themselves to a rule of thumb – if the figure is less than X, we'd better send the load now; if greater than X, meaning that we have some flexibility, then we might test some other condition before deciding whether to hold it back and re-optimize its shipments in the next run.

That "some other condition" might be something that prevented the shipment from being optimized this time, such as an incompatible time window. This time around we didn't get any benefit of optimization, but we might next time.

Example: Your most recently added shipment can't be optimized – it can't be delivered until at least a day after all of today's earlier shipments. But there's plenty of leeway on its non-optimized load, so maybe we can consolidate in <u>tomorrow's</u> batch of shipments, and gain the benefit of a break range that we couldn't get today.

'On the Dock' Continuous Optimization

A different style of continuous optimization is employed by some shippers who optimize to start building loads on their docks early in the day, but then keep re-optimizing to add new shipments to the right loads as they come in during the day, like sorting apples.

The consideration is that we want to preserve the loads assigned so far. This is an ideal use for the optimizer's "Load Preference" setting. When shipments are put on "real" loads back in the TMS, they are assigned a load ID. For each subsequent run of the optimizer, we'll use this load ID for grouping shipments.

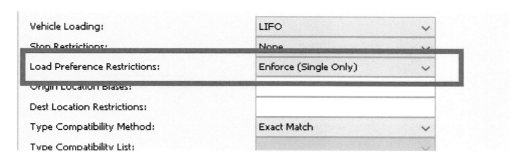

Fig. 12-2: Using load preference restrictions, we'll make sure that all shipments already assigned to a load are put on the same load in the re-optimization.

Continuous Moves

Ideally we'd like to keep trucks full instead of having to drive to a destination empty – especially if they're our own trucks. Common carriers, too, are less likely to accept tenders that involve too many empty miles or empty legs.

In a perfect world we could design <u>continuous moves</u> to keep our trucks in motion and busy. In real life this is dependent on the nature of our business. The best case is that at Stop A, we always have something to pick up and move to Stop B.

Fig. 12-3 represents the optimizer result for this kind of "milk run" scenario. The term "milk run" describes a route with short legs and many stops. (In a bygone age, milk was delivered door to door by dairy companies.)

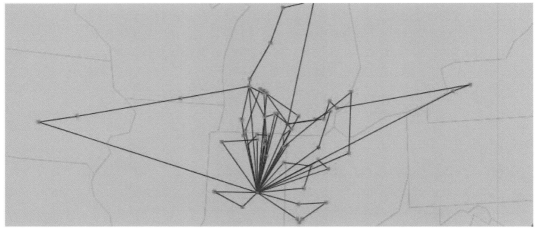

Fig. 12-3: 'Milk run' scenario involving routes with many stops.

Here's a screenshot of the "Optimizer Loads" tab for the milk run. Notice that the event sequences consist of many pickups and drops in succession:

Direct Cost:		$26,494.54				Optimized Cost:	
Optimizer Loads	Optimizer Shipments	Optimizer Events	Optimizer Rates	Optimizer Capacity			
Total Rows: 17							
Load Reference	Shipments	Stops	Events	Opt Contract	Opt Rate	Direct Rate	Savings
⊞ Load 01	15	16	PDPDDPDDPPDPDPDPD	DEDFLT (TL)	1187.23	4564.47	3377.24
⊞ Load 02	12	13	PDPDPDPDPDPDPD	DEDFLT (TL)	1227.77	3477.55	2249.78
⊞ Load 03	17	16	PDPDPDPDPDPDPDPPD	DEDFLT (TL)	991.53	5370.68	4379.15
⊞ Load 04	5	6	PPDPDPD	DEDFLT (TL)	670.84	1172.86	502.02
⊞ Load 05	11	12	PDDPPDPDPDPDD	DEDFLT (TL)	531.46	2065.87	1534.41

Fig. 12-4: Event sequence of many pickups and drops in 'milk run' optimization.

You might already be able to guess at the wizard settings for this kind of optimization:

The most obvious is "Max Stops" – in this example it was set to 16. With our own trucks we can set any limit we want; for a common carrier, max stops per route might be specified for the contract or by individual lane.

We might need to bump the "Max Out-of-Route" limit to allow for more zig-zag along our routes. In standard optimization you might remember we said this should be no higher than 1.3 or 1.4 – but for private purposes and deliberate design of continuous move routes it might be set much higher (the max is 25).

On the second wizard screen, a setting named "Stop Restrictions" might be relevant – for continuous moves, we definitely do not want the options labeled "No Multi-Pick" or "No Multi-Drop". The "Drop Bias" setting, on the other hand, encourages the optimizer to schedule drops before pickups, all else being equal, and in effect biases the optimizer toward continuous moves.

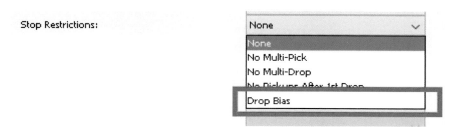

Fig. 12-5: The 'Drop Bias' setting encourages drops before pickups, biasing the optimizer before continuous moves.

The continuous move strategy also employs a high <u>backhaul bias</u>, allowing the optimizer to be more flexible about including legs turning back to the route origin. We'll talk about backhaul bias next.

Backhaul Bias

The term <u>backhaul</u> is used here with the specific meaning of <u>a return leg that moves freight</u>. This is in contrast to an empty or "deadhead" return-to-origin leg.

The guiding philosophy of looking for backhauls is that "something is better than nothing". If we earn even a dollar of revenue against a leg that was going to cost us anyway, then we've gained something.

Like the scheduling of continuous moves, backhaul opportunities depend somewhat on the nature of the business. Maybe we don't <u>have</u> loads that will help us. But if we do, we can tell the optimizer to consider them.

The third screen of the optimization wizard includes a setting labeled "Backhaul Bias". The possible settings are Off, Low, Medium and High. The higher the setting, the more likely the optimizer is to allow a backhaul leg on a route.

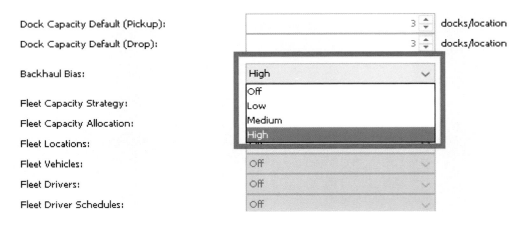

Fig. 12-6: Options for telling the optimizer how strongly to consider backhaul opportunities as it builds routes.

What's happening behind the scenes is we're telling the optimizer to think differently about what constitutes an "out of route" violation.

Remember that we are normally not allowed to go beyond a certain amount of "zig-zag" in route construction. And yet, turning back toward the origin from the furthest point of a route certainly increases zig-zag! So the higher the "Backhaul Bias" setting, the more tolerant the optimizer will be about allowing backhaul legs that are part of the same route.

Here's an example taken from a larger run. We have shipments from a couple of places in North Carolina to Tampa, and we also happen to have a shipment from Tampa to Columbia, S.C. – seemingly tailor-made for putting something on a truck heading back to North Carolina.

Owner	Primary Reference	Payment Terms	Origin Code	Origin Name	Origin City	Origin State	Origin Zip	Origin Ctry	Origin Geo	Dest Code	Dest Name	Dest City	Dest State
	Shipment 1	Prepaid	BUR	Burlington Puppy Support Center	Burlington	NC	27215	USA	36.033420,-79.490882	TAM	Tampa Puppy Rescue Inc	Tampa	FL
	Shipment 2	Prepaid	AVL	WNC Puppy Supply	Asheville	NC	28813	USA	35.552703,-82.511169	TAM	Tampa Puppy Rescue Inc	Tampa	FL
	Shipment 3	Prepaid	TAM	Tampa Puppy Rescue Inc	Tampa	FL	33606	USA	27.936563,-82.465286	CPS	Columbia Puppy Emporium	Columbia	SC

Fig. 12-7: We have two shipments bound from N.C. to Tampa – and then one from Tampa back to South Carolina. Can we put them on the same route?

However, with a "Backhaul Bias" setting of "Off", the optimizer does not see the Tampa-Columbia leg as an <u>opportunity</u>. It sees it as an unworkable combination because tacking it on after Florida would make the overall route too zig-zaggy.

To be more technical about it, the optimizer reports that putting them on the same load would constitute a Max Out-of-Route Violation, and so it builds two separate loads in the optimization.

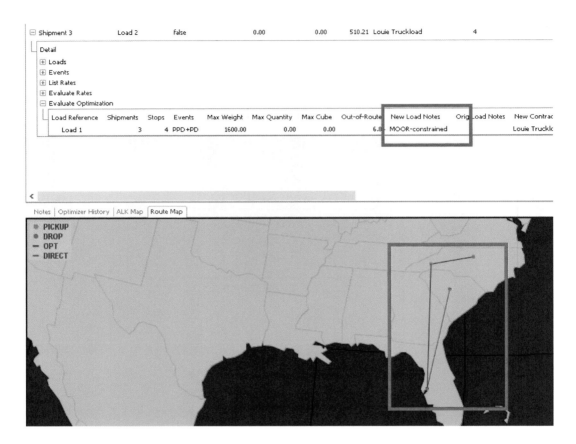

Fig. 12-8: No bias toward backhauls allowed, so the optimizer stubbornly creates a separate load (non-optimized, single-shipment) for the Tampa-Columbia movement.

Now we'll re-optimize the same shipments, this time setting the "Backhaul Bias" setting to "High". We're telling the optimizer to be extremely forgiving about legs than turn back toward the origin of a route when it comes to out-of-route restrictions.

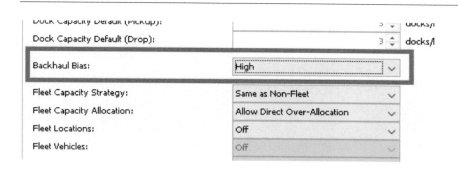

Fig. 12-9: Telling the optimizer to be as tolerant as possible about allowing bends back toward the route origin.

With the changed setting, the optimizer now is able to add Columbia as a leg on the same proposed load carrying all three shipments. If our goal was to make some money on our way back to North Carolina, then we've succeeded.

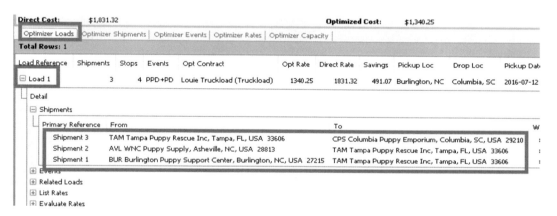

Fig. 12-10: The higher backhaul bias allowed the optimizer to put all three shipments, even the return to South Carolina, on the same route.

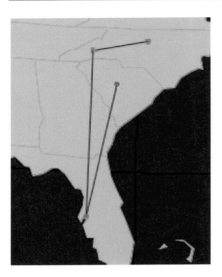

Fig. 12-11: With a higher bias in favor of backhauls, the single load route plan includes the Tampa-Columbia movement back toward the load origin.

Using backhauls helps produce a more accurate overall optimization, allows us to apply revenue against otherwise empty return legs, and reduces the number of routes and amount of total freight spend.

'Zone-Skip' Scenario

In our next example we'll use the optimizer's settings to bring about a carefully designed result – a "zone-skip" strategy that consolidates many small shipments onto long cross-country hauls, then relies on distributive pooling in the target zone via parcel delivery legs.

The point of this strategy is to avoid parcel rates that are based on movement across multiple "zones" as defined by the parcel carrier. Depending on volume and nature of the business, a zone-skip approach can save a lot of money.

In this example we're using more than 2,100 shipments ideally suited for parcel – all under 70 pounds and most just a few pounds, moving from eastern U.S. origins to the west coast.

Trying to consolidate and optimize so many small packages across the country without a pooling strategy is nearly impossible, even if we tell the optimizer to use high stop counts and a high out-of-route zig-zag to build proposed routes. Our attempt gives us either a lot of multi-zone parcel shipments or inefficient stabs at cross-country LTL routes (Fig. 12-12):

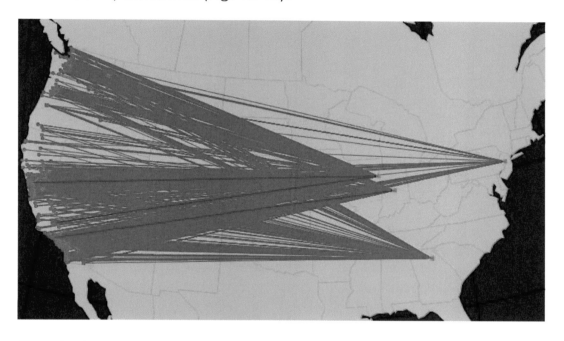

Fig. 12-12: Non-pooled, non-zone skip strategy. In this example we have 2,154 shipments with little opportunity for consolidation and negligible optimized savings.

In the next screenshot below, here are the same shipments optimized with a pooling and zone-skip strategy. Notice that now we have just a few consolidated long-hauls from the origins to designated west coast distribution points (Fig. 12-13):

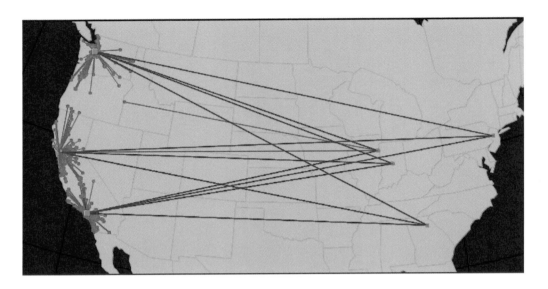

Fig. 12-13: The same 2,154 shipments from Fig. 12-12 shipped with a pooled, zone-skip strategy. We use LTL consolidation to get across the country, then distribute with local parcel delivery legs.

The difference is striking. In Fig. 12-13 we're using cross-country LTL consolidation to arrive at three west coast pool points. Because of the small, parcel nature of our shipments we're able to consolidate a high shipment count onto a few loads (Fig. 12-14):

Load Reference	Shipments	⌄ᴸ	Stops	Events	Opt Contract	Opt Rate	Direct Rate	Savings
⊞ Load 0050	227		1	PI	CNWY LTL 2010 (LTL)	237.35	18897.75	18660.40
⊞ Load 0035	154		1	PI	CNWY LTL 2010 (LTL)	197.48	12820.50	12623.02
⊞ Load 0046	112		1	PI	CNWY LTL 2010 (LTL)	154.52	9324.00	9169.48
⊞ Load 0052	102		1	PI	CNWY LTL 2010 (LTL)	175.03	8491.50	8316.47
⊞ Load 0048	98		1	PI	CNWY LTL 2010 (LTL)	204.82	8158.50	7953.68
⊞ Load 0038	93		1	PI	CNWY LTL 2010 (LTL)	318.60	7742.25	7423.65
⊞ Load 0051	89		1	PI	CNWY LTL 2010 (LTL)	173.17	7409.25	7236.08

Optimizer Loads · Optimizer Shipments · Optimizer Events · Optimizer Rates · Optimizer Capacity

Total Rows: 2207

Fig. 12-14: Optimization results sorted by shipment count on each load, showing a lot of consolidation on our cross-country routes.

Arriving at these zone-skip results took just a few adjustments to the optimizer parameters:

- Pool strategy set to "Force Pools". We want to send everything through a pool point for its final delivery leg.
- Pool assignment set to "Closest to Destination". This is an example of a "distributive" pool philosophy that we discussed in the chapter on pooling.
- Max Out-of-Route set to 1.0 – in other words, allow nothing except a straight route from origin to pool point, and from pool point to delivery.
- Max Stops = 1. In other words, go from origin to pool point, and from pool point to destination for each leg.

Given these settings, the optimizer had little choice except to give us exactly the result we wanted! And in this example, not only did we get across the country a lot more simply, but we even managed to save a few percentage points versus a non-optimized cost:

CO₂ Change:	10,430 tons		
Distance Change:	4,708,898 mi (93.8%)		
Optimized Savings:	$172,879.45 (92.5%)	No Pools:	$616.85 (4.2%)

Fig. 12-15: Results of our pooling/zone-skip strategy. Our optimization saved a lot of money versus pooling without optimization, and even saved a few percentage points versus a direct-ship scenario.

A fine illustration of zone-skipping, as well as the strong use of optimizer parameters to design the kind of result we want.

Inbound Freight Optimization

The term <u>inbound</u> freight describes shipments that are coming <u>to</u> a TMS client instead of being sent <u>by</u> that client. An example would be raw materials or components coming in to a manufacturer, or wholesale consumer goods coming to a retailer.

The term <u>inbound freight management</u> refers to the ability of these clients to control and manage their own inbound shipments – that is, to be able to arrange for themselves the routes, trucks and rates on which their inbound supplies will travel.

This is not a concept that we get to experience in our own daily lives as consumers. When we order goods online, our order gets there when it gets there, it gets there whichever way that the shipper chose to send it, and we pay what we're told to pay, period. We don't get to book our own trucks and shop for our own shipping rates, and most of us wouldn't want the hassle anyway.

But in the larger scale of business, some manufacturers, retailers and large shippers <u>are</u> able to negotiate this kind of relationship with their vendors/suppliers. In such cases the supplier's job is to make sure the goods are available at point X on date Y, and it's the TMS client that has designed the route, obtained the rate and booked the truck.

In the MercuryGate TMS, vendors of the client can have their own logins to the system, where they can view <u>purchase orders</u> that have been created by the client and assigned to them. The vendor-users then create shipment records in the TMS to fill these purchase orders, partially or completely.

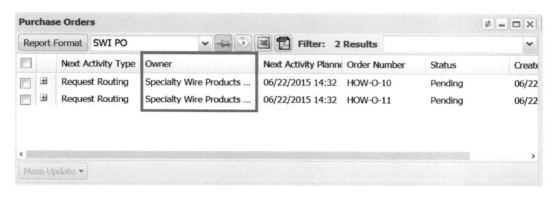

Fig. 12-16: A 'purchase order portlet' in the MercuryGate TMS in which a vendor-user sees pending purchase orders assigned to that vendor.

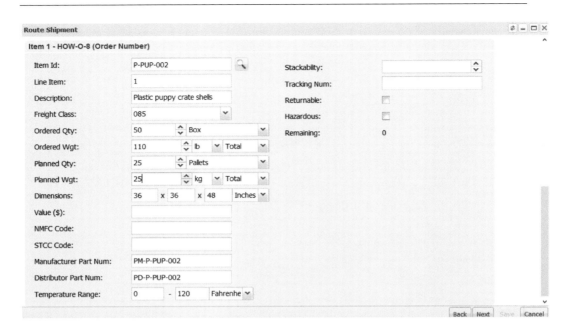

Fig. 12-17: Vendors with their own log-ins to the TMS can create shipments to fulfill their pending purchase orders.

Since the focus of this book is on optimization, we might well ask: What does all this has to do with us?

Only this: *Inbound freight is a candidate for optimization*. In fact, our standard shipper model contemplates that vendors are creating a "pool" of inbound shipments that a TMS client can consolidate, optimize and route to its own advantage, as in Fig. 12-18:

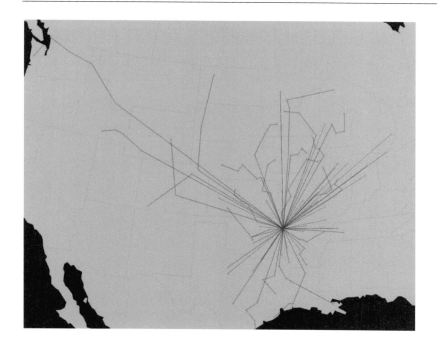

Fig. 12-18: An inbound optimization, consolidating on multi-pickup routes toward a central destination. In this example inbound optimization saved nearly 80 percent of direct-ship cost.

In fact, there is no technical difference between optimizing "inbound" and "outbound" freight – the components are the same, and the only difference is the accident of origin and destination, and thus one tends to be multi-pickup vs. multi-drop. If we are lucky enough to have a network of inbound and outbound locations that coincide or overlap, we already are close to the happy continuous-move scenario described a little earlier in this chapter.

In practice, even when inbound optimization is technically and geographically possible, the biggest challenge to adopting it has been be organizational. Traditional divisions between departments more often decide who controls what, and purchasing of inbound materials usually is considered a separate universe from the management of outbound transportation.

Discussion Questions

1. What do we mean by the term "continuous optimization"? What were the different styles of continuous optimization discussed in the chapter? Can you think of any problems that might arise from continuing to add new shipments to loads during the course of a business day?

2. Given your knowledge of optimizer parameters, think about settings that would create the <u>opposite</u> of the "zone skipping" scenario described in this chapter.

3. You work for a large company's transportation department. You want to talk your company's <u>purchasing</u> department into letting you manage the inbound goods that the purchasing department buys for the company. What are the selling points you might use? What objections should you anticipate?

###

Chapter 13: Forecasting Impacts of Change

Learning to use optimization for analysis and forecasting, and not "merely" for saving money in present-day execution, is the biggest additional bonus of an optimization tool realized over time.

We've spent the whole book stressing the importance of accurate inputs reflecting real-world conditions. Yet the tool also does a great job of testing "what-if" scenarios if we simply feed it different assumptions.

- What if fuel goes up X percent over the next year? Will that affect my choice of mode, facilities or carriers?

  Re-run the optimizer, bump the fuel adjustments on the second wizard screen, and find out!

- What if I use this other carrier's rate structure instead?

  Import the carrier's rates as a rate table, run the optimizer using that rate table instead, and compare the resulting freight spend to your previous scenario.

- Would I be better off moving my distribution center to another city?

  Add columns to your shipment data for the new location, get a valid geocode, and then use that column in the optimizer as your origin or required pool point.

You can run such scenarios again and again, changing different values each time. (Experience suggests it is best not to change too many parameters at a time, else you don't really know which change is causing the most impact.)

Remember too that the optimizer will preserve the changes from run to run, and the "Optimizer History" tab includes a summary of what's changed between runs and the relative impact on savings.

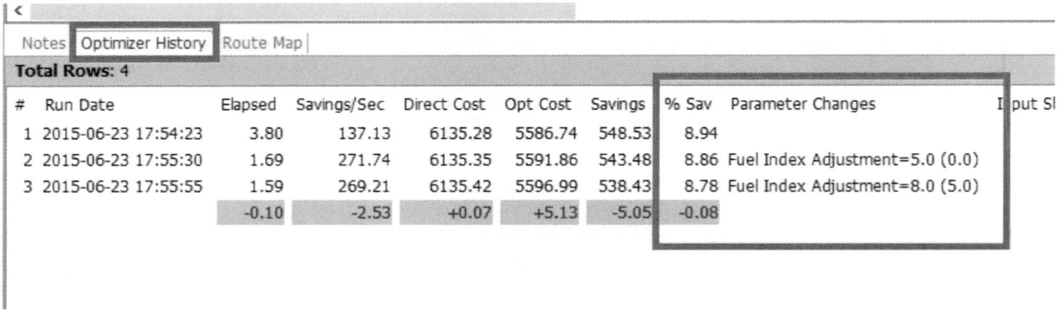

#	Run Date	Elapsed	Savings/Sec	Direct Cost	Opt Cost	Savings	% Sav	Parameter Changes	put SI
1	2015-06-23 17:54:23	3.80	137.13	6135.28	5586.74	548.53	8.94		
2	2015-06-23 17:55:30	1.69	271.74	6135.35	5591.86	543.48	8.86	Fuel Index Adjustment=5.0 (0.0)	
3	2015-06-23 17:55:55	1.59	269.21	6135.42	5596.99	538.43	8.78	Fuel Index Adjustment=8.0 (5.0)	
		-0.10	-2.53	+0.07	+5.13	-5.05	-0.08		

Notes · Optimizer History · Route Map

Total Rows: 4

Fig. 13-1: The 'history' results tab compares the results of each run of the optimizer and keeps track of changed parameters from run to run. Double-clicking a row re-launches the optimizer using the parameter settings of that run.

One important point: The effect of a combination of changes might not be obvious beforehand. An optimization is the sum of a lot of factors. It's not necessarily a simple reckoning - "If fuel goes up by X, we'll just raise our customer rates by Y."

Instead, we need to consider how changes in various cost centers affect (or don't affect!) our overall transportation <u>mix</u> – our mix of mode, of contract versus spot rates, of pooling versus non-pooling scenarios, and our preferred method of consolidation onto execution loads.

A 'Futures' Tool

Comparing one run of the optimizer to the next is fairly easy for changes to one or two parameters. However, our optimizer includes a more comprehensive modeling tool for projecting the impact of any number of parameter changes over time. This feature is known as "Mojo Futures."

Once we've completed an initial optimization to use as our baseline, notice in the right-hand "Analysis" task window that there is now a command named "Mojo Futures" (Fig. 13-2):

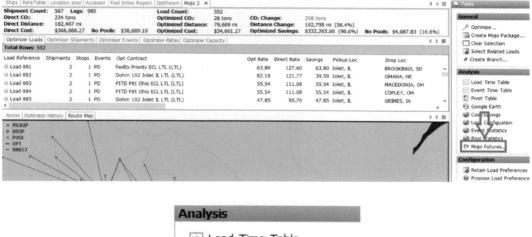

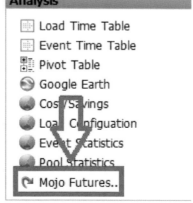

Fig. 13-2: 'Futures' command available after an intial optimization.

Clicking this command re-launches the optimization wizard – but with an interesting difference.

The wizard now skips its first screen (which mapped the columns from our shipment data). In its remaining screens, <u>only the numerical parameters</u> are available for adjustment. The remaining parameters are grayed out (Fig. 13-4, next page).

We can adjust one or many of these settings in the wizard screens to make them larger or smaller than the baseline. The optimizer then automatically runs for a requested number of loops, adjusting each parameter by the supplied increment for the changed values.

At the bottom of the final wizard screen there's a new setting labeled "Future Iterations". For all the parameters that we have adjusted up or down, the optimizer will now loop through the requested number of executions, adjusting each parameter each time by the changed amount.

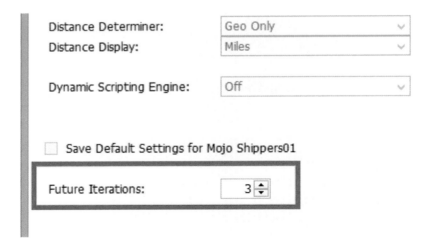

Fig. 13-3: Telling the optimizer how many 'futures' loops to run.

Mojo Optimization Wizard		

Mojo Optimization Params (Page 1)
Select your optimization options.

Rate Table:	Rate Table ⌄	
Re-Rate Table:	(None) ⌄	
Direct Rate Method:	Least Cost ⌄	
Fuel Surcharge (TL):	0 ⇕	%
Fuel Surcharge (Non-TL):	0 ⇕	%
Fuel Index Adjustment:	0 ⇕	%
Earliest Actual Date:	Use Normal Constraints ⌄ ⚠	
Strategy:	M-OOR ⌄	
Max Out-of-Route:	1.2 ⇕	ratio
Constraint Bias:	Medium ⌄	
Truckload Modes:	TL, Truckload	
Vehicle Max Weight:	42,500 ⇕	
Vehicle Max Quantity:	10,000 ⇕	
Vehicle Max Cube:	3,500 ⇕	
Truckload Max Stops:	4 ⇕	
Recommended Minimum Stop Size:	0 ⇕	%
Vehicle Loading:	LIFO ⌄	
Stop Restrictions:	None ⌄	
Load Preference Restrictions:	None ⌄	
Origin Location Biases:		
Dest Location Restrictions:		
Type Compatibility Method:	Exact Match ⌄	
Type Compatibility List:	⌄	
Non-TL Consolidation:	✓	modes only ⚠
Non-TL Transit Determination:	Same as Truckload ⌄	
Non-TL Weekend Exclusion:		modes only
Service Time Determination:	Default Only ⌄	
Service Time Base:	60 ⇕	minutes/stop
Service Time Additional:	0 ⇕	minutes/shipment
Service Time Additional:	0 ⇕	minutes/unit-quantity
Hours of Operation Determination:	Default Only ⌄	

Fig. 13-4: The wizard is presented differently for a 'futures' run, offering the ability to adjust numerical constraints only. The optimizer will loop across the requested number of iterations, adjusting the changed settings by the given increment each time.

Mojo runs the multiple interactions and displays results for each requested iteration. Each display contains its own results tab, which can be right-clicked and "floated" for a fuller view:

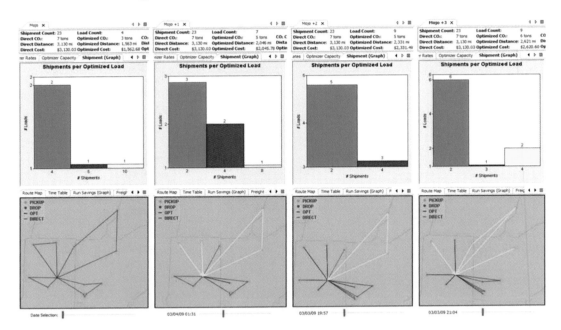

Fig. 13-5: Result of a 'futures' run with three additional iterations. Each window contains its own set of optimizer results.

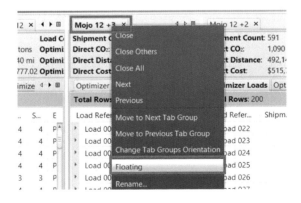

Fig. 13-6: For a better view of an individual futures window, right-click the tab header and choose "Floating" to undock the window and expand its view.

In the original results window, a new tab titled "Mojo Futures Summary" contains a line-by-line comparison of the iterations, similar to the one we saw in the "Optimizer History" tab. (You might have to scroll the frame to see the "Mojo Futures Summary" tab.)

Mojo Futures Summary ✕

Total Rows: 4   **Selected Rows:** 1

#	Run Date	Elapsed	Direct Cost	Opt Cost	Savings	% Sav	Input Ship Legs
0	2016-03-25 15:45:55	14.87	366866.27	34601.27	332265.00	90.57	985
1	2016-03-25 15:46:28	14.33	402228.44	35377.73	366850.71	91.20	986
2	2016-03-25 15:46:46	13.12	98616.61	35931.26	62685.36	63.56	703
3	2016-03-25 15:47:03	12.51	38888.49	37752.56	1135.93	2.92	567

)ista...	% Dist...	CO2 D...	Parameter Changes
)51.44	65.24	711.21	
)51.44	65.24	711.21	Fuel Index Adjustment=6.0
)51.44	65.24	711.21	Fuel Index Adjustment=12.0
)51.44	65.24	711.21	Fuel Index Adjustment=18.0

Fig. 13-7: Line by line comparison of the results of the futures interations, with a list of changes in each.

Case Study - Impact of TL Fuel Increase

In this example we want to see what the optimizer predicts about the effect of hypothetical increases in truckload versus non-truckload costs over the coming year. This might be a result of contract expirations, the disproportionate impact of facility (stop) charges, or some other mode-sensitive factor.

Our current model uses a "consider pools" scenario. We're telling the optimizer to use pool points where it makes sense.

First we perform a baseline run. In the map below the visual representation of the pooling strategy is clear. In the results summary we can see this gives us tremendous savings versus direct ship.

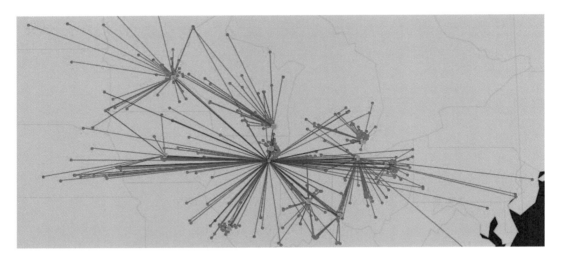

Load Count:	552		
Optimized CO₂:	26 tons	CO₂ Change:	208 tons
Optimized Distance:	79,609 mi	Distance Change:	102,798 mi (56.4%)
Optimized Cost:	$34,601.27	Optimized Savings:	$332,265.00 (90.6%) No Pools: $4,087.83 (10.6%)

Fig. 13-8: Loads recommended by the optimizer under current conditions and a 'consider pools' strategy. Note the extensive use of pool points.

Next we'll run the futures tool, telling the optimizer to assume a staggered increase in truckload costs. In this example we're using the truckload fuel adjustment factor on the first wizard screen:

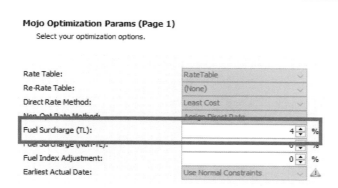

Mojo Optimization Params (Page 1)

Select your optimization options.

Rate Table:	RateTable
Re-Rate Table:	(None)
Direct Rate Method:	Least Cost
Non-Opt Rate Method:	Assign Direct Rate
Fuel Surcharge (TL):	**4 % %**
Fuel Surcharge (Non-TL):	0 %
Fuel Index Adjustment:	0 %
Earliest Actual Date:	Use Normal Constraints

Fig. 13-9: Modeling a disproportionate increase in truckload vs. non-truckload fuel cost.

We tell the optimizer to run three additional iterations in its futures model, so we'll have data modeling four quarterly calculations. We can see a striking change over time in the resulting recommended optimization in Fig. 13-10:

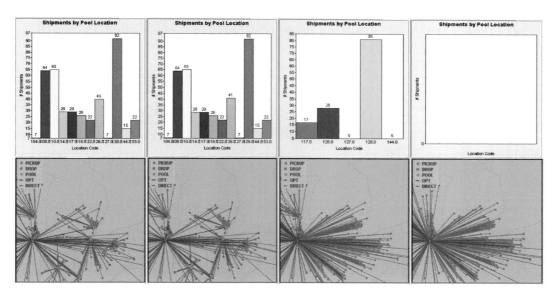

Fig. 13-10: A "futures" optimization projecting the impact of a change over time. In this example, the optimizer moves away from truckload pooling.

In Fig. 13-10, the optimizer moves from reliance on truckload pooling to more reliance on non-pooled transport.

Looking at the "Pool Statistics" analysis graphs in the top row, we see charts that confirm a decreasing reliance on pool points as the scenario progresses. Note that several pool locations were employed in our first and second runs, fewer in the third, and none in the final. As truckload rates increased, it made more and more sense to move to a non-pooling scenario.

Comparing the "Optimized Contract" display from first to last runs, the optimizer has redistributed its recommended loads, concentrating them more on non-TL carriers (Fig. 13-11):

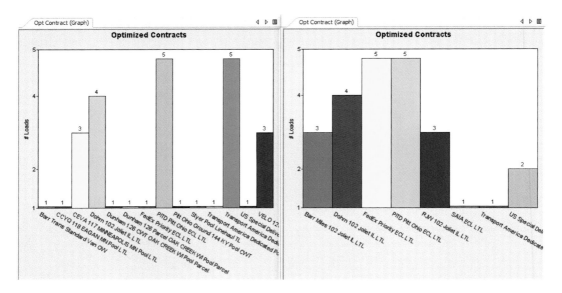

Fig. 13-11: Dramatic shift in recommended carrier contracts as the optimizer deals with the impact of projected truckload cost increases.

The lesson is that as parameters change (such as fuel costs, carbon taxes, etc.), the overall recommended execution plan can shift dramatically as the optimizer attempts to mitigate the effect of the cost increases.

Unexpected mode shifts, for example from LTL to parcel, and changes in pooling scenarios (such as shipping more direct instead of through pool points) might be the result. <u>Become aware of these possibilities early can help with carrier bids and capacity sourcing decisions.</u>

A final point: Typically, not all carrier contracts expire simultaneously! Therefore, from month to month, different carrier contracts and rating models can be in effect, making it difficult to use a single point in time to evaluate an optimization strategy. The futures tool simplifies the task of evaluating shipment data and rating models as they change throughout the year.

Discussion Questions

1. Why would some kinds of cost increases (or decreases) influence the optimizer's recommendation of which routes to take and which carriers to use?

2. What kinds of cost changes would make it more or less desirable to use pooling versus a non-pooling scenario?

3. If you wanted to test the impact of sending all your shipments through a central pool point in the optimizer, how would you go about it?

#

Chapter 14: Automating and Extending the Optimization Models

Once optimization models have been set up, today's optimizer should be able to apply them in a variety of ways.

First the optimizer should be able to run automatically as shipments are created, building loads in the background with no user interaction.

Second, dispatchers need to be able to adjust tactically as freight is picked in warehouses and staged for shipping. As loads become more complex, changing those loads becomes more difficult and error-prone. Dispatchers can make a call to the model with a subset of altered shipments, allowing a quick tool for adapting to the real-world changes.

Finally, in rare situations it might be necessary to tweak the criteria used in the decision-making process of the optimizer. The tools today allow users to extend optimizers to enhance the decision logic used in the routing considerations. This logic boost helps the system hone in on more accurate results.

The modern transportation optimizer that we've used throughout this book as our example is named "Mojo". We have seen that the optimizer may be used to analyze historical data, to test "what-if" scenarios, to forecast the effect of potential changes – and, of course, to create live loads for actual execution.

In this chapter, consistent with the needs described above, we'll discuss three variations on use of the Mojo tool that show other ways that optimization is applied in practice. These variations are:

- Mojo "Dark" – automated optimization and load creation, used for example between the MercuryGate TMS and high-volume warehouse or order-management systems.

- Mojo "Live!" – optimization on demand, performed against shipments and loads in the TMS by dispatchers.

- Mojo Scripting – optimization that can be customized with user-written scripts to reach inside Mojo's data objects to supply additional criteria for decision-making.

Mojo Dark

The process of optimization that we have seen demonstrated over and over in the preceding chapters can be fully automated, down to the creation of execution loads in the MercuryGate TMS. Typical steps would be:

1. An external warehouse or order-management system, integrated with the MercuryGate TMS, creates records in the TMS of shipments to be moved.

2. The application launches automatically on the client's local system as a scheduled task, opens a shipment report from the TMS with the shipments to be optimized, opens a rate table and any other required data, and performs the optimization.

3. The optimizer runs a filter against the resulting loads to test for errors, and creates loads in the TMS for actual execution. Once created in the TMS, loads proceed through a normal workflow, which itself might be automated for tendering, auto-accept, pickup, and tracking to delivery – a true "no-touch" system from beginning to end!

4. Optionally the application can export and email a Mojo package or spreadsheet of results from its optimization and load creation for human eyes, or back to the warehouse system to report on which shipments were placed on which loads.

The above steps represent just one way the data can flow in a Mojo Dark scenario. Another way would be for the warehouse system to get recommended loads back from the optimizer, and then to create loads in the TMS itself via integration (Fig. 14-1).

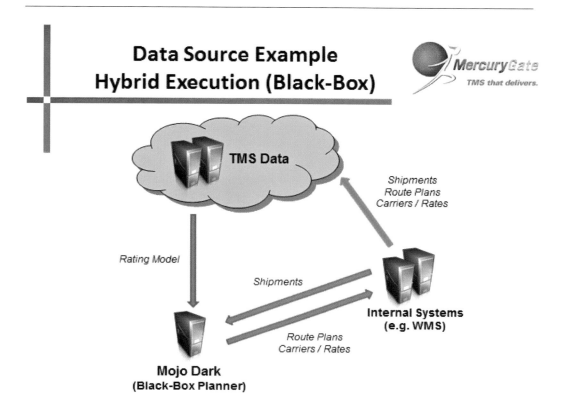

Fig. 14-1: Mojo Dark data-flow scenario in which the optimizer gets shipment data directly from a warehouse system (WMS). The optimizer sends its results back to the WMS, which creates loads in the TMS as appropriate.

The nuts and bolts of a Mojo Dark setup include creation of a scheduled <u>macro</u> in the application. A macro is a script or series of saved commands than can be executed automatically. The macro is set to run as a scheduled task on the local system.

Here's a sample optimization script, with comments preceded by a # symbol and the actual line of script indented:

```
# open a TMS shipment report, which has been set up to include the shipments we want

        open 1~Shipment~Daily Shipments

# make sure that the shipments have geocodes, using the correct column names

        geocode 1~Primary Reference|Origin City|Origin State|Origin
              Zip|Origin Ctry|Dest City|Dest State|Dest Zip|Dest Ctry|

# open contracts from the server to use for rating

        open 2~Contract~My Contracts

# open rate table from the specified contracts

        openratetable 2

# run optimization

        mojoexec 1

# run filter on load flag field – don't send any with errors

        mojoselectionfilter RouteDetail~Flags:equals::

# create server loads

        mojoupdate

# now exit for a clean desktop

        Quit
```

This script easily could be modified to export results back to the warehouse system as well.

Mojo Live!

In all our uses of Mojo so far, we've brought data into the application and launched the optimizer from there. Then we've either exported our results to packages for analysis, or sent loads back to the TMS to real execution.

Mojo Live! is a feature that instead allows optimization of loads within the TMS itself.

Users working with shipments and loads in the TMS can gather a list of candidates – anywhere from a handful to a few hundred - and optimize them on demand. As opposed to the large-scale, systematic scale of an automated warehouse optimization, Mojo Live! is better suited for ad-hoc routing by execution planners.

TMS users work in a window (called a "portlet") that displays a list of shipments or loads that should be considered possible candidates for optimization.

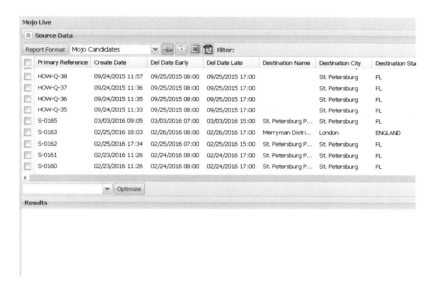

Fig. 14-2: The 'Mojo Live!' portlet in the TMS allows users to select and optimize shipments on demand.

Users select desired shipments for optimization using the checkboxes to the left of each entry in the list.

If you remember how to run Mojo externally, you might wonder how optimization works in the TMS without the optimization *wizard* – those four screenfuls of settings the user must approve before running.

The answer is that in the TMS, Mojo parameters are set <u>in advance</u>, and then uploaded to the TMS. These "pre-fabricated" settings are available for selection in the Mojo Live! window – the user can choose which group of settings to apply against the selected shipments.

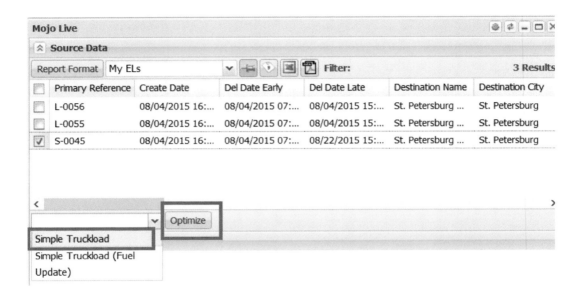

Fig. 14-3: Users choose from a list of pre-set optimization constraints and click 'Optimize'. The resulting optimized loads appear in the bottom half of the window.

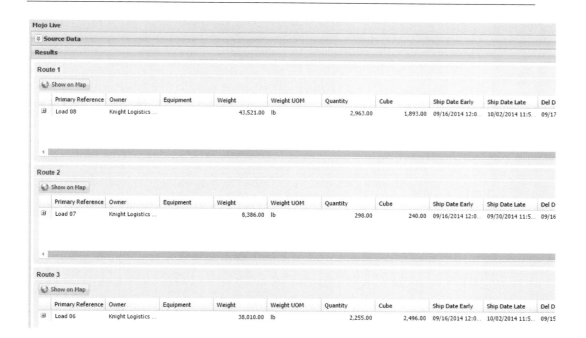

Fig. 14-4: Mojo Live! results in the lower half of the window.

Mojo Scripting

Scripting is an advanced feature that allows authorized users to write JavaScript that defines their own customized actions to execute at specified points in the optimization.

Scripts consist of functions triggered at key stages of optimization, with access to the fields of relevant objects such as shipments, loads, locations, events, and rates. Therefore script authors can create additional, flexible decision-making based on runtime conditions and values.

Only authorized users can create and edit scripts. However, once created, scripts can be shared and executed by other users via a Mojo package. Authorization requires a scripting "key" akin to a Mojo key installed in the system preferences.

For examples of script usage, we can:

- Reject a proposed load only when certain conditions about it are true.
- Create our own calculation of location hours, beyond the capacity of Mojo parameters.
  Example: At a specific pool location, hours of operation for the delivery docks differ from the pickup docks.
- Conduct a customized evaluation of dates.
- Conduct a custom calculation of carbon emissions.
- Build reports using a specialized format.

Once the scripting function is unlocked, the scripting option appears on the last page of the optimization wizard. The possible values for the wizard parameter are "Off" and "JavaScript."

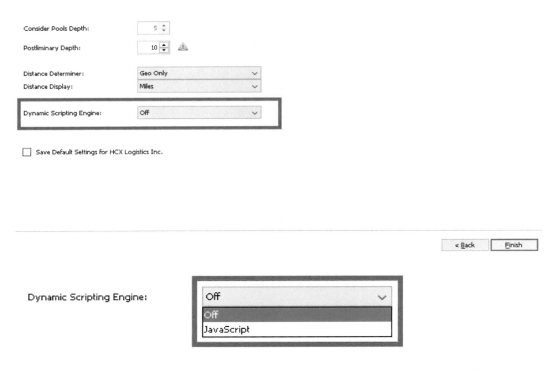

Fig. 14-4: Scripting setting on the final page of the optimization wizard.

Clicking the details ("piece of paper") icon opens a window for editing the script, which can be saved as part of a Mojo package:

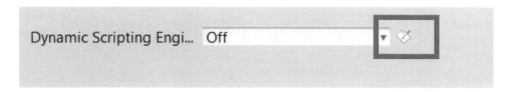

```
Dynamic Scripting Engi...   Off                              ▼  ✎
```

```
                              Mojo Scripting Engine                              ✕
1   function onRateEvaluation(load, rate) {                              ^        OK
2
3       var maxDeadheadDistance = 250;                                            Validate
4       if ("WRNN" == rate.getScac()) maxDeadheadDistance = 100;
5                                                                                 Find...
6       var shipmentsRemainingOnLoad = 0;
7       var deadheadStartEvent = null;                                            Replace...
8
9       for each (var event in load.getEvents()) {
10
11          if (deadheadStartEvent !== null) {
12              var deadheadDistance = event.getDistance() - deadheadStartEvent.getDistance();
13
14              if (deadheadDistance >= maxDeadheadDistance) {
15                  return "Deadhead distance "+deadheadDistance;
16              }
17          }
18
19          if (event.isPickup()) {
20              shipmentsRemainingOnLoad += event.getShipments().length;
21          }
22
23          if (event.isDrop()) {
24              shipmentsRemainingOnLoad -= event.getShipments().length;
25          }
26
27          if (shipmentsRemainingOnLoad == 0) {
28              deadheadStartEvent = event;
29          }
30          else {
31              deadheadStartEvent = null;
32          }
33      }
34  }
                                                        1:1    PC    Insert
```

Fig. 15-5: Editing window for scripting. The 'Validate' button tests the script for correct format, but not its programming logic.

Clicking the "Validate" button in the editing window checks the syntax of the script - whether it is formatted correctly with the right number of brackets, etc., but not its internal logic. The "Find" and "Replace" buttons are helpful in editing longer scripts with multiple functions.

Scripting Examples

The scripting API provides a list of available functions that allows users to supply scripts for actions to perform at those points in the optimization.

In the following example a script is used to alter the optimizer's decision-making when it comes to shipments flagged as hazardous. This function is executed when the optimizer proposes to create a load – the name of the function being invoked is "onShipmentCreate".

No small hazmat shipments (as measured by weight) are allowed in this scenario. Those shipments that do qualify will be assigned a "load preference" that will be used to group them together by origin and destination. Lastly, they are assigned a specialized "effective pallet size" related to their weight to use in calculations against truck capacity.

```
function onShipmentCreate(shipment) {

    // Reject small-sized hazardous shipments
    if (shipment.getType() == "HAZMAT" && shipment.getWeight() < 10 &&
shipment.getCube() < 2) {
        return "HAZMAT size too small";
    }

    // Set load preference to group shipments with the same origins and
destinations

shipment.setLoadPreference(shipment.getOrigin().getCode()+':'+shipment.ge
tDest().getCode());

    // Use "user numeric 2" field to contain a calculated effective
pallet-size
    var pallets = 3;
```

```
if (shipment.getWeight() < 1000) {
    pallets = 1;
}
else if (shipment.getWeight() < 8000) {
    pallets = 2;
}
else {
    pallets = Math.ceil(3 + shipment.getWeight() / 12000);
}

shipment.setUserNumeric2(pallets);

}
```

Although the optimizer's rating capabilities are sophisticated, scripting can be a vehicle for exceptional rating circumstances. For example, let's say an over-the-road carrier wants to provide a rate incentive for a backhaul toward the first pickup. The script function "onRateEvaluation" can evaluate the backhaul distance and add a custom negative accessorial charge to reduce the base linehaul rate.

Another application would be for custom <u>route</u> constraints. An example is the use of deadhead legs in continuous-move scenarios. The optimizer's ordinary decision-making criterion is whether the deadhead leg still produces the best cost. However, the user might want to disallow all deadhead miles, or declare a mileage limit, using the functions "onConstraintEvaluation" or "onRateEvaluation."

Here's an example of using a script for custom <u>facility</u> constraints. In a pooling facility, operating hours might vary by the direction of the load (inbound or outbound) and possibly the contents of the load (e.g., refrigeration needed). The inbound load may be allowed greater leeway in drop-off times when no refrigeration is required, but have a tighter drop-off window (nearer to the outbound load's scheduled departure) if refrigerated cargo is present because the facility itself cannot store refrigerated goods. The function "onLocationHoursLookup" can be programmed to override the default schedule lookup (by facility code) and replace it with a more detailed lookup code that allows for multiple schedules at a single location.

Here's the function:

```
function onLocationHoursLookup(load, event) {

    var newLookupCode = null;

    if (event.isPool()) {
        // For pools, perform lookup of location hours using a compound
key.
        // Key is defined as "LocCode-EventType-EquipmentType", e.g.
"MyPoolCode-Drop-Refer"
        newLookupCode = event.getLocation().getCode()+"-
"+event.getType()+"-"+load.getEquipment();
    }

    return newLookupCode;

}
```

List of Available Functions and Objects

Here are the other available function names, representing key points in the optimization at which we can supply scripting:

```
onStartup
onConstraintEvaluation
onCalculateEmissions
onRateEvaluation
onContractEvaluation
onLocationHoursLookup
onDateEvaluation
onLoadComparison
onEventSequenceComparison
onPrimaryReferenceAssignment
onReportGeneration
onUserAction
```

Notice that a script refers to fields and characteristics of available <u>objects</u> in the optimization. Look again at syntax such as:

```
if (shipment.getType() == "HAZMAT" &&
shipment.getWeight() < 10 &&
shipment.getCube() < 2) {
```

It appears that for an object of type "shipment" we are able to retrieve values with actions (in programming lingo these actions are called "methods") such as "getType" or "getWeight" and then subject those values to logical tests (equals, less than, etc.). A document available to MercuryGate clients called the Mojo Scripting API contains a list of all available fields and actions.

Here are the objects available for scripting:

```
Location
Event
Shipment
Rate
Load
Report
Edge
Java
```

###

Conclusion

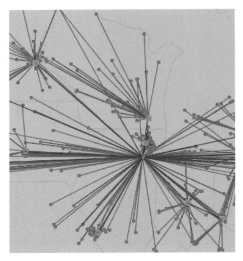

This book has dealt with the theme of the modern transportation optimizer in the business of providing logistics services. "Optimization" was defined, in general terms, as the process of designing and building loads that achieve a "better" result.

As for what exactly we mean by "better", it depends on the kind of improvement we need. Optimization can reward us with some or all of these:

- Better <u>rates</u>.
- Better and more effective <u>routes</u>.
- Better and more effective <u>loads</u>.
- Better use of our <u>network</u>.
- Better use of our planning personnel.

No paper route guide or human spreadsheet user can compete with an optimizer once volume and constraints begin to multiply.

We saw that there are many, many possible kinds of constraints – the "rules" by which our optimization must build its loads. The modern transportation optimizer not only obeys those rules, but gives us detailed data on their impact. Today's optimizer not only builds loads but also systemically shows users how it built those loads.

We saw that smart optimization can involve the accurate modeling of <u>carrier</u> and <u>facility capacity</u> in terms of available trucks, dock facilities, service times and operating hours. This is especially true when considering <u>pooling</u> scenarios. We discussed the optimization of <u>private assets</u>, trucks under our own ownership or control, and how accurate cost modeling is essential in modeling the right mix of private vs. common carrier. The tool does not require an advanced math degree, but rather, people who understand the constraints and business impacts of the alternatives.

One theme that we hope that you take away from this book is how <u>creative</u> a transportation optimizer can be. The practice of optimization challenges us to strive constantly for improvement, and requires us to think more deeply about the constraints and parameters that go into the design of our models. Optimization is a tool for analysis, for design of better networks, and for increased efficiency -- and thus better margins. The optimizer makes the organization more effective by using the constraints and rules to better align with objectives of the entire supply chain.

By allowing us to use fewer trucks, produce fewer carbon emissions, deliver the essential goods that make our society work more efficiently, and advance the mutual interests of our clients and our own businesses, today's transportation optimizers help to make better decisions faster.

\#\#\#

Glossary

accessorial charge: An additional rate on a load reflecting a charge for a specific service. Accessorials can be calculated on a variable basis (per mile, per pound, per stop, e.g.) or assessed as a flat rate.

backhaul bias: A setting telling the optimizer to be more likely or less likely to allow the construction of routes with stops that bend back toward the origin. A higher bias setting allows more backhauls.

break range: In a rate table, the declaration that a rate applies only to a given range, e.g., for shipments between 100 and 200 pounds, less than 100 miles, etc. Multiple break ranges can be declared on a lane.

capacity: General term for limits on what a carrier can carry, either in terms of per-vehicle capacity, or in terms of number of available trucks per lane, per day, per contract, or by some other measure.

consolidation pooling: A pool strategy with an emphasis on pool points closer to the origin zone, at which shipments are consolidated on loads for long hauls toward the destination.

constraint: Any limit or condition supplied to the optimizer for building loads. The more constraints placed on optimization, the more advantage a software tool has over human, manual load-building.

continuous move: Design of routes that feature a series of interspersed drop and pickup events.

continuous optimization: Frequent re-optimization as new shipments arrive. Allows reconsideration of shipments that previously could not be optimized.

cube: A volume-related measurement for shipments used both as a basis of rating or as a measurement against carrier/truck capacity.

dedicated assets: Carrier capacity owned by or under the control of the party doing the optimization, either privately owned or provided exclusively to the shipper by a common carrier.

direct cost/rate: The unimproved, non-optimized rate for a shipment that an optimizer is trying to "beat". Direct rates might be supplied in shipment data or calculated dynamically as a basis for comparison.

distributive pooling: The opposite of "consolidation pooling". A pooling strategy with an emphasis on deconsolidation into delivery legs at a pool point toward the destination.

domicile: In private-fleet scenarios, the location to which a vehicle is assigned as its home base. Routes include an initial move from domicile to first pickup, and a return to domicile after last drop.

driver, driver duty limits: The human operator of a truck, subject to legal limits on per-day and per-week operation that must be considered in optimization.

earliest actual date: When optimizing to create live loads, an instruction to the optimizer to plan events such as pickups and drops in the future. (Not set when optimizing historical or hypothetical data for analysis.)

freight class: An industry classification based on factors related to density, stowability, ease of handling and liability. Freight class designations are decimal numbers that start at 50.0 and run to 500. Freight class often is the basis of rating for LTL shipments.

geodata: A precise latitude and longitude designation for a location used in optimization. Geodata (geocodes) are required by the Mojo optimization tool, but can be calculated automatically based on existing postal codes or valid city-state combinations in the shipment data.

header row: First row of an imported spreadsheet showing column names ("Origin City", "Weight", etc.) that help the optimizer determine which columns contain what kind of information.

historical rate: A past rate actually paid for moving a shipment, contained in in historical shipment data. Can be mapped to "Direct Cost" in the wizard as the benchmark to "beat" in a re-optimization.

inbound optimization: Management of shipments inbound to the client that were originated by its vendors and suppliers, but turned over to that client for management of route planning and booking.

item, item rating: An individual freight component. Shipments consist of one or more items. The Mojo optimizer can be instructed to rate each item on a shipment individually, for greater precision, and then to "roll up" the results for the entire proposed load.

lane: The description of an origin-destination pair in a rate table against which shipments can be matched. A lane can be as specific as one five-digit zip code to another, or as general as country to country. "USA" to "USA", for example, describes a lane that would be applicable to any origin-destination pair in the U.S.

leeway: A number in the Optimizer Loads results that represents, in fractional days, how long the load could be delayed but still be delivered on time.

load optimization: An approach to optimization with a primary emphasis on efficiency of load-building, e.g., using fewest number of trucks, meeting requirements for compatible and incompatible freight, etc.

load preference: A value added to a shipment record indicating its "preferred" load. Can be used to force shipments onto the same load, or to test what-if scenarios in analysis.

location report: A spreadsheet of location data, include location codes, geodata, and columns for operating hours, service times, dock capacity and restrictions, among other fields. Opened in the application either from an imported spreadsheet or from the MercuryGate TMS.

max out-of-route (MOOR): A numerical measure of the allowed "zig-zag" of a route. A ratio of the sum of all individual legs on a route divided by the distance between its origin and destination.

macro: A saved, script-like set of instructions that can be scheduled to run automatically in the application. Macros can be scheduled to execute optimization runs and create loads, for example.

MercuryEdge: Name of a free, downloaded application for data analysis offered to clients of MercuryGate International Inc., and a platform for running the Mojo optimization tool.

mode: A category or manner of freight movement, e.g. "Truckload", "Less Than Truckload", "Rail", "Ocean", "Dray" or other options. Carrier contracts are specified by mode and service.

Mojo: Name of the proprietary software optimization tool of MercuryGate International Inc. and the optimizer used an example in this textbook.

Mojo Dark: MercuryGate's name for the automatic, "hands-off" scheduling of Mojo optimization, for example in a warehouse scenario in which shipments are brought into the TMS, loaded into Mojo, and built into loads for execution automatically.

Mojo Futures: A feature allowing users to specify any number of numerical constraints to adjust across a series of repeated optimizer runs, displaying the results of all runs for comparison.

Mojo Live!: MercuryGate's name for a feature allowing clients of the MercuryGate TMS to apply optimization within the TMS itself.

Mojo Optimization Wizard: A window with four screens of settings that guides Mojo users through the process of mapping shipment data and setting desired constraints for an optimization run.

Mojo package: A saved, multi-tabbed spreadsheet file that preserves the elements of an optimization run to share with teammates, prospects, management or for any other purpose. Mojo packages can be opened, launched and re-optimized by other users.

Mojo Scripting: An advanced feature that allows qualified clients to write and install their own JavaScript calls to fine-tune and customize Mojo decision-making.

multi-pooling: A pooling strategy in which shipments are moved across multiple pool points for the purposes of consolidation, cross-docking, reconsolidation and deconsolidation.

network optimization: An approach to optimization with an emphasis on maximum efficient use of network facilities and location requirements, pooling and cross-dock scenarios, dock capacity limitation, etc.

optimization: Designing the movement of freight with the goal of achieving an improved result in terms of cost, route efficiency, carrier and network utilization, or some other goal.

optimizer: A software tool for optimization, as opposed to the use of manual load-building by human planners.

parameter: A setting in the Mojo Optimization Wizard that either sets a constraint on load-building or provides some other instruction to the Mojo tool.

pooling, pool location: Use of intermediate locations between a shipment origin and its final destination such as a distribution center. Each part of the movement (origin to pool point, pool point to destination) is a carrier leg in the optimization.

pool strategy: The decision if and how to employ pooling in optimization. For example we might require the use of pool points, or tell the optimizer to consider pool points if they are the best option.

primary reference: A unique identifier such as a shipment or order number required for optimization. For the Mojo tool, any unique value is acceptable. Multiple lines using the same primary reference are treated as individual items on the same shipment.

private fleet, private assets: The use of privately owned assets (as opposed to for-hire common carriers) in optimization. Each truck can be assigned a home base or "domicile". A fleet optimization scenario also can include lists of drivers and driver pools. Private fleets might be used in stand-alone optimization, or considered as part of the mix with third-party carriers.

quantity: A measurement of a shipment's contents based on the sheer number of some unit, such as pallets or cartons. Quantity can be used both as the basis of rating and in calculation of vehicle capacity.

rate optimization: An approach to optimization that emphasizes the primary goal of achieving cost savings.

rate table: A line-by-line spreadsheet of carrier rates that apply to defined lanes. Each line of a rate table includes a lane calculation, a rate definition, and optional limits such as break ranges. Rate tables can be opened from imported spreadsheets or from contracts in the MercuryGate TMS.

rating count: A numerical value used to describe shipments that can represent any desired quantity, or which might have no independent meaning at all – for example, "This load is a '3' so here is the rate to charge for 3s".

report: An open spreadsheet used to supply data in Mojo optimization. A report is of a particular data type ("Shipment", "RateTable", "Location") and can be opened either from an imported spreadsheet or from the MercuryGate TMS.

route optimization: An approach to optimization with an emphasis on efficiency of routes in terms of number or mileage.

SCAC: Standard Carrier Alphanumeric Code, an assigned "call sign" unique to each carrier. Rate tables used in optimization include the SCAC of the carrier providing each rate.

service (contract): A level or grade of service specified in a carrier contract, such as "Standard" or "2nd Day Air". Each carrier contract is specified by a unique combination of SCAC, mode and service.

service time(s): Time allowed per stop at a dock facility. A base time can be assigned for every stop, as well as additional time allowances for each individual shipment or unit of quantity on a load.

shipment: Record of an individual request to move freight from an origin to a destination. Shipments are combined in optimization into carrier loads for execution. Shipment data can come from an imported spreadsheet or from the MercuryGate TMS.

total cost of ownership: In design of private fleet optimization, a figure representing all costs associated with the private truck, so that it can "compete" fairly in the rate table against common carriers. Owners often underestimate the true cost of operating private assets.

TMS: Transportation management system, used for the creation, rating, booking, tracking and invoicing of loads. Clients of the MercuryGate TMS can open their logistics data for optimization.

transit time: Estimated or claimed time, in days and portions of days, from pickup to delivery. The Mojo optimizer calculates its own transit times to build loads, based either on global standard assumptions or transit-time specifics included in rate tables.

user defined numeric: In Mojo, an all-purpose column in shipment data containing a number to match against a max allowed value in the rate table. There can be two of these columns in shipment data.

zone-skipping strategy: Optimization with the goal of avoiding parcel carrier multi-zone rates by consolidation on long-haul routes, then using a destination pool point as the origin for the delivery legs.

###

Appendix: Reference Material

MercuryEdge

MercuryEdge is a free, downloaded application that runs the Mojo optimizer and can be used for other data analysis. It is available to MercuryGate clients and to participants in the MercuryGate University program. A Mojo "key" issued by MercuryGate is required to run the optimizer.

MercuryEdge Installation

Direct a browser to:

http://<YourServerName>.mercurygate.net/MercuryGate/webstart/Launcher.html

The server designation is provided by MercuryGate. The page will validate your version of Java and provide a download link. MercuryEdge will install an icon on your desktop and then launch. Use your TMS user name and password to log in.

User Interface

The "Reports" panel opens shipment, contract, rate table and other kinds of data from the user's TMS enterprise. Otherwise use the File > Import menu command to import external spreadsheets.

Data is displayed in the central workspace contained in tabbed spreadsheets called "reports". Each report has a type such as "Shipment", "RateTable", "Location" etc. telling the application what kind of data it contains.

Tabs, Rows and Columns

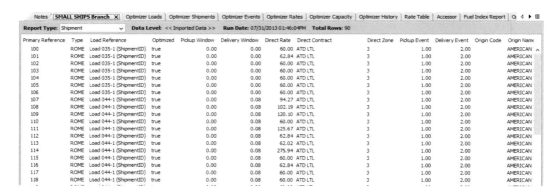

Right-clicking a tab opens a menu with options for manipulating or closing worksheets.

Right-clicking a column header opens a menu for re-ordering, formatting, renaming or deleting a column.

Clicking in a column header sorts the worksheet in ascending order of the values in the selected column. Clicking again sorts in descending order, and once again returns to the original order. This can be useful for searching for flags or error messages within a Mojo column.

Double-clicking a field in a worksheet opens an editing window for editing data in the worksheet, for example, changing the value in a rate table.

Running Mojo in MercuryEdge

To use Mojo in MercuryEdge, the user must have a valid "Mojo key" issued by MercuryGate and entered in the MercuryEdge System Preferences window. When the key is present and a Shipment report is selected on the screen, a command named "Route optimizer..." is available in the right-hand window to launch the Mojo Optimization Wizard.

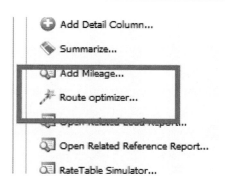

Mojo results are displayed in a new tab in the MercuryEdge application named "Mojo". Mojo results can be saved as a "Mojo package" from the right-hand commands when a Mojo tab is currently selected.

Mojo Optimization Wizard Walkthrough

Wizard Screen 1 – Mapping Columns from Shipment Data

Primary Reference: Maps to a column containing a unique identifier for each shipment. Lines with non-unique values are treated as individual items within the same shipment. Improper duplicate values can affect optimization.

Alternate Reference: Maps to a column containing user-defined contents that may be used for any purpose.

Location Codes (Origin Code, Dest Code): Maps to columns containing a unique location code for each location. Use highly recommended. Duplicate codes for different locations will result in shipments omitted from optimization.

Origin Name and Destination Name, City, State, Postal, Country, Geocode: Of these only country and geocode are required for optimization but individual rate tables might require the others. MercuryEdge uses ZIP codes (if present) or valid city-state combinations (if ZIP not present) to generate geodata. Edge does not confirm ZIP codes match the city and state.

Target Dates (Target Ship Early, Target Ship Late, Target Delivery Early, Target Delivery Late): All required. For historical data missing some values, the same column can be mapped more than once, then adjusted with the use of window extensions. Typical date format is yyyy-mm-dd hh:mm; however, MercuryEdge/Mojo usually can parse other formats.

Shipment Information (Weight, Quantity, Cube, Freight Class, Temperature Min, Temperature Max): Any or all can be used with any unit of measure (lb, kg, cu-ft, cu-m) consistent with the rate table. Quantity can be mapped to a column with a number of units of any package type (pallets, effective pallets, cartons, shipments). If SMC modules will be used for rating a freight-class column needs to be mapped. A minimum, maximum or both may be defined. Mojo will not consolidate shipments with incompatible ranges.

User Numeric Columns: These columns, if mapped, should contain numerical values that are to be compared against a maximum allowed value in the MercuryEdge rate table. This field is used entirely at the user's discretion to represent any meaning. The rate table column names must be "User Numeric 1" and (if used) "User Numeric 2."

Type: Maps to a column with a user-defined value that allows Mojo to separate incompatible shipments, e.g. dry vs. frozen, hazmat vs. non-hazmat. This column can be used any way the user prefers, for example, mapping a destination state into this field to separate shipments. For additional fine-tuned control of types, a report can control the compatibility/incompatibility of specific types. See "Type Compatibility Method" and "Type Compatibility List" under the second wizard screen.

Loading Priority: Maps to a column in the shipment data that numbers a shipment in ascending order of priority. With no priority a shipment can be loaded in any order. Only enforced if the "Vehicle Loading" parameter is set on a later wizard screen.

Equipment/Services: Maps to columns in the shipment data that name any required equipment/services, e.g., "Lift Gate". Rate tables can define optional accessorials in a contract lane. Non-optional equipment might be specified in a "Carrier Equipment" column. Both of these options must be enabled in a setting later in the wizard to be enforced.

Item fields: Maps columns with information about individual items in a shipment, when items exist on individual lines in the shipment report sharing the same primary reference. Mojo expects to find any values that it needs for quantity, weight or cube to be mapped in these fields. User-defined numerical values also can be mapped at the item level (see "User Numeric Columns" above.)

Direct/Historical: Maps to columns showing the charge and/or timeframe for actual or historical values that Mojo is trying to beat. The contract field is simply a contract identifier for reference. "Direct Carrier Mode" maps to a column to allow mode to be determined when using external or synced rates. The "Historical Charge" and "Historical Contract" columns, if used, should contain the actual charge for the item and an identifier for the contract used.

Pool Location: Maps to a column supplying a unique location code for pooling this shipment. Required for pre-assigned pooling scenarios. For no pre-assigned pool locations, do not map this column. For a mix of pre-assigned and non-pre-assigned, leave the non-pre-assigned blank. Entries with the word "none" will not be assigned. Non-pre-assigned pool locations exist in a Pool Location report.

Load Preference: Maps to a column in the shipment data containing a user-defined load preference for each shipment. Shipments with matching preferences will be consolidated. Load Preference can be enforced in various ways – only one preference in a load, a load may contain shipments with more than one preference, etc. – with the wizard parameter "Load Preference".

Shipment Options: Maps to a column containing a predefined value that overrides certain global Mojo settings for that shipment only. The codes are in a comma-delimited list. Current possible values are:

-WindowExtension	*Do not use time-window extensions for this shipment*
-WindowExtensionP	*No extensions for pickups only*
-WindowExtensionD	*No extensions for delivery only*
-NonTLConsol	*Prevent use of non-TL consolidations*
-NonTLConsolP	
-NonTLConsolD	

CL Reference: Maps to a column containing a reference value that can be used to group by <u>customer loads</u>. If the column is mapped then shipments with the same ref value will be grouped. The behavior is the same as the "Enforce (Allow Groups")" setting of Load Preference Restrictions.

<u>Wizard Screen 2 – Optimization Parameters</u>

The second screen starts the process of setting the constraints that will be used in the optimization.

Rate Table: The name of the rate table spreadsheet open in MercuryEdge to use in the optimization. If multiple reports of type "RateTable" are open be sure to use the correct one.

Re-Rate Table: Advanced feature to specify a second rate table to conduct re-rating after the initial optimization. For example, we might run a "light" optimization in a MercuryEdge rate table to build loads and routes, then conduct a more intensive server-based rating.

Direct Rate Method: The method Mojo should use to calculate the direct rate it should try to improve upon. Defaults to "Least Cost." The setting "Transit Time (LC Fallback)" tries to find a rate that meets the transit time requirements, but will fall back to least cost if none found. "Transit Time (or No Rate)" does not give the load a direct cost, and hence it cannot be optimized, if no rate is found that also satisfies the transit time.

Non-Opt Rate Method: Method used to calculate direct rate for non-optimized shipments (shipments that could not be consolidated and optimized given the stated constraints). Options are Assign Direct Rate (regardless of constraint violations), Least Cost (does not respect time/transit constraints), Transit Time (next lowest cost that respects time/transit constraints).

Fuel surcharges: A percentage uplift for quick calculations of what-if impacts of fuel-cost changes.

Fuel Index Adjustment: A global offset to apply to any fuel indexes associated with rate tables being used for rating.

Earliest Actual Date: Used to prevent Mojo from building live loads with pickup dates in the past. Example: pickup windows for shipments run from Monday to Wednesday but optimization is occurring on Tuesday.

Strategy: Adjusts Mojo's fundamental optimization strategy. The two most common options are M-OOR (Max-out-of-Route) and NOGGIN. Others include SPARR and STOCHAT. The first three have an "Hz" variant for unusual geographic features. Consult MercuryGate for uses other than M-OOR or NOGGIN.

Max-Out-of-Route: An important number that represents a ratio of the sum of the legs in a load divided by the direct distance between origin and final destination. A zigzag route would have a higher ratio. Although the maximum possible value is 25, as a practical matter carriers may reject the tenders of loads with ratios higher than 1.4. See also the MOOR looping option on the final wizard screen.

Constraint Bias: Values of high/medium/low reflect how likely Mojo is to use already-provisioned vehicles instead of new vehicles. Comes into play when the potential savings is negligible. Mojo can be instructed to run multiple constraint-bias scenarios.

Truckload Modes: Enter a comma-delimited list of terms that Mojo should use to recognize as a truckload mode, such as "TL,Truckload." Some rate tables might use other terms that should be included here.

Vehicle Max Weight/Quantity/Cube, Truckload Max Stops: Self-explanatory. These settings <u>WILL BE OVERRIDEN BY THE RATE TABLE</u> if the rate table's values are smaller. Besides reflecting real-world limits, these values can be adjusted to study the effect of what-if scenarios.

Recommended Minimum Stop Size: Tells Mojo to avoid placing relatively small drops on the same multi-stop route as relatively large ones. The idea is that a large delivery is not put at risk by a small one. The actual ratio is known as "relative effective stop size." Each drop is calculated as a percentage of vehicle capacity by weight, quantity or cube (whichever is largest). Then these ratios are compared against each other. Example: stop 1 is 3.3% of capacity, stop 2 is 95%, so the size of the first relative to the second is 3.3%/95% = 3.5%. If this figure is below the parameter setting, Mojo is discouraged from putting the two drops on the same route.

Vehicle Loading: This parameter enforces the "Loading Priority" column mapped from the shipment data. The options are "LIFO" (Last In First Out) and "Any Order." Using the LIFO setting makes loads with other, conflicting constraints subject to LIFO violations and not being optimized.

Stop Restrictions: Applies only to multi-pick/multi-stop loads. The options are None, No Multi-Pick, No Multi-Drop, No Pickups After 1st Drop, Drop Bias. Choosing "Drop Bias" tells Mojo to schedule drops before pickups when the distance is not significantly farther. In effect, this biases Mojo toward continuous moves.

Load Preference Restrictions: This setting enforces the "Load Preference" column mapped from the shipment data. The options are None, Enforce (Single Only), Enforce (Allow Groups), Bias (Normal) and Bias (Strong). The single-only option means only shipments with the same load preference may be consolidated. The allow-groups option allows shipments with different preferences to be on the same load. The bias options may split shipments with matching preferences for greater savings; a strong bias generally is more likely to leave them together.

Origin Location Bias: Enter a comma-delimited list of location codes that indicate a preference for first/earlier pickup; e.g., two warehouse locations in the same city. Only applicable to multi-pick loads. Biases Mojo toward the outcome but does not force it.

Dest Location Restrictions: Comma-separated list of location codes that must be last on a route. If a route does not have a location that is restricted, all normal routing rules apply. If a route has more than one location that is restricted, the route is invalid ("DestRestriction-constrained"). If a route has one restricted location, the last drop will be at the specified location.

Type Compatibility Method: Shipments can be consolidated according to type by requiring an exact match, or else use of a "compatibility list" or "incompatibility list" that specifies compatibility by individual types.

Type Compatibility List: If the previous field specifies use of a list, this field contains a dropdown menu list of compatibility reports open in MercuryEdge. The report type must be "OptConstraint." The report contains two columns labeled "Type 1" and "Type 2". In a compatibility list, the report specifies which types can be consolidated with each other. In an incompatibility list, shipments can be consolidated with any type *not* specified in the report. Types with blanks are treated as wildcards that can be consolidated with any other type.

Non-TL Consolidation: By default Mojo only considers "truckload" vehicles. If this option is enabled you can enter a comma-delimited list of other, non-TL modes to consider, e.g., "LTL,Parcel." Or you can enable the option and leave the list empty, meaning all contracts are eligible for consolidation.

Non-TL Transit Determination: Determines non-TL (single-stop) transit time either in the same manner as for truckload contracts or by an alternate method as follows:

☐ Using the Direct Service Days column mapped from the shipment data.

☐ Using two optional columns in the Edge rate table with the headings "Transit Method" and "Transit Value." If the entry contains the value "Service Days," Mojo uses the value (1-99) in the value column. If the method column contains the value "Zone Days," then the value column contains a value relative to the calculated zone. Example: Column = 3, value = -1, Mojo uses a value of 2 for service days.

☐ If neither of these options is used, Mojo uses a value returned from a TMS contract.

Non-TL Weekend Exclusion: By default weekend days are excluded for all carriers. This behavior can be overridden in this field by entering a comma-delimited list of only the modes for which weekends should be excluded (for non-listed modes, weekends will be included). In general, most LTL carriers will keep the exclusion; in general most intermodal carriers will include weekends; parcel tends to depend on additional contract information. This field is enabled when the previous parameter, Non-TL Transit Determination, is set to "Use Specified Values."

Service Times: The options for the "Service Time Determination" parameter are "Default Only" and the names of any Load/Unload Service Time reports open in MercuryEdge. The default-only setting uses the next three settings (Service Time Base, Service Time Additional) as global values. Shipments with a location code not listed in the report will default to the global values. The fields of a Load/Unload Service Time report are:

Location Code (mandatory)	*String*
Service Time Base	*Numeric*
Service Time per Shipment	*Numeric*
Service Time per Quantity	*Numeric*
Delivery Idle Time	*Numeric*

Hours of Operation Determination: The possible values are Default Only, Use Shipment Hours, and the names of any Location Hours reports open in MercuryEdge. The default-only setting applies the default settings of the next two parameters globally. The shipment-hours setting uses the hours specified in the shipment data. The hours of operation for each location specified in a Location Hours report will be used instead of the default. The fields of a Location Hours report are:

Location Code (mandatory)	*String*
Days	<Constant>
Hours	hh – hh, hh:mm – hh:mm

Example formats for location hours:

> Mon-Fri, Mon-Sat,Mon-Sun
> Mon,Tue,Wed,Thu,Fri,Sat,Sun
> Date: 12-25
> Date: 2012-11-22

Specific dates are considered before recurring dates; weekly or day-of-week after that. Hence a location might be open Mon-Fri except on Dec. 25. Location codes also may include *DEFAULT* (with asterisks) for all locations not listed in the report, or *GLOBAL* applying to all locations if not overridden.

Hours of Operation Enforcement: The "Arrival" option in this setting allows any arrival before a facility's closing time. "Arrival/Departure" means arrival, unloading and departure before closing.

Wizard Screen 3 – Optimization Parameters

Extend Early Ship/Late Ship/Early Delivery/Late Delivery Window: Allows Mojo to be flexible in its time windows for pickup and delivery, in increments of half-days at a time. Mojo reports how much of the available extension that it used in the "Pickup Window" and "Delivery Window" columns of the Optimizer Shipments tab. Time extensions often are used to optimize historical data where only one date column (e.g., ship-by) is available. Another common tactic is to extend the inner windows (late pickup, early delivery) to achieve better results. Individual shipments may override these extension settings in a "Shipment Options" column.

Input Date Adjustment: A global adjustment that can be applied against times in the shipment data. One example of usage would be to adjust historical shipments into the effective period of a contract for rating. Clicking the field adjusts the offset in increments of seven days, recommended to comport with any location service days constraints.

HOS/Speed Determination: If this parameter is set to "Use Lane Info," then Mojo uses the "Transit Method" column of a MercuryEdge rate table. The value in each row of the rate table should have the format: "HOS: #1/#2/#3/#4/#5" where #1 = Vehicle Speed, #2 = Driver Duty Limit, #3 = Driver Driving Limit, #4 = Driver Off-Duty Rest, #5 = Route Duty Limit. For example, "HOS: 50/14/11/10/70" for typical USDOT single-driver. An alternate form is simply "HOS: #1" where #1 = vehicle speed, with driver and route limits using wizard-based defaults in the following parameters.

Driver constraints: The defaults are set to USDOT regulations but are configurable, for instance in a tandem-driver scenario. Mojo uses these values in calculating transit times.

Allow Off-Duty Extension: Allows Mojo to include off-duty driver time as part of its calculations. Important, for example, for shipments with a short transit time that might arrive before a facility's operating hours.

Carrier Capacity Strategy: By default Mojo assumes carrier capacity is infinite. These settings allow a primary and optional secondary capacity limit (if both are specified, both are used). Options are:

Off
  -- build loads without considering capacity limits
Vehicles/Contract/Lane/Day
  -- limit per individual contract, for each day
Vehicles/Contract/Lane/Run
  -- limit per contract, for this Mojo run
Vehicles/Carrier/Origin/Day
  -- number available from one origin for one day
Vehicles/Carrier/Origin/Run
  -- number available from one origin for this Mojo run
Vehicles/Carrier/Dest/Day
  -- limit on vehicles to this destination, per day
Vehicles/Carrier/Dest/Run
  -- limit on vehicles to this destination, for this Mojo run
Vehicles/Carrier/ODPair/Day
  -- limit between this unique origin and dest, per day
Vehicles/Carrier/ODPair/Run
  -- limit between this unique origin and dest, this Mojo run
Vehicles/Carrier/Day
  -- overall limit for this carrier, per day
Vehicles/Carrier/Run
  -- overall limit for this carrier, this Mojo run

Carrier Capacity Allocation: For non-optimized shipments, whether to set direct-ship even if it over-allocates a stated capacity, or to require the direct-ship to respect declared capacity.

Carrier Capacity Enforcement: Option to enforce carrier capacity limits even on non-optimized (i.e., direct) loads. If this option is enabled and a violation occurs, a "Capacity Violation" flag is raised on the load. If it is not enabled, non-optimized loads are is assigned the direct rate automatically.

Carrier Capacity Default: If the capacity strategy is not "Off," sets the default number of vehicles available in both primary and secondary strategy. Detailed values for carrier capacity can be specified using a "Capacity" column in the ratetable itself.

Dock Capacity Strategy: Either off, or tied to a Dock Capacity report open in MercuryEdge. Names of open reports appear in the dropdown menu of this parameter. A dock-capacity report has the required columns Location Code, Pickup Docks, Drop Docks. With no dock restrictions Mojo will schedule the first route pickup as early in the day as possible. A dock capacity limits the number of vehicles that can be unloaded/loaded at the same time.

Backhaul Bias: This parameter determines how likely Mojo is to allow a route with a partial or complete return toward its origin. Settings are Off, Low, Medium, High. Lower bias results in fewer backhauls allowed in Mojo's results; higher bias, more backhauls.

Private Fleet Strategy/Private Fleet SCAC: Note that these settings might be hidden if using the "advanced" fleet setting – see next item. Options here are "Off" and, if using a private fleet, "Return Vehicle." The SCAC of the carrier should be in the "Private Fleet SCAC" parameter. This strategy may be used with or without backhaul bias. Use the "Origin Location Bias" parameter to specify a fleet origin, which must also be a shipment origin. The final return leg is identified by an "R" or "Return" in event-related fields in Mojo results.

Advanced Private Fleet Strategy: Different parameters are displayed if the Mojo option "advancedfleet" is installed in MercuryEdge system properties.

Fleet Capacity Strategy: Settings are "Same as Non-Fleet" or "Use Vehicle Assignments"

Fleet Capacity Allocation: How to allocate non-optimized fleet shipments. Options are "Allow Direct Over-Allocation" (ignores any limits on carrier capacity) or "No Over-Allocation" (assigns to a load that respects capacity).

Fleet Locations: The name of an open Location report in MercuryEdge for specifying "domicile" locations from which vehicles originate and return. Columns must include "Location Code" and "Geo" for valid geodata.

Fleet Vehicles: If using vehicle assignments, this must be the name of an open Vehicle report in MercuryEdge with columns headed "Vehicle Id", "Location Code" and "Contract Id". (Exact column names are required.) A Vehicle report can contain two optional columns, "Availability Start" and "Availability End", for example, for known upcoming maintenance downtime.

Fleet Drivers: If using driver assignments, this is the name of an open report of type "Driver" in MercuryEdge. The required columns are "Driver Id" and "Location Code" for the driver's assigned location. Optional columns "Max Weekly Duty" (numerical in hours, 60 is standard for US); "First DOW" (Mon Tue, etc.) and "Schedule Id" to assign this driver to a DriverSch report (next item).

Fleet Driver Schedules: Optionally selects an open report of type "DriverSch" that defines a schedule to which a driver or groups of drivers can be assigned.

Required columns are "Schedule Id", a unique identifier - same file can include multiple schedules; "Days" in the following allowed format:

Mon – Fri, Mon – Sat, Mon – Sun	(Weekly format)
Mon, Tue, Wed, Thu, Fri, Sat, Sun	(Day of Week format)
Date: 12-25	(Month-Day format for
recurring dates)	
Date: 2012-11-22	(Date format for specific
dates)	

And a third column, "Hours", e.g. 0900-1800,2100-2400

Fleet Driver HOS Restrictions: If using driver assignments, the options are "Vehicle Assignment Reset" and "Require Rest Reset".

Vehicle Assignment Reset - When a driver is assigned to vehicle, all existing hours of service are considered available (even if Mojo used the same driver immediately prior). Possible use case: Each Driver Id actually refers to a Driver "Group" (not defined in Mojo) for a single vehicle. It is assumed when the vehicle is used, a driver from that group would always be available with freshly reset hours of service.

Require Rest Reset - When a driver is assigned to vehicle, Mojo ensures the driver has an off-duty rest period sufficiently long to ensure a HOS reset. For example, if "Driver Off-Duty Rest" is 10 hours, a driver will never be assigned to a vehicle without a minimum of 10 hours off-duty time from the previous route completion. This occurs regardless of any HOS that may actually be still available to the driver.

International Stop Restrictions: "None" or "No Backtracking," in which routes may not return across a border once a stop is completed.

Pool Strategy: Options are Off, Consider Pools, Consider Hybrid, Force Pools. Strongly recommended to use "Force Pools" first with new data because errors such as missing rates will be flagged in results. With the "consider" options Mojo simply does not assign a pool location. The final wizard screen has an improvement option called "Consider Pools Depth".

Pool Locations: Will contain a dropdown list of any Pool Location reports open in MercuryEdge. A pool-location report is required for an optimization involving pools. The only required columns in a Pool Location report are Location Code and Geo, but other possible columns include Name, City, State, Country, Drop Modes, Drop SCACs, Pickup Modes and Pickup SCACs.

Pool Assignment: Controls the way Mojo assigns pool locations. The options are:

Pre-assigned Only:	Uses "Pool Location" column defined in mapping screen
Best Rate (Predictive):	Assign a pool loc with the lowest predicted rate.
Best Rate (Introspective):	In-depth analysis; significantly longer than predictive
Nearest to Ratetable Origin	
Nearest to Ratetable Dest	
Nearest to M-OOR Origin	Nearest pool that passes the M-OOR constraint...
Nearest to M-OOR Dest	... may leave unassigned if no location qualifies
Nearest to Origin	

Max Pool Hold Time: Limits time allowed for a shipment at a pool location. Increasing hold time generally improves optimization opportunities. This global setting can be overridden for individual locations with a "Max Pool Hold Time" column in a Pool Locations report.

<u>Wizard Screen 4 – Optimization Parameters, Looping Improvements</u>

Besides the selection of some final parameters, this screen also sets "looping" options for repeated runs, automatically incrementing the value of certain variables. Another way is to use "Mojo Futures" to step across changes in multiple variables at once.

Equipment/Services Enforcement: When enabled, these options enforce the equipment and/or services column mapped from the shipment data in the first screen of the wizard. Equipment and services in the rate table are specified in columns headed "Carrier Equipment" and "Carrier Services."

Pickup/Drop Clustering: Allows pickup and/or drop events to be limited by specified radius/radii. Pickup radius determined by first pickup location. Drop radius determined by last drop location. Limits may be defined by SCAC or mode (use comma-separated lists). Up to four distinct limits may be defined.

Green Methodology/CO2: For calculating estimated CO2 savings, sets a truckload baseline and calculates other modes as a percentage relative to the baseline. Enter a comma-separated list of modes in the right-hand column to which this calculation should apply. (The question marks in the default values exist to prevent interference with any existing calculations. Remove them if you want the calc to apply to that mode.) "Carbon Tax" adds a "CO2" accessorial on all ratetable-derived rates based on CO2 usage. Typical values are $10-$50 per ton.

Max Out-of-Route: The first looping improvement option tells Mojo to run multiple M-OOR scenarios with the specified number of loops and the increment to use in each loop. Example: the Max Out-of-Route parameter on the second wizard screen is set to 1.4, then on this screen the settings are 3 additional loops with an increment of 0.1. Mojo runs loops at values of 1.4, 1.3, 1.2 and 1.1. The best option will be listed in the "Notes" tab of Mojo results.

Max Stops: Tells Mojo how many times to consider a new maximum-stop value and how much to increase that value on each loops.

Constraint Bias: Conduct multiple runs with each possible constraint bias, low, medium and high.

Savings Gambit: Potentially finds fewer loads but an overall savings is not guaranteed. At initial settings of 4 loops and initial value of $1,000, Mojo finds loads that each save a minimum of $1,000, then $667, then $333, then finally all remaining loads with any savings.

STOCHAT Depth: Sets Mojo's depth when using the "STOCHAT" strategy. Valid range is 1-4 with default of 2.

Consider Pools Depth: How deep to search in pooling scenarios. Possible values are 1-10 with a default of 5. At a setting of 2, Mojo considers only two runs, all shipments forced through a pool and none forced through a pool. Intermediate settings reflect additional combinations of pooled and non-pooled shipments.

Postliminary Depth: How deep to look overall. Possible values range from 0 to 100. A value of 0 performs no adjustments to Mojo's original solution. Values between 10 and 20 usually provide the best compromise between optimizer time and overall savings. Large datasets (>5000 shipments) will most likely perform unacceptably with values above 5.

Distance Determiner: Tells Mojo whether to use server-based or cached distance calculations instead of its faster, default geocode-based calculation, which is usually sufficient. Options are Geo Only, Distance Table Cache (zip-to-zip distances), Server-Lite (combination of server and non-server distances) and Server (slowest option).

Distance Display: Set to miles or kilometers. Distance columns are labeled "Distance." To revert to earlier label of "Mileage," use optimization parameter "outputversion=2" or lower.

Dynamic Scripting Engine: If enabled, allows authorized users to enter and edit JavaScript to modify optimization decisions.

Save Default Settings: All wizard settings are saved for the current company. Remember that saving Mojo results as a Mojo Package also preserves the settings used for the run.

Finish: Tells Mojo to conduct an optimization based on the settings chosen in the wizard.

Mojo Options (System Preferences)

This section describes possible comma-separated values to include in the "Mojo Options" field of the System Preferences dialog of the MercuryEdge application.

NOTE: After changing a preference you must exit the cell before saving. That means clicking in another cell or hitting the tab key. Simply typing or changing a setting and clicking "OK" does not save your changed preference.

Mojo Key	••••
Mojo Close Confirm	false
Mojo Options	advancedfleet,multipool
ALK Map Key	
Schedule Optimizer Key	
Rating Debug	
Rating Parallelism	3
Rating Submit Size	120

advancedfleet	Enables Mojo options related to private fleet
-DupLocCheck	Disables enforcement of unique location codes
-leeway	Suppresses "Leeway" column in results. See Results Reference just below for definition.

outputversion=1	Disables Weight, Quantity, Cube columns in event results
outputversion=2 (or lower)	Disables Leeway column in Mojo results. Also uses older "Mileage" label instead of the newer "Distance"
outputversion=3 (or lower)	Disables "User Number 1" and "User Number 2" columns in load, shipment, event results
outputversion=4 (or lower)	Disables "CL Reference" columns in output (CL = Customer Load)

The reason for suppressing certain output columns is so that features added to Mojo more recently do not disrupt existing integration setups that rely on an earlier format.

Mojo Results Reference

After a Mojo run a new tab labeled "Mojo" (with a number reflecting the number of different runs) opens in Mercury Edge. At the top of the panel the statistics for the last completed run include:

Shipment Count
Load Count
CO2 Change
Direct Distance
Optimized Distance
Distance Change
Direct Cost
Optimized Cost
Optimized Savings

In a pooling optimization, figures are included for pooled versus non-pooled.

Optimizer Loads tab

Shows a view of the loads created by Mojo. The number of rows in the report is listed at the top of the panel. Columns in the report for each load are:

Load Reference
Shipments- *Number of shipments in load*

Stops- *Number of stops*
Events- *Sequence of events, e.g. PPDD*
Opt Contract- *Carrier contract*
Opt Rate- *Optimized rate*
Direct Rate-*Direct rate*
Savings- *Direct-minus-optimized*
Pickup Loc
Drop Loc
Pickup Date
Leeway - Estimate of how long pickup could be delayed and still have on-time delivery. Assumes carrier capacity is available. Useful in continuous-optimization scenarios for indicating a load should be sent now instead of remaining in the pool. This column can be suppressed with Mojo Option "outputversion=2" (or lower) or Mojo Option "-leeway".
Drop Date
Trns Days
Max Weight
Max Qty
Max Cube
Max User Numeric 1
Max User Numeric 2
OOR- *Strategy Out-of-route calculation*
RTO- *Return to origin calculation Backhaul Bias*
#PE- *Number of pickup events*
#DE- *Number of drop events*
Equipment Service- *Equipment & services, if any*
Type- *Shipment type*
Temp Min
Temp Max
Opt Distance
Direct Distance
Distance Diff
CO2 Change
Payment Terms
Flags- *Check for error conditions/flagged shipments*
Server Rate
Hist Rate

Each load listed in the Optimizer Loads tab is preceded by a plus-mark icon. Clicking a load's icon opens a new submenu of available details:

Shipments-Details on each shipment in the load
Events- Details on each pickup/drop
Related Loads- Details on loads related to this load or its shipments, e.g. legs

List Rates-Details on rate including contract, lane, rate, service days, etc
Evaluate Rates -Line-by-line description of evaluation vs. available contracts

When one or more loads are selected, the tab header will display totals for weight, quantity, cube and direct rate for the selected loads.

Optimizer Shipments tab

This tab presents a shipment-level view of the optimization result. Each row in the report corresponds to a shipment in the original shipment report that was optimized. The total number of rows in the report is listed at the top of the panel. The columns in the Optimizer Shipments report are:

Primary Reference- From original shipment report
Notes- Check for error conditions, missing rates, etc.
Load Reference- Load to which this shipment was assigned
Optimized- True, or false if unsuccessful
Pickup Window- Extension used? Time Window Extensions
Delivery Window
Direct Rate
Direct Contract
Direct Days
Direct Zone
Pickup Event- Order of occurrence of event
Delivery Event
Origin Code- Location code of shipment origin
Origin Name
Origin City
Origin State
Origin Zip
Origin Ctry
Origin Geo
Dest Code
Dest Name
Dest City
Dest State
Dest Zip
Dest Ctry
Dest Geo
Target Ship (Early)
Actual Ship
Target Ship (Late)
Target Delivery (Early)
Actual Delivery

Target Delivery (Late)
Weight
Quantity
Cube
User Numeric 1
User Numeric 2
Class
Temp Min
Temp Max
Equipment
Services
Type
Priority
Payment Terms
Rating Count
Alt Ref
Load Preference- Load Preference
CL Reference-Customer load reference
Options
Hist Rate
Hist Contract

In addition, each shipment listed in the Optimizer Shipments report is preceded by a plus-mark icon. Clicking the icon reveals a submenu of details:

Loads- Details on this shipment's load
Events- Details on pickups/drops for this shipment
List Rates- Details on contract, lane, rate, service days, charges
Evaluate Rates- Line-by-line narrative of evaluation of each contract
Evaluate Rates- Evaluation of this shipment vs. each possible load

When one or more shipments in the list are selected, the tab header will display totals for weight, quantity, cube, direct rate and pool rate (if any) for the selected shipments.

Other results tabs

Optimizer Events: The report in this tab lists every event in the optimization, with the total number of rows reported at the top of the panel. Columns for each event are:

Load Reference
Type- Pickup, drop, etc
Seq Num- Ordinal of this event in the load's event sequence
Distance- Distance in the route where this event occurs

Weight
Quantity
Cube
User Numeric 1
User Numeric 2
Code- Location code of event
Name
City
State
Zip
Ctry
Geo
Actual Date
Service Time
Loc Hours
SCAC
Mode
Service
Ship Refs- List of shipments involved in this event

In addition each event listed in the Optimizer Events tab is preceded by a plus-mark icon. Clicking the icon reveals a details submenu with these options:

Hours of Operation
Shipments- *Details on shipments involved in this event*

Optimizer Rates tab: For each load, this report lists the contract, SCAC, mode, service, lane, total rate, and item/accessorial rates.

Optimizer Capacity tab: For each day in the overall time window covered by the optimization, for each SCAC and its origin code, the carrier capacity used that day. If dual capacity strategy is used, there also will be an "Optimizer Capacity 2" tab.

Map Tab

Route Map tab: Visual display of loads created in the optimization. Interactively highlights loads/shipments in the results tabs by clicking on routes in the map, and vice versa. Map can be dragged with cursor. Map window can be resized by click-dragging on border of window.

ALK Map Tab

ALK is an additional map option available by subscription. If a valid ALK key is installed in the System Preferences window an ALK map will be displayed in this tab, with more sophisticated user options for markup and overlay management.

History Tab

Optimizer History tab: For each initial optimization and subsequent re-optimization of the results in the same Mojo tab, this tab shows a result line with these columns, followed by a summary comparison of the latest runs:

> Run Date
> Elapsed
> Savings/Sec
> Direct Cost
> Opt Cost
> Savings
> % Sav
> Input Ship Legs
> Opt Ship Legs
> PL Adj- *Postliminary adjustments made — also listed in Notes*
> Total Loads
> Opt Loads
> Direct Miles
> Opt Miles
> % Mile- *Percentage reduction in direct vs. optimized mileage*
> CO2 Diff
> Parameter Changes- *Which wizard settings were changed between runs*

Clicking on the row of a previous run in the Optimizer History tab re-launches it.

Notes Tab

This tab contains a report on the last run including performance statistics, summary of the results, a list of the wizard settings applied, and Mojo version information. The "Warnings" line at the top of the report should be checked after each run; any warnings will be listed in the report.

General Commands

Optimize

Launch a new optimization run on the current Mojo results and parameters. Re-launches the wizard for the chance to adjust settings.

Create Mojo Package

Save results of the last Mojo run as a multi-tabbed spreadsheet file, including any charts, etc. generated during post-run analysis. The file-save dialog will include different file types in the dropdown menu:

> Standard- *Includes all content*
> Input- *Saves input data, not results*
> Flash- *Also saves Mojo's calculations for instant re-load*
> Auto-flash- *Saved automatically after each run*

Flash packages can be retrieved via the MercuryEdge menu: Tools -> Mojo Tools -> Recover Auto-Flash.

Clear Selection

Un-highlights any individual or groups of rows selected, for example from the "Select Related Loads" command, which might have selected non-contiguous rows throughout the report.

Select Related Loads

In a pooling scenario, select all loads related to the currently selected loads. "Related" loads are all loads on a multi-leg shipment, for example, the pool inbound and pool outbound load. Repeated clicks on this command will find all secondary relations, then tertiary, etc. It is good practice to choose Select Related Loads before creating server loads to avoid creating only part of the multi-leg shipment execution plan.

Create Branch

Create a separate Mojo run for the currently selected subset of data for use in what-if analysis or just ease of analysis. Re-launches the optimization wizard with the new results and the branch data displayed in new tabs in MercuryEdge. Does not change original data.

Analysis Tasks

Load/Event Time Tables

Load Time Table: Adds a "Time Table" tab to Mojo's results showing pickups, dock time and deliveries graphically for each load. Useful in identifying timetable problems. Light-shaded areas represent the service time base; dark areas represent additional service time on a per-shipment or per-unit basis.

Event Time Table: Adds a "Time Table" chart to Mojo's results with an event-level view. Color code: Green, pickup; red, drop; blue, optimized; magenta, direct.

Pivot Table

Opens an spreadsheet-style pivot table for results analysis. Drag columns from the available list to add them to the table.

Cost/Savings

Adds tables labeled "Run Savings," "Freight Spend" and "Load Savings" showing graphical analysis of results. Run Savings plots the amount saved by optimization versus elapsed time; useful in determining whether looping improvements are worth the extra time. Freight Spend analyses spending by carrier contract. Load Savings charts the optimized loads by the percentage of savings they represent.

Load Configuration

Adds tabs to Mojo's results with charts for shipments per optimized load, weight, quantity and cube by optimized load, vehicle capacity used and contract-related information.

Event Statistics

Adds tabs to Mojo's results with charts for loads by event types ("PDD" for "pickup-drop-drop, "O" outbound, "I" inbound, etc.)," loads by number of stops, optimized mileage per load and backhaul statistics.

Pool/Fleet Statistics

Adds new tabs with charts breaking down loads by pool location and shipments broken down by pool hold duration, or by fleet usage.

Mojo Futures

Selecting this command after an initial Mojo run re-runs the optimization wizard, allowing user to adjust any number of numerical parameters. On the final screen, users specifies a number of future loops to run. Mojo executes the requested number of times, stepping through the changed parameters, and presents a comparison of all results.

Google Earth

Generates an interactive Google Earth route layer using the selected loads. Use Google Earth's timeline feature to narrow the displayed date ranges. Using Google Earth for business purposes requires a license from the Google website.

Configuration Tasks

Load Preferences

These options allow us to save, change or clear load preferences to run additional scenarios. We can save current loads, select loads and propose a new load preference for them, or clear existing preferences. A load preference column is added to (or cleared in) the shipment data.

Modify Shipment Endpoints

Change the origin or destination for shipments selected in the Mojo results window. Requires a location report to be open in MercuryEdge. Opens a dialog with a list of available options. Because the source shipment data is changed, this option creates a new branch.

Modify Shipment Pools

Dynamically reassign pool locations for the selected shipments from a list in a dialog window. Options are to retain pool selection, disable pool selection (sets the value to "None"), clear pool selection, or assign a new pool location from a list in a location report.

Integration Tasks

Sync Direct Rates

Installs in the shipment data the direct rate as calculated by Mojo. Useful in using server-based rates to save time on subsequent runs. Mojo adds three columns to the original shipment report (if not present) headed "Direct Rate," "Direct Contract" and "Direct Days."

Load/Shipment/Event Filters

Opens the Selection Filter Wizard to screen optimized loads by user-chosen criteria. The left side contains three fields: a dropdown list of columns, a list of operators (such as "equals" or "contains"), and the value to use in the filter. Click "Add" to add the criterion to the filter and "Finish."

Create Server Loads

Creates the optimized loads in Mojo's results for actual execution in the TMS. The TMS generates its own primary reference for each load, adds a server re-rating to the "Server Rate" column in the Optimized Loads tab, sets the status to "Rated" if successfully rated against a contract in the TMS or "Edge-Rated" if not, sets plan dates and adds a column to the Load and Shipment reports headed "RunID" with a unique identifier for the Mojo run used. Once loads are created they can be tendered or auto-tendered.

Mojo Dark Reference

Menu Commands

Menu: Edit -> Preferences -> System

NOTE: <u>After changing a preference you must exit the cell before saving. That means clicking in another cell or hitting the tab key. Simply typing or changing a setting and clicking "OK" does not save your changed preference.</u>

Macros Dir:	Default directory for saving/retrieving macros
Macro Login ID: Macro Login Pwd	Enter id & pwd to avoid login during automatic execution
Menu: Tools -> Macro Editor	Opens Macro Editor window, if not visible
Menu: Tools -> Macro Log	Displays log of macro runs in a new tab in MercuryEdge

Requirements for Macro Scripts

- Only one command per line

- Comments start with #

- Starting a line with @ suppresses any visual output

- For unattended execution, add "Quit" as the last line

<u>Opening Macros</u>

Click the folder icon in the editor window, or macros stored in the home directory (as set in System Preferences) are visible in the Reports window in MercuryEdge

<u>Macro Command Syntax</u>

Open a report

```
open [tab index]~<Reports window tab name>~<report name>
```

Example:

```
open 1~Shipment~My Shipments
```

Import a file

```
import filename~true
import filename~false
```

Example:

```
import C:\Users\John\Documents\MercuryEdge\
                MyShipments.xls~true
```

The true/false flag indicates whether the file has a header row.

Open a rate table

```
openratetable <tab index>
```

Example:

```
openratetable 1
```

Add GeoData:

```
geocode <tab index>~<list of column names>
```

Example:

```
geocode 1~Primary Reference|Origin City|Origin State|
                Origin Zip|Origin Ctry|Dest
                City|Dest State|Dest Zip|Dest Ctry
```

Using the names of columns in the report that needs geodata.

Filter

```
filter [new tab index\~<index of tab to
     filter>~<column name>:<operator>:value:
```

Example:

```
filter 4~1~Dest City:equals:OMAHA:
```

Optimize

```
mojoexec <index of tab to optimize>
```

Example:

```
mojoexec 1
```

Create Mojo Package

```
mojopackage <index of Mojo tab>~<filename>
     ~<package type>
```

Example:

```
mojopackage 4~C:\Users\John\Documents\MercuryEdge
     \MyMojoPackage.xls~MojoStandardPackage (.xls)
```

Clear Selection

```
mojoclearselection
```

Select Related Loads

```
mojoselect related
```

Retain Load Preferences

```
mojoretainloadprefs
```

Load Selection Filter

```
mojoselectionfilter RouteDetail~<column
    name>:<operator>:value
```

Example:

```
mojoselectionfilter RouteDetail~Flags:not equals::
```

Create Server Loads

```
mojoupload
```

Create Branch

```
mojobranch
```

Override Wizard
Parameter

```
<parametername>~key~value
```

(See export formats, Optimizer Parameters, for list of names)

Timestamp

{timestamp}

Example: 20130806142756

Timestamp

{longtimestamp}

Example:

2013_08_06_14_27_56

MercuryEdge Macro Reference

Macro Format

- Each macro script is contained in a text file on a local or remote filesystem.
- Macros stored in the "Macros Dir" System Preference are also available in the Edge GUI under the Reports / Main / Macros section.
- Macro scripts may only contain one macro command per line.
- Lines prefixed by # are considered comments and are not processed.
- Commands prefixed by @ will suppress generated report from opening in the Edge GUI or external viewer (e.g. spreadsheet).
- For unattended macros, always use Quit command to exit Edge GUI upon completion

Macro Configuration

- To launch any macro external from the Edge GUI, configure the "Macro Login ID" and "Macro Login Pwd" to suppress login prompts.
- Macro logs are available under the "Tools / Macro Log" menu option and in the Edge home directory.
- Externally launched macros perform additional logging in the TMS audit logs (see "Audit Log Report Data Fields" document).
- Additional macro logs may be generated using the TmsLog command. If externally launched, TmsLog will also send log entry to TMS audit log.

Macro Launcher Options
- For examples of unattended scheduling, see "Edge Macros – Scheduling" document.

Option	Notes
-J-Xmx1200m	Changes Java memory usage – See "Adjusting MercuryEdge Memory" document
-J-Djnlp.homedir=C:/myhome	Changes default user home directory (creates "MercuryEdge" folder under homedir)
-J-Djnlp.headless=true	Forces Edge to run "headless". Headless operation suppresses all input prompts, dialog boxes and alert pop-ups to ensure macro completes without manual intervention.
-J-Djnlp.headless.timeout=<seconds>	Optional. If headless, terminates Edge execution after specified inactivity. Used to detect "stuck" macros. Diagnostic log written to current directory upon termination.
-J-Djnlp.mutex=true -J-Djnlp.mutex=<port number>	Checks for another running instance of Edge (which was also launched with mutex=…). Exits immediately if another instance already running.

	Uses default socket port of 4063 to claim mutex. May override using <port number>.

* Example

```
javaws -J-Djnlp.headless=true -J-Djnlp.headless.timeout=1800 -J-
Djnlp.homedir=C:/myhomedir
https://MY_DNS_NAME.mercurygate.net/MercuryGate/webstart/LauncherD
ark.jnlp
-open "C:\MyMacroPath\MacroName.edge"
```

Macro Variables

Variable	Notes
{timestamp}	* timestamp in format yyyyMMddHHmmss
{longtimestamp}	* timestamp in format yyyy_MM_dd_HH_mm_ss
{dirimportfile}	** Full name of import file (e.g. C:\docs\mydata.xls)
{dirimportfile.absolutepath}	** (Same as {dirimportfile})
{dirimportfile.parent}	** Directory component of import file (e.g. C:\docs)
{dirimportfile.name}	** Name component of import file (e.g. mydata.xls)
{dirimportfile.prefix}	** Name component (w/o extension) of import file (e.g. mydata)

* timestamp values are initially determined at start of Macro and remain static during entire run
** dirimportfile variables are populated using DirImportFile macro command.

Macro Command Table

Command	Arguments
Company	New Company Name
Open	New ReportKey, Report Type, Report Name
Merge	New Report Key, ReportKey #1, Report Key #2, Merge Col #1, Merge Col #2, Merge Type, true/false for outer join
Summary	New ReportKey, ReportKey #1, Group Columns, SortColumns, Filters
OpenRateTable	Contract Report Key #1
RelatedNotes	New ReportKey, Report Key #1
Reorder	New ReportKey, ReportKey #1, Column List
Filter	New ReportKey, ReportKey #1, Filter List
AddDetailColumns	ReportKey #1, Column List
AddFormulaColumn	Report Key #1, Expression, New Column Name
AddDupeColumn	Report Key #1, Column List
AddRegexColumn	Report Key #1, delimited column list , Delim, Expression, New Column Name
Pricesheet	New Report Key, Report Key #1, Carrier?, Cust?, 1 Row?, Acc Total?, Acc Summ?, Acc Edi Code List [or empty], Selected Only?
InvoicePriceSheet	New Report Key, Report Key #1, Report Type, Acc Summ?, Acc Edi Code List [or empty]
RelatedShipments	New Report Key, Load Report Key #1
Items	New Report Key, Report Key #1, Source Pri Ref Column (optional)
References	New Report Key, Report Key #1, Object Type
ShipUnits	New Report Key, Report Key #1, Source Pri Ref Column (optional)
OpenInternationalDetails	Report Key #1
Contacts	New Report Key, Report Key #1, Source Pri Ref Column (optional)
OpenMarginReport	Report Key #1
LineItems	New Report Key, Report Key #1, Source Pri Ref Column (optional)
Mileage	Report Key #1, Column Maps
CreateFuelIndex	New Report Key, Report Key #1
LeastCostCarrier	New Report Key, Report Key #1
LeastCostCustomer	New Report Key, Report Key #1
RateByContract	New Report Key, Report Key #1, Colon-separated Contract Oids
RenameColumn	Report Key #1, Orig Column Name, New Column Name
OpenBidPricesheetReport	Report Key #1
InvoiceAllocations	New Report Key, Report Key #1
GeoCode	Report Key #1, Column List
Convert	Report Key #1, Converter Name
Append	Report Key #1, Report Key #2
RemoveColumn	Report Key #1, Column Name

Charge	Report Key #1, Report Key #2
PrimaryLoc	New Report Key, Report Key #1
CarrierLoc	New Report Key, Report Key #1
MasterItem	New Report Key, Report Key #1
Extract	Report Key #1, Output File Path, use CSV quotes?
Import	Import File Path, true/false Header Row Flag
DirImportFile	* Import File Directory, true/false Header Row Flag
WizardParam	** WizardName, Key, Value
MojoExec	
MojoBranch	
MojoClearSelection	
MojoSelectRelated	
MojoRetainLoadPrefs	
MojoSelectionFilter	Report, Filter
MojoAnalysis	Analysis Tool
MojoUpload	
MojoPackage	File Type, Package Filename
SubmitNews	Summary, Type, Sequence, Details, Start Date, End Date, Attachment FilePath
Email	To, From, Subject, Body, AttachmentFile (optional)
RenameFile	SourceFile, DestFile
CopyFile	SourceFile, DestFile
TmsLog	Ok? (true/false), message
Quit	

* Use DirImportFile to import the FIRST csv/xls/xlsx file in specified directory. To process all files in directory, move the file to another directory using RenameFile which will allow the next file to be processed in a subsequence macro run.

** For Mojo, use WizardName = "mojo". Refer to _Mojo Import-Export Format.doc_ for all parameter descriptions.

Mojo Import / Export Formats

Mojo Version 8.2+

Import Data Overview

Mojo accepts import files in ".xls" (preferred), ".xslx" and ".csv" formats. The data may be contained in multiple files or in a multi-worksheet spreadsheet. Format types are identified by a standardized worksheet name.

Input Data	Shipments
Worksheet Name	Shipment - nnnnnn
Usage	Mandatory
Description	The shipment file contains the point-to-point movements for optimization. Each row is generally identified by a unique identifier (Primary Reference) and contains the basic location, date and physical parameters of the shipment. Shipments with multiple items are identified by repeating rows using the same Primary Reference. * For shipment data, column names are mapped using the Mojo wizard.

Column Name*	Usage	Data Type	Notes
Primary Reference	Mandatory	String	Unique Shipment Identifier
Alternate Reference		String	User-defined Optional Identifier
Origin Code		String	Unique Location Identifier
Origin Name		String	
Origin City		String	
Origin State		String	
Origin Postal		String	
Origin Country	Mandatory	String	
Origin Geo	Mandatory	Lat/Long (dd.dddddd,dd.dddddd)	If unknown, may be generated using Edge wizard
Dest Code		String	Unique Location Identifier
Dest Name		String	
Dest City		String	
Dest State		String	
Dest Postal		String	
Dest Country	Mandatory	String	
Dest Geo	Mandatory	Lat/Long (dd.dddddd,dd.dddddd)	If unknown, may be generated using Edge wizard
Target Ship (Early)	Mandatory	yyyy-mm-dd hh:mm	
Target Ship (Late)	Mandatory	yyyy-mm-dd hh:mm	

Target Delivery (Early)	Mandatory	yyyy-mm-dd hh:mm	
Target Delivery (Late)	Mandatory	yyyy-mm-dd hh:mm	
Weight	Mandatory	Numeric	
Quantity		Numeric	
Cube		Numeric	
Freight Class		Numeric	
Temperature Min		Numeric	
Temperature Max		Numeric	
Type		String	
Loading Priority		Numeric	
Equipment		String	
Services		String	
User Numeric 1		Numeric	
User Numeric 2		Numeric	
Item Weight		Numeric	
Item Quantity		Numeric	
Item Cube		Numeric	
Item Freight Class		Numeric	
Item Temperature Min		Numeric	
Item Temperature Max		Numeric	
Item ID		String	
Item Quantity UOM		String	
Item Length		Numeric	
Item Width		Numeric	
Item Height		Numeric	
Item Dimension UOM		String	
Item User Numeric 1		Numeric	
Item User Numeric 2		Numeric	
Payment Terms		String	
Rating Count		Numeric	
Direct Carrier Charge		Numeric	
Direct Carrier Contract		String	

Direct Carrier Mode		String	
Direct Service Days		Numeric	
Pool Location		String	
Shipment Options		Constants (CSV)	-NonTLConsol, -NonTLConsolP, -NonTLConsolD -WindowExtension, -WindowExtensionP, -WindowExtensionD
Load Preference		String	
Historical Charge		Numeric	
Historical Contract		String	

Input Data	Base Rates
Worksheet Name	RateTable – nnnnnn
Usage	Mandatory – Identified by Rate Table Parameter
Description	The rate file describes the cost structures for the carriers. The rate table is composed of one or more contracts that contain the carrier information, services lanes, required equipment and base rate details. Contracts are identified and grouped by "Contract Id". Each contract may return (at most) one rate for a specified shipment or load.

Column Name	Usage	Data Type	Notes
Contract Id	Mandatory	String	Contract Id used to group rows
SCAC	Mandatory	String	
Mode	Mandatory	String	
Service	Mandatory	String	
Effective Date	Mandatory	yyyy-mm-dd	
Expiration Date	Mandatory	yyyy-mm-dd	
Lane Calc	Mandatory	Constant1-Constant2	ZONE, LOC, 5ZC, 3ZC, CSC, SC, CTRY, ANY
Rating Zone		String	
From LocCode		String	
From City		String	
From State		String	
From Zip		String or String1-String2	Zip ranges supported
From Country		String	
To LocCode		String	
To City		String	
To State		String	
To Zip		String or String1-String2	Zip ranges supported
To Country		String	
Carrier Services		String	
Carrier Equipment		String	
Break 1 Field		Constant	Weight, Mileage, Class, Quantity, Cube, ItemCount, ItemUOM, ItemId, Stops, Equipment, Services
Break 1 Min		Numeric	
Break 1 Max		Numeric	
Break 2 Field		Constant	Weight, Mileage, Class, Quantity, Cube, ItemCount, ItemUOM, ItemId, Stops, Equipment, Services
Break 2 Min		Numeric	
Break 2 Max		Numeric	
Break 3 Field		Constant	Weight, Mileage, Class, Quantity, Cube, ItemCount,

			ItemUOM, ItemId, Stops, Equipment, Services
Break 3 Min		Numeric	
Break 3 Max		Numeric	
Rate Field	Mandatory	Constant	Weight, Mileage, Class, Quantity, Cube, ItemCount, Stops
Rate Calc	Mandatory	Constant	Per, Pct, Flat, Flat-Conditional
Rate	Mandatory	Numeric	
Accessorial Profile		String	Foreign Key to Accessorial Rates
Total Min		Numeric	
Total Max		Numeric	
Max Stops		String	
Capacity		Numeric	
Capacity2		Numeric	
Use Server	Mandatory	Constant	false or true
SMC Module		String	
SMC Discount		String	
SMC MC Discount		String	
Transit Method		Constant	Service Days or Zone Days
Transit Value		Numeric	1 – 99 for Service Days, -1 – 99 for Zone Days
User Numeric 1		Numeric	
User Numeric 2		Numeric	

Input Data	Accessorial Rates
Worksheet Name	AccessorialProfile - nnnnnn
Usage	Optional – Implicitly linked to Base Rates
Description	The accessorial file describes the accessorial cost structures for the base rate contracts. Accessorials are identified and grouped by "Accessorial Key". Each contract may return multiple accessorials charges.

Column Name	Usage	Data Type	Notes
Accessorial Key	Mandatory	String	Accessorial Key used to group rows
Accessorial Effective Date	Mandatory	yyyy-mm-dd	
Accessorial Expiration Date	Mandatory	yyyy-mm-dd	
Accessorial Break Field	Mandatory	Constant	Weight, Mileage, Class, Quantity, ItemCount, ItemUOM, ItemId, Stops, Equipment, Services
Accessorial Break Condition	Mandatory	String	
Accessorial Break Field Min	Mandatory	Numeric	
Accessorial Break Field Max	Mandatory	Numeric	
Accessorial Rate Field	Mandatory	Constant	Weight, Mileage, Class, Quantity, ItemCount, Stops
Accessorial Rate Method	Mandatory	Constant	Per, Pct, Flat, Flat-Conditional
Accessorial Rate Value	Mandatory	Numeric	
Accessorial Rate Min		Numeric	
Accessorial Rate Max		Numeric	
Accessorial Code		String	

Input Data	Fuel Indexes
Worksheet Name	Fuel Index - nnnnnn
Usage	Optional – Implicitly linked to Accessorial Rates
Description	The fuel index file describes the variable fuel index parameters. Indexes are grouped by "Name" and always have a time component.

Column Name	Usage	Data Type	Notes
Name	Mandatory	String	Name used to group rows
Effective Date Start	Mandatory	yyyy-mm-dd	
Expiration Date End	Mandatory	yyyy-mm-dd	
Value	Mandatory	Numeric	

Input Data	Location Hours
Worksheet Name	Location - nnnnnn
Usage	Optional – Identified by Hours of Operation Determination Parameter
Description	The location hours file describes the hours of operation for each location. Locations are identified by Location Code. Omitted locations use the global default hours specified in the wizard parameters.

Column Name	Usage	Data Type	Notes
Location Code	Mandatory	String	Unique Location Identifier
Days		Constant	Mon – Fri, Mon – Sat, Mon – Sun, DOW, etc…
Hours		hh – hh, hh:mm – hh:mm	

Input Data	Load/Unload Service Time
Worksheet Name	Location - nnnnnn
Usage	Optional – Identified by Service Time Determination Parameter
Description	The service time file describes the loading/unloading time required at each location. Locations are identified by Location Code. Omitted locations use the global default service times specified in the wizard parameters.

Column Name	Usage	Data Type	Notes
Location Code	Mandatory	String	Unique Location Identifier
Service Time Base		Numeric	
Service Time per Shipment		Numeric	
Service Time per Quantity		Numeric	
Delivery Idle Time		Numeric	

Input Data	Dock Capacities
Worksheet Name	Location - nnnnnn
Usage	Optional – Identified by Dock Capacity Strategy Parameter
Description	The dock capacity file lists the available pickup and drop-off docks at each location. Locations are identified by Location Code. Omitted locations use the global default dock capacities specified in the wizard parameters.

Column Name	Usage	Data Type	Notes
Location Code	Mandatory	String	Unique Location Identifier
Pickup Docks		Numeric	
Drop Docks		Numeric	

Input Data	Shipment Compatibility Types
Worksheet Name	OptConstraint - nnnnnn
Usage	Optional – Identified by Type Compatibility List Parameter
Description	The list contains the rules used to determine shipment-type (in)compatibilities

Column Name	Usage	Data Type	Notes
Type1	Mandatory	String	
Type2	Mandatory	String	

Input Data	Pool Locations
Worksheet Name	Location - nnnnnn
Usage	Optional – Identified by Pool Locations Parameter
Description	The pool locations file lists the available pool locations and their carrier restrictions. Locations are identified by Location Code.

Column Name	Usage	Data Type	Notes
Location Code	Mandatory	String	Unique Location Identifier
Name		String	
City		String	
State		String	
Postal Code		String	
Country		String	
Geo	Mandatory	Lat/Long (dd.dddddd,dd.dddddd)	If unknown, may be generated using Edge wizard
Drop Modes		String	
Drop SCACs		String	
Pickup Modes		String	
Pickup SCACs		String	
Max Pool Hold Time		Numeric	

Input Data	Fleet Locations
Worksheet Name	Location - nnnnnn
Usage	Optional – Identified by Fleet Locations
Description	The fleet locations file lists the available domiciles for fleet vehicles and drivers

Column Name	Usage	Data Type	Notes
Location Code	Mandatory	String	Unique Location Identifier
Name		String	
City		String	
State		String	
Postal Code		String	
Country		String	
Geo	Mandatory	Lat/Long (dd.dddddd,dd.dddddd)	If unknown, may be generated using Edge wizard

Input Data	Fleet Vehicles
Worksheet Name	Vehicle - nnnnnn
Usage	Optional – Identified by Fleet Vehicles
Description	The fleet vehicles file lists the available vehicles and their associated contracts and domiciles

Column Name	Usage	Data Type	Notes
Vehicle Id	Mandatory	String	Unique Vehicle Identifier
Location Code		String	Fleet Locations Foreign Key
Contract Id	Mandatory	String	
Availability Start		yyyy-mm-dd hh:mm	
Availability End		yyyy-mm-dd hh:mm	

Input Data	Fleet Drivers
Worksheet Name	Driver - nnnnnn
Usage	Optional – Identified by Fleet Drivers
Description	The fleet driver file lists the available drivers and their associated domiciles

Column Name	Usage	Data Type	Notes
Driver Id	Mandatory	String	Unique Driver Identifier
Location Code	Mandatory	String	
First DOW		Constant	Mon, Tue, Wed, Thu, Fri, Sat, Sun
Max Weekly Duty		Numeric	
Schedule Id		String	Driver Schedule Foreign Key

Input Data	Fleet Driver Schedules
Worksheet Name	DriverSch - nnnnnn
Usage	Optional – Identified by Fleet Driver Schedules
Description	The fleet driver schedules controls driver date/time assignments

Column Name	Usage	Data Type	Notes
Schedule Id	Mandatory	String	Unique Schedule Identifier
Days	Mandatory	Constant	Mon – Fri, Mon – Sat, Mon – Sun, DOW, etc…
Hours	Mandatory	hh – hh, hh:mm – hh:mm	

Input Data	Mojo Parameters
Worksheet Name	OptParam
Usage	Optional – If included, parameters in OptParam override company or Mojo defaults
Description	Key / Value pairs used to configure the Mojo Wizard prior to Mojo execution. Also used for Mojo macro configuration.

Wizard Field	OptParam Key	Data Type	Default Value	Valid Values
Primary Reference	priref	String		*Shipment Report Column*
Alternate Reference	altref	String		*Shipment Report Column*
Origin Code	oloccode	String		*Shipment Report Column*
Origin Name	oname	String		*Shipment Report Column*
Origin City	ocity	String		*Shipment Report Column*
Origin State	ostate	String		*Shipment Report Column*
Origin Postal	ozip	String		*Shipment Report Column*
Origin Country	octry	String		*Shipment Report Column*
Origin Geo	ogeo	String		*Shipment Report Column*
Dest Code	dloccode	String		*Shipment Report Column*
Dest Name	dname	String		*Shipment Report Column*
Dest City	dcity	String		*Shipment Report Column*
Dest State	dstate	String		*Shipment Report Column*
Dest Postal	dzip	String		*Shipment Report Column*
Dest Country	dctry	String		*Shipment Report Column*
Dest Geo	dgeo	String		*Shipment Report Column*
Target Ship (Early)	eshipdate	String		*Shipment Report Column*
Target Delivery (Early)	edeliverdate	String		*Shipment Report Column*
Target Ship (Late)	lshiplate	String		*Shipment Report Column*
Target Delivery (Late)	ldeliverlate	String		*Shipment Report Column*
Weight	weight	String		*Shipment Report Column*
Quantity	quantity	String		*Shipment Report Column*
Cube	cube	String		*Shipment Report Column*
Freight Class	class	String		*Shipment Report Column*
Temperature Min	temperature_min	String		*Shipment Report Column*
Temperature Max	temperature_max	String		*Shipment Report Column*
Type	shiptype	String		*Shipment Report Column*
Loading Priority	loadingpriority	String		*Shipment Report Column*
Equipment	equipment	String		*Shipment Report Column*
Services	services	String		*Shipment Report Column*
Payment Terms	payment_terms	String		*Shipment Report Column*
Rating Count	rating_count	String		*Shipment Report Column*

User Numeric 1	usernumeric1	String		*Shipment Report Column*
User Numeric 2	Usernumeric2	String		*Shipment Report Column*
Item Weight	itemweight	String		*Shipment Report Column*
Item Quantity	itemquantity	String		*Shipment Report Column*
Item Quantity UOM	itemuom	String		*Shipment Report Column*
Item Cube	itemcube	String		*Shipment Report Column*
Item Length	length	String		*Shipment Report Column*
Item Width	width	String		*Shipment Report Column*
Item Height	height	String		*Shipment Report Column*
Item Dimension UOM	dimensions_uom	String		*Shipment Report Column*
Item ID	itemid	String		*Shipment Report Column*
Item Freight Class	itemclass	String		*Shipment Report Column*
Item Temperature Min	itemtemperature_ min	String		*Shipment Report Column*
Item Temperature Max	itemtemperature_ max	String		*Shipment Report Column*
Item User Numeric 1	itemusernumeric1	String		*Shipment Report Column*
Item User Numeric 2	itemusernumeric2	String		*Shipment Report Column*
Direct Carrier Charge	carriercharge	String		*Shipment Report Column*
Direct Carrier Contract	carriercontract	String		*Shipment Report Column*
Direct Service Days	servicedays	String		*Shipment Report Column*
Direct Carrier Mode	mode	String		*Shipment Report Column*
Historical Charge	historicalcharge	String		*Shipment Report Column*
Historical Contract	historicalcontract	String		*Shipment Report Column*
Pool Location	poolloc1	String		*Shipment Report Column*
Shipment Options	shipopts	String		*Shipment Report Column*
Load Preference	Load Preference	String		*Shipment Report Column*
CL Reference	CL Reference	String		*Shipment Report Column*
Rate Table	RateTable	String		*RateTable Report Name*
Re-Rate Table	ReRateTable	String		*RateTable Report Name*
Direct Rate Method	Direct Rate Method	String	Least Cost	Least Cost, Transit Time (LC Fallback), Transit Time (or No Rate)
Non-Opt Rate Method	Non-Opt Rate Method	String	Assign Direct Rate	Assign Direct Rate, Least Cost, Transit Time (or Direct)
Fuel Surcharge (TL)	Fuel Surcharge TL	Numeric	0	0.0 – 999.0

Fuel Surcharge (Non-TL)	Fuel Surcharge LTL	Numeric	0	0.0 – 999.0
Fuel Index Adjustment	Fuel Index Adjustment	Numeric	0	-999.0 – 999.0
Earliest Actual Date	Earliest Actual Date	String	Use Normal Constraints	Use Normal Constraints, Now + 1hr, Now + 2hr, Now +4hr, Now + 8hr, Now + 12hr, Now + 24hr
Strategy	Strategy	String	M-OOR	M-OOR, NOGGIN, SPARR, M-OOR/HZ, NOGGIN/HZ, SPARR/HZ, STOCHAT, STOCHAT/A
Max Out-of-Route	Max Out-of-Route	Numeric	1.2	1.0 – 25.0
Constraint Bias	Constraint Bias	String	Medium	Low, Medium, High
Truckload Modes	Truckload Modes	String	TL, Truckload	CSV List
Vehicle Max Weight	Max Truck Weight	Numeric	45000	0 – 999999
Vehicle Max Quantity	Max Truck Quantity	Numeric	10000	0 – 999999
Vehicle Max Cube	Max Truck Cube	Numeric	3500	0 – 999999
Truckload Max Stops	Max Stops	Numeric	5	1 – 999
Recommended Minimum Stop Size	Minimum Stop Size	Numeric	0	0 – 100
Vehicle Loading	Vehicle Loading	String	LIFO	LIFO, Any Order
Stop Restrictions	Stop Restrictions	String	None	None, No Multi-Pick, No Multi-Drop, No Pickups After 1st Drop, Drop Bias
Load Preference Restrictions	Load Pref Restrictions	String	None	None, Enforce (Single Only), Enforce (Allow Group), Bias (Normal), Bias (Strong)
Origin Location Biases	Origin Location Bias	String		CSV List
Dest Location Restrictions	Dest Location Restriction	String		CSV List
Type Compatibility Method	Shipment Type Compatibility Method	String	Exact Match	Exact Match, Compatibility List, Incompatibility List
Type Compatibility List	TypeCompatibilityTable	String		OptConstraint Report Name
Non-TL Consolidation	LTL Consolidation	String	false	true, false

Non-TL Consolidation	Non-TL Consol Modes	String		*CSV List*
Non-TL Transit Determination	Non-TL Transit Time Method	String	Same as Truckload	Same as Truckload, Use Specified Values
Non-TL Weekend Exclusion	Non-TL Weekend Exclusion Modes	String		*CSV List*
Service Time Determination	Service Time Method	String	Default Only	Default Only, *Location Report Name*
Service Time Determination	ServiceTimeList	String		*Location Report Name*
Service Time Base	Service Time (Shipment)	Numeric	45	0 – 2000
Service Time Additional	Service Time (Stop)	Numeric	15	0 – 2000
Service Time Additional	Service Time (Unit Qty)	Numeric	0	0 – 2000
Hours of Operation Determination	Hours of Operation Method	String	Default Only	Default Only, *Location Report Name*
Hours of Operation Determination	HoursOfOperationList	String		*Location Report Name*
Hours of Operation Enforcement	Hours of Operation Enforcement	String	Arrival Time	Arrival Time, Arrival & Departure Time
Hours of Operation (Default)	Hours of Operation (Open)	String	06:00	00:00, 01:00, 02:00, … , 22:00, 23:00
Hours of Operation (Default)	Hours of Operation (Close)	String	22:00	01:00, 02:00, 03:00, … , 23:00, 24:00
Hours of Operation (Default)	Days of Operation	String	Mon - Sun	Mon - Fri, Mon - Sat, Mon - Sun
Extend Early Ship Window	Extend Ship Early	Numeric	0.0	0.0 – 99.0
Extend Late Ship Window	Extend Ship Late	Numeric	0.5	0.0 – 99.0
Extend Early Delivery Window	Extend Delivery Early	Numeric	0.5	0.0 – 99.0
Extend Late Delivery Window	Extend Delivery Late	Numeric	0.0	0.0 – 99.0
Input Date Adjustment	Input Date Adjustment	Numeric	0.0	-999.0 – 999.0
HOS / Speed Determination	HOS / Speed Determination	String	Default Only	Default Only, Use Lane Info
Vehicle Speed	Vehicle Speed	Numeric	50	1 – 9999
Driver Duty Limit	Driver Duty Limit	Numeric	14	1 – 999

Driver Driving Limit	Driver Driving Limit	Numeric	11	1 – 999
Driver Off-Duty Rest	Driver Off-Duty Rest	Numeric	10	0 – 999
Route Duty Limit	Route Duty Limit	Numeric	70	1 – 999
Allow Off-Duty Extension	Allow Off-Duty Extension	String	false	false, true
Allow Off-Duty Extension	Off-Duty Extension Max	Numeric	84	1 – 999
Carrier Capacity Strategy (Primary)	Capacity Strategy	String	Off	Off, Vehicles/Contract/Lane/Day, Vehicles/Contract/Lane/Run, Vehicles/Carrier/Origin/Day, Vehicles/Carrier/Origin/Run, Vehicles/Carrier/Dest/Day, Vehicles/Carrier/Dest/Run, Vehicles/Carrier/ODPair/Day, Vehicles/Carrier/ODPair/Run, Vehicles/Carrier/Day, Vehicles/Carrier/Run
Carrier Capacity Strategy (Secondary)	Capacity Strategy (Secondary)	String	Off	Off, Vehicles/Contract/Lane/Day, Vehicles/Contract/Lane/Run, Vehicles/Carrier/Origin/Day, Vehicles/Carrier/Origin/Run, Vehicles/Carrier/Dest/Day, Vehicles/Carrier/Dest/Run, Vehicles/Carrier/ODPair/Day, Vehicles/Carrier/ODPair/Run, Vehicles/Carrier/Day, Vehicles/Carrier/Run
Carrier Capacity Allocation	Carrier Capacity Allocation	String	Allow Direct Over-Allocation	Allow Direct Over-Allocation, No Over-Allocation
Carrier Capacity Enforcement	Capacity Enforcement	String	Optimized Loads Only	Optimized Loads Only, All Loads
Carrier Capacity Default	Capacity Default	Numeric	10	0 – 999999

Dock Capacity Strategy	Dock Capacity Strategy	String	Off	Off, On
Dock Time Requirements	Dock Time Requirements	String	Full Service Time	Full Service Time, Shipment Service Time
Dock Capacity Default (Pickup)	Dock Capacity Default (Pickup)	Numeric	3	0 – 999999
Dock Capacity Default (Drop)	Dock Capacity Default (Drop)	Numeric	3	0 – 999999
Private Fleet Strategy	Private Fleet Strategy	String	Off	Off, Return Vehicle
Private Fleet SCAC	Private Fleet SCAC	String	PFLT	*Single SCAC*
Backhaul Bias	Backhaul Bias	String	Off	Off, Low, Medium, High
Fleet Capacity Strategy	Fleet Capacity Strategy	String	Same as Non-Fleet	Same as Non-Fleet, Use Vehicle Assignments
Fleet Capacity Allocation	Fleet Capacity Allocation	String	Allow Direct Over-Allocation	Allow Direct Over-Allocation, No Over-Allocation
Fleet Locations	Fleet Locations	String	Off	*Location Report Name*
Fleet Vehicles	Fleet Vehicles	String	Off	*Vehicle Report Name*
Fleet Drivers	Fleet Drivers	String	Off	*Driver Report Name*
Fleet Driver Schedules	Fleet Driver Schedules	String	Off	*Driver Schedules Report Name*
Fleet Driver HOS Restrictions	Fleet Driver HOS Restrictions	String	Vehicle Assignment Reset	Vehicle Assignment Reset, Require Rest Reset
International Stop Restrictions	International Stop Restrictions	String	None	None, No Backtracking
Pool Strategy	Pool Strategy	String	Off	Off, Force Pools, Consider Pools, Consider Hybrid
Pool Locations	LocationsTable	String		*Location Report Name*
Pool Assignment	Pool Assignment	String	Pre-Assigned Only	Pre-Assigned Only, Best Rate (Introspective), Best Rate (Predictive), Nearest to Rateable Origin, Nearest to Rateable Dest, Nearest to M-OOR Origin, Nearest to M-

				OOR Dest, Nearest to Origin, Nearest to Destination
Pool Date Policy	Pool Date Policy	String	Normal	Normal, Strict
Max Pool Hold Time	Max Pool Hold Time	Numeric	2.0	0.1 – 99.0
Equipment Enforcement	Equipment Enforcement	String	false	false, true
Services Enforcement	Services Enforcement	String	false	false, true
Pickup Clustering	Pickup Radius Limit 1	Numeric	0	0 – 999999
Pickup Clustering	Pickup Radius Carriers 1	String		*CSV List*
Pickup Clustering	Pickup Radius Ident 1	String	Off	Off, Modes, SCACs
Pickup Clustering	Pickup Radius Limit 2	Numeric	0	0 – 999999
Pickup Clustering	Pickup Radius Carriers 2	String		*CSV List*
Pickup Clustering	Pickup Radius Ident 2	String	Off	Off, Modes, SCACs
Drop Clustering	Drop Radius Limit 1	Numeric	0	0 – 999999
Drop Clustering	Drop Radius Carriers 1	String		*CSV List*
Drop Clustering	Drop Radius Ident 1	String	Off	Off, Modes, SCACs
Drop Clustering	Drop Radius Limit 2	Numeric	0	0 – 999999
Drop Clustering	Drop Radius Carriers 2	String		*CSV List*
Drop Clustering	Drop Radius Ident 2	String	Off	Off, Modes, SCACs
TL Vehicle Efficiency	Vehicle Efficiency	Numeric	5.0	1.0 – 99.0
TL CO2 Emissions Factor	CO2 Emissions Factor	Numeric	22.37	1.0 – 99.0
Green Factor LTL	CO2 Factor LTL	Numeric	80	0 - 9999
Green Factor LTL	CO2 Modes LTL	String	LTL?	*CSV List*
Green Factor Rail	CO2 Factor Rail	Numeric	286	0 – 9999
Green Factor Rail	CO2 Modes Rail	String	Rail?	*CSV List*
Green Factor Intermodal (Rail)	CO2 Factor Intm Rail	Numeric	238	0 – 9999

Green Factor Intermodal (Rail)	CO2 Modes Intm Rail	String	Intermodal?,IM?	*CSV List*
Green Factor Ocean (Container)	CO2 Factor Ocean	Numeric	769	0 – 9999
Green Factor Ocean (Container)	CO2 Modes Ocean	String	Ocean?	*CSV List*
Green Factor Air	CO2 Factor Air	Numeric	10	0 – 9999
Green Factor Air	CO2 Modes Air	String	Air?	*CSV List*
Carbon Tax	Carbon Tax	Numeric	0	0.0 – 999.0
Max Out-of-Route	Max Out-of-Route Iter	Numeric		1 – 25
Max Out-of-Route	Max Out-of-Route Step	Numeric		1 – 25
Max Stops	Max Stops Iter	Numeric		1 – 25
Max Stops	Max Stops Step	Numeric		0.01 – 5.00
Constraint Bias	Constraint Bias Improvement	String	false	false, true
Savings Gambit	Savings Gambit Iter	Numeric		1 – 25
Savings Gambit	Savings Gambit Max	Numeric		0 – 50000
STOCHAT Depth	STOCHAT Depth	Numeric	2	1 – 6
Consider Pools Depth	Pool Consideration Iter	Numeric	5	2 – 10
Postliminary Depth	Postliminary Depth	Numeric	10	0 – 100
Distance Determiner	Distance Determiner	String	Geo Only	Geo Only, Distance Table Cache, Server-Lite, Server
Distance Display	Distance Display	String	Miles	Miles, Kilometers

Export Data Overview

Mojo extracts export data in a multi-worksheet spreadsheet called a "Mojo Package". The package contains a copy of all input data, the optimized results and any analysis graphs and charts generated by the user. The version number indicates at which output version the value is supported. To specify the output version, configure the Mojo Option "outputversion=n". For example, to freeze the output at version 1, configure "outputversion=1". If not configured, values of all versions are extracted. The formats of the non-derivable optimized results are detailed below:

Output Data	Optimizer Loads
Worksheet Name	RouteDetail - Optimizer Loads
Description	Each row lists the configuration of every load created by the optimization process. Loads are uniquely identified by the "Load Reference" column.

Column Name	Version	Usage	Data Type	Notes
Load Reference	1	Always	String	Unique Load Identifier
Shipments	1	Always	Numeric	
Stops	1	Always	Numeric	
Events	1	Always	Dynamic Constant	P = Pickup, D = Drop, I = Inbound, O = Outbound - = Deadhead, + = Continuous Move
Opt Contract	1	Always	String	
Opt Rate	1	Always	Numeric	
Direct Rate	1	Always	Numeric	
Savings	1	Always	Numeric	
Pickup Loc	1	Always	String	City, State
Drop Loc	1	Always	String	City, State
Pickup Date	1	Always	yyyy-mm-dd hh:mm	
Leeway	3	Always	Numeric	
Drop Date	1	Always	yyyy-mm-dd hh:mm	
Trns Days	1	Always	Numeric	
Max Weight	1	Always	Numeric	
Max Qty	1	Always	Numeric	

Max Cube	1	Always	Numeric	
Max UN1	4	Always	Numeric	User Numeric 1
Max UN2	4	Always	Numeric	User Numeric 2
OOR	1	Always	Numeric	1.00 – 25.00 (Out-of-route)
RTO	1	Always	Numeric	0.00 – 1.00 (Fractional Return-to-origin)
# PE	1	Always	Numeric	Number of pickups
# DE	1	Always	Numeric	Number of drops
Equipment	1	Always	String	
Services	1	Always	String	
Type	1	Always	String	
Temp Min	1	Always	Numeric	
Temp Max	1	Always	Numeric	
Opt Mileage / Opt Distance	1 / 3	Always	Numeric	Column renamed in version 3
Direct Mileage / Direct Distance	1 / 3	Always	Numeric	Column renamed in version 3
Mileage Diff / Distance Diff	1 / 3	Always	Numeric	Column renamed in version 3
CO2 Change	1	Always	Numeric	
Payment Terms	1	Always	String	
Flags	1	Always	Dynamic Constant	MT = Mileage Table, PMT = Partial Mileage Table
Server Rate	1	Always	Numeric	Populated after server load creation
Hist Rate	1	Always	Numeric	

Output Data	Optimizer Shipments
Worksheet Name	Shipment - Optimizer Shipments
Description	Each row lists the configuration of every shipment used in the optimization process. For non-pooling scenarios, shipments are uniquely identified by the "Primary Reference" column. Pooled shipments are listed using two rows – the inbound shipment and the outbound shipment. The "Load Reference" and/or the "Pool Direction" column may be used to distinguish the inbound/outbound legs.

Column Name	Version	Usage	Data Type	Notes
Primary Reference	1	Always	String	Unique Shipment Reference
Notes	1	Always	String	
Load Reference	1	Always	String	Optimizer Loads Foreign Key
Optimized	1	Always	Constant	true or false
Pickup Window	1	Always	Numeric	
Delivery Window	1	Always	Numeric	
Direct Rate	1	Always	Numeric	
Direct Contract	1	Always	String	
Direct Zone	1	Always	String	
Direct Days	1	Conditional	Numeric	*servicedays Mojo option
Pickup Event	1	Always	Numeric	Optimized Events Foreign Key
Delivery Event	1	Always	Numeric	Optimized Events Foreign Key
Pool Dir	1	Conditional	Constant	Used in pooling scenarios (In or Out)
Pool Loc	1	Conditional	String	Used in pooling scenarios
Pool Hold	1	Conditional	Numeric	Used in pooling scenarios
Pool Zone	1	Conditional	String	Used in pooling scenarios
Pool Direct Rate	1	Conditional	Numeric	Used in pooling scenarios
Pool Direct Contract	1	Conditional	String	Used in pooling scenarios

Origin Code	1	Always	String	
Origin Name	1	Always	String	
Origin City	1	Always	String	
Origin State	1	Always	String	
Origin Zip	1	Always	String	
Origin Ctry	1	Always	String	
Origin Geo	1	Always	Lat/Long (dd.dddddd,dd.ddddd)	
Dest Code	1	Always	String	
Dest Name	1	Always	String	
Dest City	1	Always	String	
Dest State	1	Always	String	
Dest Zip	1	Always	String	
Dest Ctry	1	Always	String	
Dest Geo	1	Always	Lat/Long (dd.dddddd,dd.ddddd)	
Target Ship (Early)	1	Always	yyyy-mm-dd hh:mm	
Actual Ship	1	Always	yyyy-mm-dd hh:mm	
Target Ship (Late)	1	Always	yyyy-mm-dd hh:mm	
Target Delivery (Early)	1	Always	yyyy-mm-dd hh:mm	
Actual Delivery	1	Always	yyyy-mm-dd hh:mm	
Target Delivery (Late)	1	Always	yyyy-mm-dd hh:mm	
Weight	1	Always	Numeric	
Quantity	1	Always	Numeric	
Cube	1	Always	Numeric	
User Num 1	4	Always	Numeric	User Numeric 1
User Num 2	4	Always	Numeric	User Numeric 2
Class	1	Always	Numeric	
Temp Min	1	Always	Numeric	
Temp Max	1	Always	Numeric	

Equipment	1	Always	String	
Services	1	Always	String	
Type	1	Always	String	
Priority	1	Always	String	
Payment Terms	1	Always	String	
Rating Count	1	Always	Numeric	
Alt Ref	1	Always	String	
Options	1	Always	String (CSV)	Lists recognized input "Shipment Options"
Load Preference	1	Always	String	
CL Reference	5	Always	String	
Hist Rate	1	Always	Numeric	
Hist Contract	1	Always	String	

Output Data	Optimizer Events
Worksheet Name	PlanEvent - Optimizer Events
Description	Each row lists the configuration of every event (pickup, drop-off, pool-point) used in the optimization process. Events are uniquely identified by the "Load Reference" and "Sequence Number".

Column Name	Version	Usage	Data Type	Notes
Load Reference	1	Always	String	Optimizer Loads Foreign Key
Type	1	Always	Constant	Pickup or Drop
Seq Num	1	Always	Numeric	Optimized Shipments Foreign Key
Distance	1	Always	Numeric	
Weight	2	Always	Numeric	
Quantity	2	Always	Numeric	
Cube	2	Always	Numeric	
User Num 1	4	Always	Numeric	User Numeric 1
User Num 2	4	Always	Numeric	User Numeric 2
Code	1	Always	String	Location Code
Name	1	Always	String	
City	1	Always	String	
State	1	Always	String	
Zip	1	Always	String	
Ctry	1	Always	String	
Geo	1	Always	Lat/Long (dd.dddddd,dd.dddddd)	
Off-Duty Ext	1	Conditional	Constant	true or false
Actual Day	1	Always	Constant	Mon, Tue, Wed, Thu, Fri, Sat, Sun
Actual Date	1	Always	yyyy-mm-dd hh:mm	
Service Time	1	Always	Numeric	
Loc Hours	1	Always	hh:mm – hh:mm	
Docks Used	1	Conditional	Numeric	Used with dock capacity scenarios
Dock Capacity	1	Conditional	Numeric	Used with dock capacity scenarios
Dock Arrival	1	Conditional	yyyy-mm-dd hh:mm	Used with dock capacity scenarios
Dock Departure	1	Conditional	yyyy-mm-dd hh:mm	Used with dock capacity scenarios
SCAC	1	Always	String	
Mode	1	Always	String	

Service	1	Always	String	
Ship Refs	1	Always	String	List of shipment primary references (max 25)

Output Data	Optimizer CLs
Worksheet Name	Transport - Optimizer CLs
Description	Each row lists the configuration of every customer load. This output report is OPTIONAL and is generated only if customer loads are configured in the shipment input map.

Column Name	Version	Usage	Data Type	Notes
CL Reference	1	Always	String	
Load References	1	Always	String (CSV)	
Loads	1	Always	Numeric	
Shipments	1	Always	Numeric	
Stops	1	Always	Numeric	
Events	1	Always	Dynamic Constant	P = Pickup, D = Drop, I = Inbound, O = Outbound - = Deadhead, + = Continuous Move
Pickup Loc	1	Always	String	City, State
Drop Loc	1	Always	String	City, State
# PE	1	Always	Numeric	Number of pickups
# DE	1	Always	Numeric	Number of drops
Weight	1	Always	Numeric	
Quantity	1	Always	Numeric	
Cube	1	Always	Numeric	
Distance	1	Always	Numeric	
Ship Refs	1	Always	String	List of shipment primary references (max 25)

Output Data	Optimizer Rates
Worksheet Name	PriceSheet - Optimizer Rates
Description	Each row shows the contract, lane and charge details for associated Load

Column Name	Version	Usage	Data Type	Notes
Load Reference	1	Always	String	Optimizer Loads Foreign Key
Contract	1	Always	String	Base Rates Foreign Key or User-Defined
SCAC	1	Always	String	
Mode	1	Always	String	
Service	1	Always	String	
Lane	1	Always	String	
Total	1	Always	Numeric	
(Charge Detail #1)	1	Conditional	Numeric	0 – N columns – one column for each unique charge type or EDI code
(Charge Detail #N)	1	Conditional	Numeric	

Output Data	Optimizer Capacity
Worksheet Name	Log - Optimizer Capacity
Description	Each row shows number of vehicles dispatched for configured location and timescale strategy

Column Name	Version	Usage	Data Type	Notes
Date	1	Conditional	yyyy-mm-dd	
Day	1	Conditional	String (day of week)	Only returned if Date configured
SCAC	1	Conditional	String	Either SCAC or Contract & Lane is returned
Origin Code	1	Conditional	String	Only one column in group is returned
Dest Code	1	Conditional	String	Only one column in group is returned
OD Pair	1	Conditional	String	Only one column in group is returned
Contract	1	Conditional	String	Either SCAC or Contract & Lane is returned
Lane	1	Conditional	String	Either SCAC or Contract & Lane is returned
Capacity Used	1	Always	Numeric	
Capacity Max	1	Conditional	Numeric	Returned if capacity restrictions are enabled
Capacity %	1	Conditional	Numeric	Returned if capacity restrictions are enabled

Output Data	Optimizer Fleet
Worksheet Name	Log - Optimizer Fleet
Description	Each row shows the Vehicle/Driver assigned to Load. Report generated only when Fleet Vehicles are configured.

Column Name	Version	Usage	Data Type	Notes
Vehicle Id	1	Always	String	Fleet Vehicles Foreign Key
Driver Id	1	Always	String	Fleet Drivers Foreign Key
Load Reference	1	Always	String	Optimizer Loads Foreign Key
Location Code	1	Always	String	Fleet Locations Foreign Key
Driver Week	1	Always	yyyy-mm-dd hh:mm	
Duty Hours	1	Always	Numeric	
Start Duty	1	Always	yyyy-mm-dd hh:mm	
End Duty	1	Always	yyyy-mm-dd hh:mm	

Troubleshooting

Contents:

(1) No 'Route optimizer...' command
(2) Too few shipments reported in results
(3) Shipments won't optimize
(4) No rating results
(5) Data quality
(6) Constraints not being respected (max weight, etc.)
(7) Optimization taking too long
(8) 'History' tab not recording new runs

(1) No 'Route optimizer' command is present in MercuryEdge.

-- A valid Mojo key must be installed in System Preferences. Remember that to change a preference, you must enter the value and exit the field before saving – click in another field or hit the tab key before clicking OK.
-- The key is case-sensitive and must be entered exactly as provided.
-- Re-login is required after entering the key.
-- A valid Shipment report must be the currently selected tab in MercuryEdge. Be sure the report type is recognized as 'Shipment' and not 'Import'.
-- If MercuryEdge has lost its connection to the server, re-login and re-open the shipment report.

(2) Fewer shipments are reported in optimizer results than were submitted.

-- Check for multiple uses of same shipment primary reference number. The optimizer treats all multiple lines with the same primary reference as items on the same shipment.
-- Check for incorrect duplicate location codes (same code used for multiple locations). Check Warnings section of Notes tab.
-- Corrupted or incorrect geodata. Re-selected "Add Geodata" command to update and re-optimize.

(3) Shipments won't optimize.

-- Shipment could not be optimized with given constraints, e.g. a 35,000 pound shipment with truck max capacity set to 30,000 pounds. See "Notes" column in the 'Optimizer Shipments' tab.

-- This shipment has unworkable time windows or other settings that prevents this shipment from being compatible with any other.

-- No direct contract rate was found that applied to this shipment so it could not be optimized. Check for whether the shipment's "Direct Rate" field in the Optimizer Shipments tab is blank or zero. See section "No Rating Result" below.

(4) No Rating Results

-- A report of type "RateTable" must be open in MercuryEdge and specified in first setting of the second wizard screen.

-- Rate table might be expecting a Quantity, Cube, Freight Class or other field that is not being supplied by the shipment data (mapped on first wizard screen).

-- Shipment dates fall outside effective date range of contracts.

-- Shipment requires a service or equipment that is not available in the rate table – are we enforcing this requirement on the last screen of the wizard?

-- No modes are available in the rate table for which optimization is permitted. Check the setting on the second wizard screen, "Truckload Modes", to make sure all mode designations that should be considered as truckload are listed. Check the setting, "Non-TL Optimization" to make sure optimization is enabled for all non-TL modes, or a list of modes you want.

-- Problem with the format of shipment or rate table data – see "Data Quality" section below.

- <u>IMPORTANT NOTE ON BREAK RANGES</u>: If your shipments with round numbers are not getting rated (100 pounds, 200 pounds, etc.) check the rate table's break ranges – a common error is to declare ranges such as "0-100", "101-199", etc. – which is actually SKIPPING the value of 100. Rate table break ranges must be defined like this: 0-100, 100-200, etc. – the second value is the ENDPOINT of the range <u>and is not captured by that range</u>. (This is different from TMS rate tables.)

(5) Data Quality

-- Shipment reports must have geocodes or else Mojo will report that it cannot optimize. MercuryEdge can install geocodes with the "Add Geodata…" command in the right-hand task window.

-- Geocodes rely on valid ZIP codes, or in the alternative, valid city-state combinations without ZIP codes. (If there is a ZIP code but it does not match the city and state, Mojo uses the ZIP code anyway, so be careful.)

-- If a spreadsheet file is dropping the leading zero from ZIP codes, then before importing, re-format those cells as zip codes in the spreadsheet, or put a leading apostrophe in front of the entries involved (e.g., '01234).

-- Shipment reports must have at least a <u>weight column</u> mapped. Other columns such as Quantity and Cube might be needed depending on the needs of the rate table.

-- Make sure the rate table is being recognized as type "RateTable".

-- <u>Rate table column headers must be exactly as specified</u>, case-sensitive, with exact spelling, spacing and capitalization. "ZIP" does not match "Zip". See file formats and headers in earlier appendix section.

-- Origin and destination location codes are recommended and are mandatory in some scenarios. Again, make sure the spreadsheet is not omitting leading zeroes if you are using numerical codes.

-- Location codes should be unique. If two locations have the same city, state and zip code, they must have different location codes. (One trick in this situation is to map the location's street address as the location-code column in the optimization wizard.)

-- Are country codes consistent, e.g. "US" vs. "USA"? Inconsistent uses between the shipment data and rate table is a common reason for not getting back rates.

-- This might seem like a "duh" statement, but be sure to select <u>only the shipments you want to optimize</u> – for example, in executing live loads, don't re-optimize loads already in transit.

-- MercuryEdge treats columns that contain only digits as a column of numerical values, but treats a column with any mix of digits and non-digits as a column of text values. If you're trying to compare strings to numbers, make sure the numbers are being treated as text – right-click the column header and choose the command, "Format as Text". If you're trying to use text as numbers, make sure the values contain only digits.

(6) Constraints not begin respected for max weight etc.)

-- No shipment data was supplied to calculate against the limit. Example: "Max Quantity" set to 60, but no "Quantity" column was mapped from shipment data.

-- Often these are non-optimized shipments already be outside allowed limits, e.g., already above max weight, quantity or cube allowed for a single load. Shipment is flagged in "Notes" column, resulting load is flagged "Flags" column for violating constraints.

- Rate table values on a per-lane basis can override the optimizer's global setting

(7) Optimization taking too long

-- Main reason is calls to external servers for rating
-- Where possible use rates in rate table as opposed to server calls

-- After initial run, use the 'Synch Direct Rates' command to save the calculated direct cost rates – no need to repeat these server calls on every subsequent run

- Reduce use of any looping options on final wizard screen, set Postliminary depth to 10 or less.

- Use smaller dataset until the model you want is built.

(8) History tab not capturing subsequent runs

- To re-optimize after a Mojo run, with the Mojo tab selected choose the first command in the right-hand window, "Optimize". This re-launches the Mojo wizard and the results of the run are added to the History tab

-- The other way is to select the original Shipment report and click "Route optimizer…." in the right-hand window. This is treated as a new, separate run of Mojo, with a separate tab of Mojo results, and its History now starts with the new run.

###

About MercuryGate International Inc.

MercuryGate International was founded in 2000 and has grown steadily since its creation. The company provides a highly scalable platform that supports all modes of transportation (parcel, LTL, truckload, air, ocean, rail, intermodal) enabling companies to centrally manage transportation across divisions and business units with control tower visibility.

MercuryGate's solutions assist clients in procurement, planning, optimization, execution and settlement of freight movements. MercuryGate's clients span the full logistics industry universe, and its products form an interconnected system that enables them to reach across that universe.

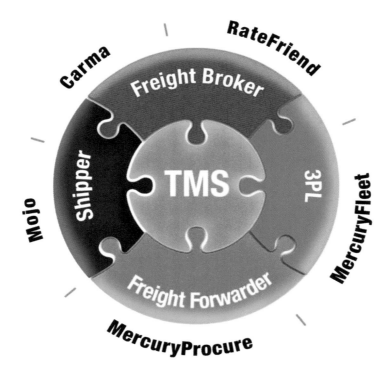

MercuryGate University

Investing in the future of the industry, MercuryGate is partnering with universities, colleges and other institutions across the continent in a program called "MercuryGate University." The company makes available its TMS and other software tools, including the Mojo optimizer, for the study of supply-chain management.

Those institutions are putting MercuryGate tools to work in their own supply-chain programs, demonstrating to students actual business solutions to real transportation problems.

###

60542539R00179

Made in the USA
Charleston, SC
30 August 2016